Basics of Indian Philosophy

Basics of Indian Philosophy

ShashiPrabha Kumar

With a Foreword by
Arvind Gupta

Vivekananda International Foundation

DK PRINTWORLD
Publishers of Indian Traditions

Cataloging in Publication Data — DK
[Courtesy: D.K. Agencies (P) Ltd. <docinfo@dkagencies.com>]

Kumāra, Śaśiprabhā, 1951- **author.**
Basics of Indian philosophy / Shashiprabha Kumar.
pages cm
Includes passages in Sanskrit (roman).
ISBN 9788124612460 (HB)

1. Philosophy, Indic. 2. Hindu philosophy.
I. Vivekananda International Foundation
(New Delhi, India) publisher. II. Title.

LCC B131.K86 2025 | DDC 181.4 23

ISBN: 978-81-246-1246-0 (Hb)
Lectures presented at Vivekananda International Foundation, New Delhi, during 2021-22.
First Published in India in 2025

Author: ShashiPrabha Kumar (b.1951)

Published by:
Vivekananda International Foundation
3, San Martin Marg, Chanakyapuri
New Delhi — 110021
Phones : (011) 24121764, 24106698

and

D.K. Printworld (P) Ltd.
Regd. Office : "Vedaśrī", F-395, Sudarshan Park
ESI Hospital Metro Station, New Delhi - 110015
Phones : (011) 4172 2626, 98713 94815
e-mail : indology@dkprintworld.com
Web : www.dkprintworld.com

Printed by: D.K. Printworld (P) Ltd., New Delhi

Foreword

THE Vivekananda International Foundation (VIF) is delighted to present Professor ShashiPrabha Kumar's book *Basics of Indian Philosophy*. She is a renowned Sanskrit scholar, well-versed in classical Indian philosophy. She is presently the Chairperson of the Indian Institute of Advanced Study, Shimla and a former Vice-Chancellor of Sanchi University of Buddhist–Indic Studies. A Distinguished Fellow with the VIF, she recently authored a unique book *Vedic Prayers for Global Peace and Universal Well-being* published by the VIF on India's presidency of G-20 in September 2023.

In 2020, the VIF requested Professor ShashiPrabha Kumar to deliver a few lectures on ancient Indian philosophy for the benefit of our researchers and scholars who are specialists in international relations but have little or no knowledge about Indian philosophical traditions. It was felt that our scholars, who study contemporary global issues, should also have awareness about ancient Indian thought to help them see global issues from an Indian perspective. Ancient Indian philosophy, which is comprehensive and rich in content, provides an alternative analytical framework and some correction to the Western-dominated thinking on contemporary issues. Familiarity with the basics of Indian philosophical thought will help develop an Indian narrative for contemporary global issues.

Professor ShashiPrabha Kumar agreed to our request and delivered ten fascinating lectures during 2020-21. This happened during the dreaded corona period when all of us were confined to our respective homes. It seemed that the humanity would come to an end. Despondency and anxiety were all pervasive. Technology came to our rescue. The VIF organized a series of webinars including those on ancient Indian philosophy. Professor ShashiPrabha Kumar not only introduced the participants to the essentials of Indian philosophy, her lectures also provided solace during the troubled times. Senior members of Indian strategic community including former diplomats, retired armed forces officials, academics, and experts and scholars attended the lectures. The interaction between a scholar of Indian philosophy and the strategic community proved to be extremely rewarding. It was then decided that since the lectures have lasting value, they should be published in the form of a book.

The book not only introduces the six schools of the Indian philosophy viz. Nyāya, Vaiśeṣika, Sāṁkhya, Yoga, Mīmāṁsā and Vedānta, but also covers the Vedic literature, philosophy of the Upaniṣads, besides the traditions of Cārvāka, Buddhism and Jainism.

There are several takeaways from the book. Knowledge is highly regarded in Indian thought. The word *veda* signifies knowledge. Questioning is essential as a methodology to acquire knowledge. The mind has to be kept open. Absolutism is eschewed. It is recognized that while Truth is one but the paths to attain it are many. The Vedāntic tradition lays great stress on the unity between the human and the divine. The divine is present in all forms of creation, living and non-living. The atheistic philosophy of Cārvāka is accommodated in the overall theme of Indian thought. A balance between materialism and spiritualism is advocated.

In the contemporary global discourse on environment, human rights and feminism are critical issues. The book brings out that in the Indian thought, these subjects have been discussed extensively and openly. The forces of nature are to be respected and pacified. Sustainable development is inherent in Indian thinking. There is a yearning for peace within, and peace in the world and in the cosmos. The concept of *vasudhaiva kuṭumbakam* (one earth, one family) underlies the ancient Indian philosophy.

Woman occupies central place in ancient Indian philosophy. She is seen as the fount of knowledge and is worth worshipping. She is regarded as pure and pious and also as the epitome of power. She is brave and kills the demons when required. She compliments the man and the gods and her contribution is pivotal to creation and creativity. Without woman, creation is incomplete.

The Upaniṣads are the jewels of Indian philosophical thought. The book introduces the reader to the essentials of the eleven Upaniṣads: *Īśa*, *Kena*, *Kaṭha*, *Praśna*, *Muṇḍaka*, *Māṇḍūkya*, *Aitareya*, *Taittirīya*, *Chāndogya*, *Bṛhadāraṇyaka* and *Śvetāśvatara*. They engage in great depth with the eternal questions of metaphysics, epistemology and ethics.

Buddhism and Jainism originated from the Indian soil. Millions of people follow them even today. Although they arose as a reaction to ancient Hindu thinking, there is an underlying unity in essentials among Hinduism, Buddhism and Jainism. They form an integral part of the Indian philosophical tradition. One chapter introduces the readers to Bauddha and Jaina philosophy.

Naysayers and non-believers are not to be ignored. Atheism is not to be taken lightly. The Cārvāka philosophy, which epitomizes materialism and negates the other schools, also finds place in the Indian philosophical thought.

The lectures were intended for the international relations specialists. It is hoped that the readers will be able to develop a framework to understand and analyse contemporary international discourse around peace, welfare, environment, friendship, culture, feminism, sustainable development, materialism and spiritualism, education and knowledge and other issues taking a cue from the quintessentials of Indian philosophy.

Specialists live and work in silos. Philosophy delves into difficult questions of human existence. The encompassing, wide-ranging ancient Indian philosophy helps individuals to come out of narrow thinking.

I am confident that the book will be welcomed by experts in various disciplines who are interested in understanding the significance of ancient Indian thought and how it engages one with perennial questions of human behaviour, ambitions, achievements and follies.

New Delhi
Nirjalā Ekādaśī
18 June 2024

Arvind Gupta
Director, VIF

Prologue

THE book in hand is a testimony and a tribute to human perseverance despite difficult times due to the pangs of pandemic Corona. It was during the lockdown period after the spread of this dreaded disease that Dr. Arvind Gupta, Director, Vivekananda International Foundation, New Delhi asked me to deliver a few online lectures on Indian philosophy for beginners.

These monthly lectures started in July 2020 and concluded in July 2021. Total ten online lectures were delivered by me and each of the lecture was followed by an intense question — answer session which further motivated me to continue the series of lectures. During the course of lectures, it was decided by VIF that these would be published in the form of a book. Accordingly a transcript was later made available to me and preparation of the book commenced. Evidently this book is not an ordinary one, rather it is extraordinary in many respects. First of all, the journey for this book began in the most testing times for humanity across the world. Second, the participants were not ordinary students of Indian philosophy, these so-called beginners were in fact not even ordinary persons but the distinguished members of VIF fraternity including former ambassadors, diplomats, defence officers and senior scholars in different domains.

Needless to say that I enjoyed every bit of the journey. On the one hand it was my initiation into the web world and on the other hand it was a refreshing of my own understanding of Indian philosophy. Topics for these ten lectures were: Common Characteristics of Indian Philosophy; Environmental Awareness in Vedas; Vedic Feminism; Introduction to Vedic Literature;

Philosophy of Upaniṣads; Cārvāka Philosophy; Bauddha and Jaina philosophy; Nyāya and Vaiśeṣika Philosophy; Sāṁkhya and Yoga Philosophy; and Mīmāṁsā and Vedānta Philosophy.

However, it must be clarified that the present book is not meant for scholars or regular students of philosophy but it will definitely fill a lacunae among genuine seekers of the subject and will guide them for an advanced study in this domain. The book will also provide help for exploring the original sourcetexts and secondary readings in different areas covered in it. The best and unique aspect of this extraordinary book is the original interactive deliberations appended after each lecture. It is therefore that although a few revisions have been made in the main content of the lectures delivered but the question–answer session has been retained as it is. An epilogue at the end of the book will give additional information to those who are interested in going further in the field.

I am highly obliged to Sri S. Gurumurthy, Chairman, VIF for his constant support and encouragement. I am extremely grateful to Dr Arvind Gupta and his team at VIF for giving me this opportunity for self-enrichment in more ways than I had expected. Dr. Gupta has not only advised me at every step but has also obliged by writing a Foreword. My personal thanks are due to Ms Anuttama Ganguly, Secretary, VIF for her patience and cooperation during period of preparation for the book. Mr Susheel K. Mittal deserves due credit for a fine production.

17 May 2024

ShashiPrabha Kumar
"Abhyudaya"
295/15-A, Noida - 201301

Contents

Common Characteristics of Indian Philosophy

At the outset, let us dwell upon a few common characteristics of Indian philosophy which underlie its edifice. But even before we go to these common characteristics, let us remember that Indian philosophy is not philosophy in its literal sense. The word philosophy signifies love of wisdom (*philos+sophia*). It was an intellectual quest for the West, but in India the word was *darśana* (दर्शन) from the root *dṛś* (दृश्). It means "to see" but this seeing is not just physical seeing because if it is merely seeing or looking, then even the animals look at various objects in the world. Incidentally, the Sanskrit word for an animal is *paśu — paśyati iti paśuḥ* (one who merely sees is a *paśu*) while human beings are called *manu — manute iti manuḥ*, so we have to evolve from *paśu* and we have to grow, we have to rise up to the level of *manu*.

Darśana is not merely seeing or looking physically, rather it is reflecting, it is having an insight, it is based on observation as well as introspection, so the first contrast between Indian philosophy and Western philosophy is that *darśana* is not just looking at things but also reflecting upon their essence. It is not just a view of life for the Indian philosophers, but it is a way of life as well. As we shall see during the course of discussion, all the systems of Indian philosophy were propounded by the sages who were not known as scholars, professors or doctors, they were all the ṛṣis, *maharṣis*, and the very word *ṛṣi* is derived from the root *dṛś*: *ṛṣirdarśanāt* (*ṛṣiḥ darśanāt*). A *ṛṣi* is the seer who has realized the truth, it has to be a seer with the vision and then there has to be a seeker with the quest; when these two meet — the seer with the vision and the seeker with a quest — then philosophizing takes place in Indian tradition.

There are many other contrasts between Indian philosophy and Western philosophy as will be discussed below. Arvind Sharma once delivered a lecture and he dwelt upon an analytical contrast between Indian philosophy and Western philosophy. I would like to quote him:

> Western philosophy focuses on this world, while Indian philosophy is other-worldly. It not only focuses on this world but it also talks beyond this world. Then there is a relation between religion and philosophy. In the West, religion is totally different and philosophy is totally different. While in India all the religions have a philosophical background. Their essence is hidden in the philosophy beneath and then the religion is based on the practices. Philosophy is based on the precepts and religion is based on those very precepts, but it is practical in orientation.
>
> — 2020: p.16

In ancient Indian scenario, as long as religion and philosophy were working together, there were debates, disputes and divergences, but there was no clash like what we see today. Differences were there but they were only intellectual differences, there were only academic clashes; this blend between religion and philosophy was another hallmark of Indian philosophy (Bhāratīya Darśana).

In the context of this contrast between Indian and Western philosophy, let me quote Hiriyanna:

> Philosophy in India did not take its rise in wonder or curiosity as it seems to have been in the West; rather it originated under the pressure of a practical need arising from the presence of moral and physical evil in life. It is the problem of how to remove this evil that troubled the ancient Indian most, and *mokṣa* in all the systems represents a state in which it is, in one sense or another, taken to have been overcome. Philosophic endeavour

> was directed primarily to find a remedy for the ills of life and the consideration of metaphysical question came in as a matter of course. — 2005: 18-19

In the above background, when we begin to acquaint ourselves with the Indian philosophical thought, first we divide all the thinkers and their theories into two types — one is Vedic schools and the other is non-Vedic schools. Mostly people use the words orthodox and heterodox (*āstika* and *nāstika*) for this division but that is not appropriate because *āstika* primarily means a theist and *nāstika* means an atheist while this division in Indian philosophy is based on the authority of Vedas. Many of those schools who follow the authority of the Vedas, even they do not propound theism and they do not accept the existence of God like Mīmāṁsā and Sāṁkhya, even then they are known as Vedic. They do not clearly accept the existence of God but they are classified as Vedic because they follow the authority of Vedas. So, there are the Vedic schools and non-Vedic schools, and out of the non-Vedic schools, with the exception of the Cārvāka — Jainism, Buddhism and *ṣaḍ-darśanas* (six schools) as we call them, all of them have some inherent features or some essential common characteristics which are being presented in the following pages.

We can discuss below a few points in this regard:

I. *Saprayojanatā* (*Purposiveness*) — The Indian mind is basically purposive. Everything in the world has a purpose. Kumārila Bhaṭṭa says:

> *prayojanamanuddiśya mando 'pi na pravartate* ।
> — *Ślokavārttika* 19.55

> If there is no purpose, then even a dull person will not indulge in any activity.

Every activity and every human endeavour is based on some purpose and same is true of all the Indian philosophical schools. Purpose of life is to get rid of suffering and this getting rid of suffering is known through different terms, different concepts; different ideas, different roads and different paths have been charted out for reaching at this goal, but the goal is there. All of them have this goal in mind, be it Jainism, Buddhism, Sāṁkhya, Nyāya or Vaiśeṣika. We have different terms for this goal in different schools like *mukti*, *mokṣa*, *kaivalya*, *apavarga* and *nirvāṇa*. When we come to these concepts we shall discuss different viewpoints propounded by different schools and thinkers. Even within a school, there are different views of different scholars regarding this idea. So the first common characteristic is that there is a purpose of philosophizing and there is a purpose of life as well.

II. *Sātmakatā* (*Spirituality*) — The next point is that Indian philosophy is essentially spiritual (*ādhyātmika*) and it includes a belief in the *ātman*; *ātman* is different from matter. Matter is visible, so nobody needs to prove it but *ātman* is not visible, still everyone experiences him or herself; everyone knows the world through this *ātman* only, so there are arguments and counter arguments regarding the nature of *ātman* — whether this *ātman* is eternal or non-eternal; whether there is one *ātman* in all of us or there are different *ātmans* in different bodies, but all of them believe that *ātman* is there. The Sanskrit term for the first characteristic, will be *saprayojanatā* — that there is a purpose and the second one will be *sātmakatā* or *ādhyātmikatā* (spirituality).

III. *Sakāraṇatā* (*Causality*) — The third common characteristic will be *sakāraṇatā*. All the schools in Indian tradition except Cārvāka propound that everything has a cause behind it, nothing happens without a cause. But the theory of causality is different; according to Buddhism, it is called *pratitya-samutpāda*, for Nyāya–Vaiśeṣika and others, it is called Asatkāryavāda or Ārambhavāda. It is different according to Sāṁkhya–Yoga, it is known as Satkāryavāda or Pariṇāmavāda. It is different for Vedānta which calls it Vivartavāda. So theories of causation may be different but all of them agree that there is a cause behind every act, every effect and every incident.

IV. *Sātatya* (*Continuity*) — The theory of causation leads us to the theory of *karma* because this world is diverse and different. For example, a family has two kids, maybe twins, but their fortunes are different, their aptitudes are different and their interests are different. They are born in the same family with the same genes, they are brought up in the same environment, but they are different, why so? Somebody has interest in academics and the other has interest in music and the third one might have interest in aeronautics. How their attitudes or inclinations are determined, why somebody is rich and somebody is poor, somebody is healthy and somebody is weak? According to Indian philosophy, this is due to *karma* or *karma-vaicitrya*: difference in our *karma* leads to this difference in our life, so this theory of causality gives rise to the theory of *karma* which is also acceptable to all the systems across religions: Hinduism, Jainism or Buddhism. Theory of *karma* takes us to another corollary that is known as re-birth (*punarjanma*). In fact, all the schools and all the thinkers agree on this basic pre-supposition of Indian thought, for the Bhāratīya Darśana this world is not the *be all and end all* of life, whatever we do in this life will lead us to the next life and whatever we are in this life are due to the previous actions performed by us in our previous lives; so there is a chain of causality, there is a series of consequences that everything we do will have to be borne by us:

> *avaśyameva bhoktavyaṁ kr̥taṁ karma śubhāśubham* ।
>
> — *Brahmavaivar-tta Purāṇa* 1.44.74

one has to bear the fruit of actions performed-good or evil.

To recapitulate, the first feature of all the systems of indian philosophy is *saprayojanatā* (purposiveness). Next is *sātmakatā*, spirituality (*ādhyātmikatā*), the third is *sakāraṇatā* (causality), the fourth is *continuity* and this continuity is determined by the theory of *karma*, theory of *karma* leads to the theory of *punarjanma* because *karma* and *punarjanma* are intrinsically related to each other.

V. Sadācāratā (Morality) — Then comes the aspect of morality because, as mentioned earlier, Indian philosophy is not just a view of life, it is a way of life. It is not like the teachings of Western philosophers who propounded something but they led a life which was totally unrelated to their thought, while in India they were not called *ṛṣis* without a reason. For example, Kaṇāda is the propounder of Vaiśeṣika: *kaṇānattīti kaṇādaḥ*. The name Kaṇāda is a given name because he propounded the theory of atoms, *kaṇas* or *paramāṇus*, and he also lived his life like that: he had stopped eating except the grains whichever had fallen in the fields; he was so engrossed in thinking that whatever *kaṇas* he got to eat, with that only he could sustain himself. Kaṇāda, Kapila and then Jaimini, Gautama all were *ṛṣis* and they were living a life of self-restraint, *ātmasaṁyama* and *sadācāra* (morality). Morality is an essential ingredient of Indian philosophy. If a person is not moral, if a person is not restrained in his behaviour, he cannot be an ideal person, he cannot be a role model for the society while these *ṛṣis* were the role models of society; they were propounding different schools of thought, they were the thinkers par excellence for generations and they propounded their own *sampradāyas*.

Significantly, these days, we use the word *sampradāya* in a very different and negative sense, while in Indian philosophy the term *sampradāya* has been explained in a logical and positive manner by Nyāya scholar Uddyotakarācārya. He has written a text called *Nyāyavārttika*. According to him a *sampradāya* is when the teacher and the student (*ācārya* and *śiṣya*) are continuously carrying forward a tradition; because this tradition has been an oral tradition in ancient times: one generation directly transmitted the knowledge to the next generation; when *ācārya* and *śiṣya* are continuously transmitting the knowledge of their tradition from one to other, then it is known as *sampradāya*.[1] Accordingly, Gautama propounded one *sampradāya*, Kaṇāda another *sampradāya* and Kapila started another *sampradāya*.

---

1 *sampradāyo nāma śiṣyācāryasambandhasyāvicchedena śāstraprāptiḥ* — *Nyāyavārttika*, p. 21

Therefore, continuity was there but this continuity was based on morality or self-restraint or to say it more clearly, all the systems in Indian philosophy, all the scholars of Indian philosophy, they were practising and preaching; they were not preaching and practising. In other words, they were first practising and then preaching. For example, take *yoga* — we have Hindu *yoga*, Jaina *yoga* and Buddhist *yoga*. What is this *yoga*? *Yoga* is not just physical exercise, *yoga* is the *sādhanā*, *yoga* is the control of sense organs, *yoga* is the restraint of mind, so we may also call this as *sadācāratā yogaparāyaṇatā* or *naitikatā* which was inherent in all the systems of thought in India. This idea of morality comes naturally when the teacher is directly teaching his students and they are evolving into a *sampradāya*. But, at the same time, there remains a possibility of becoming just blind followers like it happens even today, the people flock to listen to *ācāryas*, saints and *sādhus*. This is, therefore, alleged that Indian philosophy is more of a religion than that of philosophy. Some of the Western scholars allege that Indian philosophy is not proper philosophy, specially the Hindu philosophy. In their opinion, it is not rational, it is not logical because they follow whatever the earlier *ācārya* has said without arguing; without examining; but this allegation is not correct at all. It is true that in Indian philosophy, verbal authority or the tradition was respected; there was a reliability of certain speakers because they were not ordinary persons; their reliability depended upon their *āptatā (reliability)*. These systems are also known as *ārṣa*, propounded by the *ṛṣis* and therefore we believe in their reliability, we do not question them. This is *śraddhā* (faith) of course but this is not blind faith, because rationality is very much ingrained in Indian philosophy. On the one hand, we have reliability or the verbal testimony or the authority of the *ācārya*; on the other hand, we have the rationality, logic or epistemology of each of the systems in Hindu thought or Jaina philosophy or Buddhist philosophy for that matter.

Accordingly, we have total eight *pramāṇas* (means of knowing): *śabda* is one of them. It is not that we believe everything that the teacher utters. There are eight means of knowing, i.e. eight *pramāṇas*: Cārvāka believed in only one *pramāṇa* – perception; Buddhist and Vaiśeṣika believe in two *pramāṇas* – perception and inference; then we come to the third that is analogy (*upamāna*). Fourth one is *śabda-pramāṇa*. It is true that *śabda-pramāṇa* (verbal authority of Vedas) and the *ācārya* is highly venerated, but it is because we have already examined his reliability; there is a test of reliability, of an *āpta*. Who is a reliable person? We get an answer that a reliable person is one who is knowledgeable and committed to the cause of learning. For example, if I am a teacher or student of philosophy, you will believe what I say but for other branches of learning, if Dr Arvind Gupta will speak about strategy or diplomacy, we shall believe because he is an expert in that area; so reliability depends on the knowledge attained by the person and also his selfless intention to transmit correct knowledge. We have reliability, but we have rationality as well.

VI. *Seśvaratā* (*Theism*) – Next comes the logical theism (*seśvaratā*) – belief in the existence of God; not all of the schools in Indian philosophy, but most of them believe in God; they also argue for the existence of God. Arguments and debates do take place. In fact, there is a Nyāya scholar, viz. Udayanācārya, who has authored a separate book just to prove the existence of God known as *Nyāya-Kusumāñjali.* This book is a specimen of Indian theism. Udayana gives eight arguments for proving the existence of God, so this is termed as logical theism; I would call it *seśvaratā*; they have propounded the existence of God but why do we need God? What are the arguments for believing in God that we are propounding? Udayanācārya has given all those arguments and the three arguments that are usually given in the West, they have also been included in those eight arguments; but this theism is logical and this is not dogmatism. So, Indian philosophy is not dogmatic, it does not negate the scope for arguments or reasoning. Nyāya philosophy is, in fact, known as the science of reasoning and there are different aspects of debates and dialectics that have been described in it in detail.

VII. *Satarkatā* (*Rationality*) — This brings us to the most important feature of Indian philosophy that it is very rational in its approach, but also liberal or tolerant in its purview; so liberal that almost all the texts of Indian philosophy have been written in a particular style. What is that style — first of all the opponents' arguments are taken up — this is known as *pūrva-pakṣa*; as the name itself suggests that this is the opponents' view; opponent is given primacy — he has the first right to present his views in full detail. Thereafter, the proponents will give their own arguments; after examining each argument of the opponent, the *siddhānta-pakṣa* or the *uttara-pakṣa* will be explained. Suppose I am writing a text of Nyāya philosophy, first I will take Sāṁkhya, Cārvāka and Bauddha views — all these will be *pūrva-pakṣas*. For example, in Udayana's text *Nyāya-Kusumāñjali*, he gives several *pūrva-pakṣas* there: Sāṁkhya, Cārvāka, Bauddha and Jaina — they are all the opponents; after positing the *pūrva-pakṣas* and giving their arguments, he responds to each of the arguments and refutes them and then posits his own standpoint, that is *siddhānta-pakṣa*. In the process there are arguments, counter arguments and further arguments; if somebody says I do not agree, then he will be given a chance to present another argument.

Actually, the growth and development of Indian philosophy has been a story of arguments and counter arguments. But these arguments have enriched the Indian philosophical thought and they have also enriched the science of dialectic. It is a whole tradition, we call it Vādaśāstra (technique of debate). There are set rules for debating. There are referees appointed. There are parameters in place and if you do not argue according to that then there are fallacies; we also study the fallacies that are known as *hetvābhāsas*. They are taught in detail in Nyāya philosophy.

To reiterate, Indian philosophy is liberal, it is tolerant but it is also based on reason — so *tarka* and *śraddhā* both go hand in hand here. When we discuss the philosophy of Upaniṣads, we shall see that Upaniṣads propound *śraddhā*, they ask us to have faith because there are some things which cannot be debated; there are certain things about which we can debate but there has to be an end to the debating process, otherwise, we cannot reach a conclusion if we just debate for the sake of debating. The purpose of debate is to reach a conclusion, first we have to have a hypothesis and further we present thesis and anti-thesis, but then finally we have to arrive at some conclusion. Therefore, there are set rules for debate but if one goes on arguing and arguing without reaching a conclusion, then there will be a fallacy known as *anavasthā doṣa* (infinite regress).

VIII. *Mokṣaparāyaṇatā (Pursuit of the Ultimate Goal)* — In the last stage, all of the systems and thinkers of Indian philosophy, they have a synthetic approach and they all believe that there is a final goal of their search. This life is not meant for only enjoying and indulging in the sensual objects, there is a higher purpose in life and that has to be pursued by different methods, different modes and different processes that have been delineated upon in each of the system. In this context, I would like to quote Kālidāsa who is a very well-known Sanskrit poet, he says:

> *bahudhāpyāgamairbhinnā panthānaḥ siddhihetavaḥ* ।
> *tvayyeva nipatantyoghā jāhnavīyā ivarṇave* ॥
>
> — *Raghuvaṁśa* 10.26
>
> (Oh Lord!) Just as different rivers go on flowing and ultimately they all merge in the ocean, similarly all the paths, leading to different standpoints they all have to merge in you, the Ultimate Reality.

So the search for Ultimate Reality, the pursuit of final goal, the quest for perfection — this is where all the thinkers and all the systems of Indian philosophy come together for understanding the nature of Ultimate Reality. They also study other traditions and that is very important because if a Nyāya scholar is writing a book of Nyāya, he has to know all the *pūrva-pakṣas* which have been presented before him; unless he is aware of all the viewpoints, he cannot do justice to the topic. This is what we do in present-day research methodology as well. We do a survey of researches in the field that we are going to work upon. Similarly, a scholar of Indian philosophy is supposed to have an understanding of all the *pūrvapakṣas*. He has to study different branches of learning. That is what has been stated by Bhartṛhari, a great scholar of Sanskrit grammar. In the *Vākyapadīyam*, he says:

> *prajñā vivekaṁ labhate bhinnairāgamadarśanaiḥ* ।
> *kiyadvā śakyamunnetuṁ svatarkamanudhāvatā* ॥
>
> — *Vākyapadīyam*, 2.489

> One's intellectual understanding acquires discriminating power when it comes in contact with different viewpoints; otherwise, how much can one elevate if he/she is only pursuing one's own reasoning?

It means that if you are only harping on the same tune, if you are reading only what you know, then you will not grow further — your knowledge will not be of any use to humanity because you have to come face to face with other branches of learning. If a Sanskritist, like me, does not try to have an exposure to other branches of learning, then there is a limitation. Therefore we have to enrich ourselves with whatever is lacking in our understanding. Bhartṛhari says, if you are only following your own tradition, then you will not reach anywhere; the intellect gets sharpened and it gets discriminating power only when it reaches out to different traditions. So, the philosophers in India were having a synthetic approach — A Mīmāṁsaka would study Buddhism although there is a long debate between the Buddhist and the Mīmāṁsaka; there is a long debate between the Jaina and the Vaiśeṣika, but they have all studied each other's tradition minutely, they have argued against these drawbacks and then they have propounded their own theories. In this process, they have not only developed their own system, and enriched their own understanding, but they have also given new dimension to the treasure of wisdom that India has developed. So, these are the basic features. There are many more features which can be listed but one thing is certain that all the systems of Indian philosophy follow a certain pattern; although they are dealing differently, they are dealing with the same concepts.

All of them are talking about the goal of knowing and whatever we are going to know, we are supposed to know that the ultimate aim of all philosophizing in India has been *mokṣa* (liberation). People may ask what is the relevance of *mokṣa* today? Who is bothered about *mokṣa*? While nobody is bothered about *mokṣa* anymore, everybody is definitely bothered about getting released from suffering – physical and mental – including the fear of the corona virus today. Mental health has become such an important issue. So what is the goal of knowing? The goal of knowing is *mokṣa*. *Mokṣa* in the traditional sense is release from the cycle of life and birth and rebirth, but *mokṣa* in contemporary sense is the release from suffering, release from ignorance. There are different dimensions to *mokṣa*, but all of them accept this as the ultimate goal of knowing. More importantly, this idea of *mokṣa* has not been discussed anywhere in Western philosophy. This is the greatest contribution of Indian philosophy that all the thinkers talk of this ideal concept of *mokṣa*, albeit in different terms.

IX. *Sapramāṇatā* (*Epistemology*) – The next characteristic of Indian philosophy is that all the Indian philosophers discuss various means of knowing. As mentioned above, all the schools of Indian philosophy discuss and define the means of knowing. Sāṁkhya will say we adopt only three means, Nyāya will say we have four means of knowing. Mīmāṁsakas will add the fifth one and Vedānta will add the sixth while the Paurāṇikas will add two more and they will say that there are eight *pramāṇas*. Several means of knowing have been defined and discussed, this is a very logical and rational process of knowing. It is not that somebody is just lecturing and the students are believing in whatever is being said, they will all apply these means of knowing to test the knowledge that is being imparted to them and then be the propagators of this knowledge further. They all have their own methods of knowing as well.

X. *Saprameyatā* (*Ontology*) – The schools of Indian philosophy also discuss different objects of knowing. For the Cārvākas, only four material objects are there, known as the four *mahābhūtas* – *pṛthvī*, *jala*, *teja* and *vāyu* – the Cārvākas do not believe in the existence of *ākāśa*. According to them, only matter is there and no spirit or *ātman* (consciousness)exists. Only four objects of material nature are there for them. For Nyāya, there are sixteen reals or objects of knowing, for Vaiśeṣika, there are seven objects of knowing, for Sāṁkhya basically there are two – *prakṛti* and *puruṣa*; then there are many evolutes of *prakṛti*, so in total there are twenty-five and when *yoga* joins in, it adds one more, i.e. God, and there are twenty-six. To put it more precisely, the objects of knowing have been defined and they have been discussed differently in various schools. In fact, the method of knowing will be useful only when we start to know something as an object; some have delineated upon the method in detail, some have not, but then they will follow what the others are following. For example, the Nyāya methodology has been adopted mostly by different schools. Vedānta follows the Nyāya methodology while dealing with the other opponents, so the methods of knowing are there and the agent or the subject – the *pramātā* the conscious agent of it is there; unless there is an agent or a subject who will be the knower, knowledge cannot be gained.

In brief, there have to be four essential components: there has to be a knower, the knowable objects, the means of knowing and a result of knowing, and that result of knowing is known as *pramā* (valid knowledge). Valid knowledge (*tattva-jñāna*) is the ultimate criterion for being eligible to reach the ultimate goal of life because this knowledge is the means to *mokṣa*. The *Gītā* says that without knowledge, *mokṣa* is not possible. Some others may talk of blending knowledge with action (*jñāna-karma-samuccaya*); there are people like Mīmāṁsakas, who say *karma* is the only way to *svarga*. For Vedānta, *jñāna* is the only means of liberation and for some of the

Mīmāṁsakas *jñāna-karma-samuccaya* (amalgamation of *jñāna* and *karma*) is the way to liberation. Thus, all these aspects have been discussed in various ways in different systems by several scholars.

Finally, it must be mentioned that the inter-school debate has been there, of course, in the form of *pūrva-pakṣa* and *uttara-pakṣa,* but intra-school debates are also there. The Indian philosophical schools are not dogmatic, because although they follow what their teachers tell them, they belong to that particular *sampradāya,* even then they can question, they can raise their objections. For example, within the Nyāya — Vaiśeṣika tradition, we had a scholar known as Raghunātha Śiromaṇi in the sixteenth century who questioned the categories or the number of *padārthas* which have been propounded by sage Kaṇāda, the propounder of Vaiśeṣika. Therefore, inter-school debates and intra-school debates — both have been described in these classical texts. As Bhartṛhari, the poet (this is another one, not the grammarian, quoted above), says:

> *yadā kiñcijjño'ham dvipa iva madāndhaḥ samabhavaṁ*
> *tadā sarvaiño'smītyabhavadavaliptaṁ mama manaḥ* ।
>
> *yadā kiñcitkiñcidbudhajanasakāśādavagataṁ*
> *tadā mūrkho'smīti jvara iva mado me vyapagataḥ*
> — *Nītiśataka* 8

> When I had little knowledge, then I had become blind by pride, like an elphant. I felt proud thinking that I am an omniscienl. But as and when I realized a bit by bit in the company of wise persons, then my pride withered away like fever subsides. — I realized that I am a fool actually.

It means, when we know little, we think that we know a lot, but when slowly and slowly we start learning, then we realize that actually we do not know anything. It means that a person who does not know anything, he thinks that he knows a lot but when he goes and sits with the senior scholars and starts learning day by day, then he realizes his limitations. Finally, he comes to know that there is still so much to be known.

Besides, there are thousands of texts in Indian philosophical tradition which have all been written mostly in Sanskrit, many of them are lying in the form of manuscripts. They need to be edited and translated and there are many more which are yet to be brought to light, so it is a very vast and rich treasure of wisdom that needs to be explored and expounded.[2] There are lakhs and lakhs of manuscripts which are lying unexplored; we do not even know which topics are there in these manuscripts. We have a very rich treasure which we should not only protect but also study and propagate.

Question and Answer Session (13 August 2021)

I think if I am able to generate a little interest in Indian philosophical thought today, then the purpose of Vivekananda International Foundation in organizing this lecture series would be achieved. If I have been able to ignite that interest I will enjoy travelling with you all in this journey towards the thinkers, their thoughts and theories.

Now we are open for questions:

DR ARVIND GUPTA: Thank you very much ShashiPrabhaji for this lecture. I think all those who have listened to you today would agree that it was an extremely clear exposition of the basics of Indian philosophy and two of the things that you dwelt upon would certainly help. You talked about the differences between Western philosophical systems and Indian philosophical systems and the absence of the idea of *mokṣa*, the need to know the Ultimate Reality that is missing in the Western philosophy, whereas that is the driving force of Indian philosophy and that makes all the difference. I think that is something which has come out very clearly and this is what we must appreciate. That itself distinguishes us from the

---

[2] Whenever I used to suggest topics to my students at Jawaharlal Nehru University, I always suggested them to go to the National Mission for Manuscripts and find out a manuscript of their area of specialization and try to read it.

rest. Second, you talked about the systems and what is common among them, there is a lot of debate but the commonalities also you brought out, I think this is what is relevant even today. So I think studying all the systems together and to find solutions to the problems of today's world would be very important; then you also talked about the lot of manuscripts which are still unexplored.

Now this is a very interesting and somewhat sad commentary that we do not seem to have many people who can and actually are very well known on this side. When there is so much which is original in the philosophical systems, am I correct to say that not enough work has been done, as a result some stagnation has also come in. Is there any need to refresh ourselves, look into these systems and also link it up with today's realities and see what the application is and finally I think I am very glad that we brought you here on this platform. I am sure what you have said is known to your students and people in the philosophical discipline and domain but if this is appreciated in strategic domain and some of its lessons can be drawn and as you said if it can ignite some minds, then we can become a little more inquisitive, particularly in the scientific domain. Many experts are here who have experience in that area but how to apply this knowledge to the strategic problems that would be a great beginning. So I will now open the floor for discussion.

AMB. SATISH CHANDRA: I would like to compliment Dr ShashiPrabha Kumar. Perhaps this is the success of India's culture that without having been aware or formally studying philosophy many of things that you said are known to me at a preliminary level. I am fully conscious about the concept of *mokṣa*, the concept of *ātman*, in my own home with parents we have learnt about many of these. That you have given it a formal underpinning which is really essential and I think the other thing which comes out is an understanding of why we are uniquely a tolerant culture and you mentioned about the liberal nature and tolerant nature in Indian philosophy; this really makes me think. Also the point you made about the need to attend to our own documents that are in original and what you ask your students to do I think this was a topic I was talking the other day. Many of us including those who do not know Sanskrit at all, this is important for us all at Vivekananda International Foundation (VIF), New Delhi.

My final point is a request to you from what the director has said, because all of us, rather many of us at VIF find that philosophy has practical underpinnings. This is a practical problem which led you discuss some of the concepts which you developed. So I would look for a future lecture in which you can touch upon some of that. Thank you very much. My deepest compliments to you for an outstanding talk.

One question here — based on the current limitless economic growth and consumption, based on Western approach has led to global problems of climate change and environmental degradation. Is there anything in Indian philosophy on how we can address an environmental problem associated with Western economic growth model?

SPEAKER: Yes Sir, there are a lot of materials in Indian tradition for meeting these concerns. In fact, I can go on lecturing for hours on environmental consciousness and the concern for protection and for optimal utilization of natural resources according to Indian philosophy. But the second part of the question that how can one address the concern related with the Western economic model that is the challenge. I suppose that is where we have to apply our minds but I can give a lot of material on the first part of the question. One of my forthcoming lectures can be scheduled on environmental consciousness in Vedas itself.

AMB. SATISH CHANDRA: Actually we do not accept Western economic growth model. Our own model for economic development is what Dr ShashiPrabha stated that optimal development strategy was not that of consumption for consumption's sake which we got from the Western model. So, I was saying that this will be useful if your subsequent lecture is on the application of Indian principles to development, whether they are of political or of economic nature, that would be useful. I suspect the answer is that our own economic model from Indian philosophy would be quite different from Western one and it would be honest optimal type of utilization which as the speaker said on environment, there are best of materials in our own philosophy. We should indicate how it could be addressed?

RAKESH KUMAR SINGH: Thank you madam for this nice presentation on Indian philosophy. I would like to go with the concern of Dr Arvind Gupta that contemporary Indian philosophers need to philosophize on the contemporary problems: social, political, strategic and others with the deep metaphysical issues. Thanks a lot.

ARVIND GUPTA: I would like to add one more question from my own side. What is the state of teaching of philosophy and research in philosophy in India. I know there is a council for Indian philosophical research and we have interacted with them also but we do not hear much from that side, so what are their views on the current issues, etc. So, maybe you could give some idea about the state of teaching and research in Indian philosophy.

SPEAKER: Yes Sir, in fact, most of the Indian universities in philosophy departments till now or a few years back, they were not teaching source texts of Indian philosophy in a substantial manner. There were parts of syllabi, that had inputs from Indian philosophy but they were not being taught properly. Twenty per cent to 25 per cent of the syllabus was from Indian philosophy but lately, the tide has turned, and now the research and studies on Indian philosophy are taking primary place in most of the departments. Most of the texts of Indian philosophy are written in Sanskrit so we have the study of Indian philosophy more in Sanskrit departments of universities rather than in the philosophy departments till now. But now with the incentives provided by the Indian Council of Philosophical Research; I am also associated with it, researches are also being done mainly on Indian philosophy. Then, of course, there are people who are dealing with these contemporary problems, ethical issues and the issues of economic growth. Gunjan Sinha is here, she has worked on ethics and *dharma* in governance. Likewise, other people have focused on Indian studies, Indian problems, but very few of them. I wish and I think that now it will grow more and more with the government support and with the global awareness also, now that Indian philosophical thought is being studied across the world, not only in India but outside India also. People are getting interested to know more about this wealth that we have as was mentioned by Amb. Satish Chandra ji. He mentioned very clearly that we have a wealth of wisdom but that wealth of wisdom should be made available to all. It was also because the knowledge of Sanskrit had been marginalized, that is the main reason, unless we know the language of these texts — the real essence of these texts will not come out. So, specially for teaching and learning the texts of Indian philosophy one not only has to learn the language; one has to be conversant with the problems of philosophy also; there has to be a two-pronged approach: one is learning the language on one side and for that we have to make it more text-based but the second step is that these texts need to be contextualized; unless the text is contextualized it will be of no use. So, we have to study the text and also to relate it with the current scenario. I think that is the need of the hour and that is precisely the idea behind VIF and its efforts to explore Indian wisdom. I remember, I first came here to participate in one of the conferences organized by VIF and that was about Indian Ethos in Management. I had myself never studied Vedas from the management point of view but when the topic was given to me, Vedas and Vedic ethos on management, I found that there was so much of material in it. In fact if we go on searching, we can get enough material from the source texts but we have to reinterpret it, we have to represent it and we have to contextualize that material in modern idiom and in modern perspective.

DR ARVIND GUPTA: Now that the government has approved the New Education Policy, I do hope some of what you have said is included in that policy. Otherwise, you would miss the chance once again.

Two more comments — one is from Col. Gautam and the other from Gunjan.

COL. GAUTAM: There are three short ones: first is concept of soul and Buddhism; second is what about *ānvīkṣikī* and third is what is Navya-Nyāya philosophy.

Speaker: Yes, your questions are short but answers to these cannot be short.

First is *ātman* in Buddhism — You see that the Buddha had never propounded the concept of *ātman*, he does not talk of it, he does not even negate. The only question is that of the continuity or the eternity of *ātman*, so the Buddha said *sarvam anityam*. The idea of *ātman* is there, the idea of continuity is there in the form of *pratītya-samutpāda*, but the concept of an eternal *ātman* is not there. That idea is not in Buddhism so that is what we call *anātma*; many people like to call it Anātmavāda, but it is not Anātmavāda like that, idea of *ātman* is there, the continuity is there, *punarjanma* is there, *karma* theory is there, but the eternity of *ātman* is not there in Buddhism.

Second question is about *ānvīkṣikī* — that is the other name for Indian logic or Nyāya Darśana, if I just go by the derivative sense because I am a Sanskritist *anvīkṣā* has two terms - *anu* and *īkṣā: anu* means after, *īkṣā* means thinking or contemplating. From *anvīkṣā* the word *ānvīkṣikī* has been derived so *anvīkṣā* means thinking after; once we see something and just keep on thinking about it, reflecting upon it, that is *anvīkṣā* — very much like the word *anumāna*: *anu* means after perception and *māna* is reasoning which takes place after the sense organ and object contact is over. Suppose I have seen something but I cannot see something beyond my eyes and later on I think about that and I reflect upon that, that is *anumāna*, and that is what *anvīkṣā* is and from *anvīkṣā* the word *ānvīkṣikī* is derived. It is the science of *anvīkṣā* which means it is the science of reasoning and argumentation, that is what the *Nyāyaśāstra* is.

As regards your third query, Navya-Nyāya is actually a later school of the Nyāya only. The ancient Nyāya almost ends up to twelfth century and from twelfth century a new style arose, a new style of writing and expressing the abstruse ideas; this was purely mathematical style. So we call them both as Prācīna Nyāya and Navya-Nyāya — the later one was devised simply to argue and to debate with the Buddhists. It was so exact and so meticulous as mathematics is, so this was a sort of code language, a style which gave rise to Navya-Nyāya. In other words, Navya-Nyāya is a branch of Nyāya only and chronologically Prācīna Nyāya was simple and direct; like in computer there are different languages, now windows is not much in use. Similarly, the Prācīna Nyāya style was not sufficient to argue with the opponents, so they devised a new style which required a lot of mental gymnastics and then only one could understand the arguments. So, this is just a new style of the same old school.

GUNJAN: Good evening madam, it is mostly to respond to Amb Satish Chandra's question. Whenever talking about practical morality, one of the things we deal with as a problem in the West is consequently portrayed as practical and not rational. We must realize that in the Indian system rationality and practicality are intertwined; what is not rational cannot be practical.

Second is the point which you talked about *ānvīkṣikī* which was in response to Col. Gautam. He must have read it that Kauṭilya considered a compulsory education for all practitioners especially in the administrative and bureaucratic field, including ambassadors. So those kind of things, the method that even we do not and are not able to immediately access that they should be brought to the forefront. As to the method in which we learnt that and in which we debated within the system and intra-system, there was the practice of *ahiṁsā*. It was not just as a moral principle, but it was being used even as the method of acquiring knowledge.

As regards the question in economic concern, there is very big difference between the West and the East. The West is more on the line of profit model; however we talk on the model of *lābha* (prosperity). Now prosperity is moral with the values like *vasudhaiva kuṭumbakam*, however *lābha* (profit) is centred around single human being and we call it being centred on homocentrism. So, taking the community together in economic progress and that way the economic progress is also ethical. So our system is completely different in economic vis-à-vis the West; that little bit I wanted to point out. And I just hope that Dr ShashiPrabha would agree to this point of view. Thank you.

KAJARI: Kauṭilya's *Arthaśāstra* invokes Sāṁkhya–Yoga and Cārvāka as types of philosophy. These schools rely on sense perception, verbal testimony and inference, the missing means of knowing here is analogy as you mentioned in your talk so my question is which *darśana* talks about analogy and how is it a source of knowledge.

Speaker: Yes, this will require another lecture actually but I can only say that analogy (*upamāna*) is explained in the Nyāya and also in Mīmāṁsā, but both of them differ in their explanation and definition of *upamāna*; both of them accept *upamāna* as a *pramāṇa*, but their conception of *upamāna* is different. When I will discuss Nyāya and Mīmāṁsā, then I will talk about the *pramāṇas* in detail. Basically *upamāna* is based on the similarity between two objects.

ARVIND GUPTA: Ok I think there are no more questions and we are also now near the end of the session, so I want to thank Dr ShashiPrabha Kumar again and also all the participants for joining in this talk. I think we had a very good beginning and I am sure you would have a lot of interesting things coming in the future lectures and with that I want to close the session. Thank you very much.

Environmental Awareness in Vedas

AT THE outset, I would like to quote the definition of environment which has been given in the Environment Protection Act, 1986, as follows:

> Environment includes water, air and land and the interrelationship which exists among and between water, air, land and human beings, other living creatures, plants, micro-organisms and property.

In this background, environment has been classified into several types, but mainly and broadly, into three types: the solid, liquid and gaseous; this is also known as the lithosphere, hydrosphere and atmosphere besides biosphere. The Sanskrit word for environment is *paryāvaraṇa* which is different from *vātāvaraṇa* because *vātāvaraṇa* connotes only atmosphere; this is related to air while environment (*paryāvaraṇa*) is all that encompasses us. In Hindu philosophy, we basically have the notion of five elements: earth, water, air, fire and sky; beyond these there are many aspects of nature and interrelation with these aspects of nature has been the distinctive feature of Vedic philosophy. Vedic philosophy envisages that each entity of the universe – be it a stone or a human being – is intertwined and interconnected; nothing exists in isolation. In view of this, Vedas propound that all of us, especially the human beings, because we are the most intelligent ones (although there is unmanifest consciousness in the trees also that has been accepted in Indian sourcebooks, but mainly the human beings) are obliged to have a friendly relation with each aspect of nature. It is not only care, concern or fondness of nature like we are doing it today in the form of a fashion, rather it is the emotional bonding with nature which has been emphasized as in the following verse from the *Yajurveda* (*YV*):

> *mitrasyāhaṁ cakṣuṣā sarvāṇi bhūtāni samīkṣe* ।
> *mitrasya cakṣuṣā samīkṣāmahe* ॥ — 36.18

I should look at everything with a friendly eye and all the aspects of nature should also look at me with a friendly eye.

The *Atharvaveda* (*AV*) goes beyond that and says:

> *yāṅśca paśyāmi yāṅśca na teṣu mā sumatiṁ kr̥dhi* । — *AV*, 17.1.07

Those which I can see and even those which I cannot see — I should have a goodwill towards every being.

In fact, there are countless aspects of nature, some of them are visible and some are not. "I should have goodwill towards everything around me"; it is not just a selfish concern for an individual's progress which will lead us to a happy family and healthy society. It has to be a genuine goodwill and a sincere concern for everything around us. In Indian way of life, there has been this tradition of reciprocal approach towards the cosmic existence. When we approach nature, we should do it with reverence and not as a resource with an indulgent attitude. The experience of indulgence and gratification is not denied in Vedic view but this has to be restrained and respectful. The very first verse of the *Īśāvāsyopaniṣad,* which is also the 40th chapter of the *Yajurveda,* says:

> *tena tyaktena bhuñjīthā mā gr̥dhaḥ kasyasvid dhanam* ।
> — *YV*, 40.01

Enjoy the material world with a sense of renunciation; do not be greedy. To whom do the riches belong?

There are three statements in the above verse:

- First is *tena tyaktena*: We should seek the material pleasures, we should enjoy the natural resources but with the feeling of renunciation. *Tena tyaktena bhuñjīthā* is what Mahatma Gandhi preached and practised; In fact the aspect of *aparigraha is* implied in it. Various systems of Indian philosophy proclaim that we should cultivate, collect and enjoy as much as we need, not beyond that, because that will make us greedy. So we should enjoy with *tyāga-bhāva*, *bhoga* and *tyāga* are to be practised together.

- Second statement is: *mā gr̥dhaḥ*, it explicitly says that one should not have greed towards natural resources.
- And the third statement is: *kasyasvid dhanam* because the money does not (permanently) belong to anybody.

Natural resources are not in the form of money only, they are of course the natural wealth but this natural wealth is not created by us. This is not just for us, we have to share it with others since there is an interconnection among various forms of life. Therefore, we should share it with everybody around us.

It is worth mentioning here that *R̥gveda* (*R̥V*) is the oldest and the first among literary documents in the history of humankind and this has been accepted by UNESCO in its "Memory of the World Register 2007". Vedas are generally known as a scripture of Hindus. However, being the earliest literature in the history of humankind, they transcend far beyond their identity. It needs to be clarified that although Vedas are associated with a particular religion, i.e Hinduism, when we are talking about environmental awareness in Vedas, it is not just as a scripture of a particular religion. We have to go beyond the borders of religion, beyond the borders of a country transcend geographical boundaries and we have to go beyond many other boundaries; we have to explore all those aspects which are valuable for the whole human kind, for the cosmic existence and cosmic harmony, especially in view of the post-Corona situation that the world is facing. Corona virus has proved that there is no geographical limit. We in India were always proclaiming *vasudhaiva kuṭumbakam*, but now this pandemic has demonstrated, albeit in a negative situation, that the whole earth is one family. When the nature comes of its own, there is no limit, there is no distinction — if somebody makes a mistake somewhere, everybody will be affected across the globe. So, we have to have a broader outlook and search for such ideas which can help us in these troubled times.

There is one of the hymns of the *Atharvaveda,* which is often quoted in this regard, it is the Pṛthvī Sūkta (*Atharvaveda*, chap. 12). This has sixty-three verses, but more inportantly, earth here is not only invoked as a geographical entity or the physical earth, but it is symbolic of everything that grows and exists on earth and in this hymn there are many more valuable ideas worth emulating. First of all, it signifies that there are many aspects of existence; the Vedic view in general is holistic and it encompasses all the aspects of life. The Pṛthvī Sūkta of the *Atharvaveda* is a good example of that. The human beings, natural elements like earth, water, air, fire and sky; insects, serpentiles, animals, birds, rivers, mountains, seasons, trees and forests, physical as well as non-physical aspects, have all been described and invoked in this hymn. But anybody can say as to what is so novel about it; there are descriptions of nature in many literatures of the world. The most distinctive feature of this hymn is that here it is not only the depiction of these aspects but the underlying emotional bonding between human beings and various aspects of nature is expressed in an incomparable manner.

There is another verse in the *Ṛgveda* which says:

dyaur vaḥ pitā pṛthvī mātā somo bhrātā । — *Ṛ*V, I.191.6

Earth is your mother, moon is your brother and the sky is your father.

Obviously here is a personification of natural forces in these verses, not just personification as a literary figure of speech but as a way of life; this is not just a view of life that is being propounded. The Veda says that the seers get their wisdom awakened only at the valley of the mountains and at the confluence of rivers:

upahvare girīṇāṁ saṅgame ca nadīnām ।
dhiyā vipro ajāyata ॥ — YV 26.15

The wisdom of sages is generated in the solitude of valleys, in the high mountains and confluence of rivers.

Three spheres of the universe have been enumerated in Vedic philosophy and these are — (i) the ground or the solid earth (*pr̥thvīsthānīya*), (ii) the intermediary or the mid-space (*antarikṣasthānīya*), and (iii) the uppermost or the celestial (*dyusthānīya*) — these three are not only present around us, they are also present within our body. There is another concept of Vedic philosophy which is subtle and important. This is *yathā piṇḍe tathā brahmāṇḍe. Piṇḍa* is this body, so whatever exists within this body, the same exists outside in the *brahmāṇḍa* and there is a parity between the *piṇḍa* (microcosm) and *brahmāṇḍa* (macrocosm). In this background, the earth is not just the locus of everything, it is also the mother of everything, it nourishes everything. It nurtures everything, and everything happens on this earth.

As regard to the Vedic ideas which are important for today, we must remember three basic ideas from the Vedic philosophy:

- first, there has to be a reciprocal approach. If we just go on exploiting nature and its resources for our enjoyment, one day the same severe consequences will have to be faced by humanity that we are facing today. Mere exploitation of natural resources will not work.
- We have to replenish the resources too.
- We have to take care of the resources, we have to take as much as we need and we do not have to, we should not, we cannot afford to waste these natural resources as we are doing carelessly today. We are wasting, we are polluting and we are not at all grateful to these divine forces of nature. In this scenario, if we go on wasting natural resources, then we have to face the fierce form of Nature.

There are two aspects of nature. One is benign (*saumya*) and the other is fierce (*ugra*). The Sanskrit poets like Kālidāsa, Vālmīki and Vyāsa have described both these aspects of nature. This fierce form of nature is not natural, this is not normal, this is something exceptional and this is, in fact, a warning to humanity. The laws of nature have to be respected and if we keep on disturbing the benign being of nature, then we have to face very serious consequences in the form of natural disasters like Corona virus.

As already stated, there are sixty-three verses in the hymn to earth and the first verse gives a clue in the form of six factors which can sustain this earth. The first line of the first verse of Pṛthvī Sūkta is as follows:

> *satyaṁ bṛhad ṛtam ugraṁ dīkṣā tapo brahma yajñaḥ pṛthvīṁ dhārayanti* । — *AV* 12.1.1
>
> Great truth, formidable right, consecration, penance, ever-evolving knowledge (*Brahman*) and sacrifice sustain the earth.

These six factors sustain the earth and as mentioned earlier, earth is not just a geological entity here; earth is symbolic of all the natural phenomena and all the forms of life. Now let us discuss these six factors:

i. *Satyaṁ bṛhat*: *Satyaṁ* means truth but not just truth, *bṛhat satyaṁ* is the greater truth. What is the greater truth? When I only deal with my own personal motive and selfish interest, then it is *satyaṁ*, but when I care for others around me, then it becomes *bṛhat satyaṁ*, and Pṛthvī Sūkta is talking of the whole earth, it says that consecration for cosmic harmony is the greatest truth of them all, so we have to take care, we have to prepare our self to this greater truth, for the common causes.

ii. *Ṛtam ugram*: *Ṛtam* is an important concept of Vedas, which suggests the rhythm of nature: please note the resonance between rhythm and *ṛtam*. *Ṛtam* is the cosmic law which permeates through all forms of existence. This *ṛtam* is the controller of the universe but here an adjective is also added *ugraṁ ṛtam*. *Ugraṁ* means fierce. The concept of *ṛtam* signifies that the sun rises in the east every morning, it sets in the west every evening; there is a regular cycle of climate and change of seasons. The rain is happening at a particular time, similarly, between the summer and the winter, there is a regular cycle. They all follow the cosmic law and that is known as *ṛtam* but these days we are seeing various violations of natural laws and therefore *ṛtam* has become *ugram.* If we cross the line of *ṛtam* then we reap the fierce consequence in the *ugra* form of *ṛtam*. In other words, the fear from fierce laws of nature is implied in the *ṛtam ugram,* we must be afraid of this and should not waste the natural resources.[1] We cannot even imagine the massive wastage that we are doing today, while thousands and crores of people are sleeping hungry everyday in our country. We are wasting food, water and all the natural resources, while there is scarcity of all these resources. So, this is what *ṛtam ugram* suggests that we should be afraid of such wasteful acts, these are sinful acts. If we cross the laws of cosmic laws, cosmic norms, then we have to bear the brunt of *ṛtam ugraṁ.*

iii. *Dīkṣā*: *Dīkṣā* is the dedication for maintaining ecological balance. You see the word ecology was coined very recently, then came the term deep ecology, followed by the GAIA theory but all these are only associated with the development of the nineteenth and twentieth century. Vedas were composed thousands of years earlier, so this is not just for one particular section of humanity, these are the universal

---

[1] I remember that when we were young, our grandmother would tell us that नमक भूमि पर नहीं गिराना, नहीं तो पलकों से उठाना पड़ेगा; पानी नहीं फैलाना, नहीं तो पाप लगेगा। Whenever we were wasting some food or water, we were told that खाना झूठा नहीं छोड़ना, नहीं तो पाप लगेगा (या अन्न देवता का अपमान होगा).

guiding principles which have been charted and given to us long ago. In short, dedication or mission for maintaining ecological balance is *dīkṣā*.

iv. *Tapas*: *Tapas* is the perseverance for fulfilment of the above pledge or *dīkṣā* that we have undertaken. *Tapas* means concentrated effort towards a mission. When we take a mission, we have to fulfil that mission and efforts for fulfilling that mission come under *tapas*.

v. *Brahma*(*n*): Notably, there are two words — one is Brahmā and other is *Brahma*(*n*). There is a huge difference and a gap of thousands of years between these two words and their connotation. In Vedas, we find the word *Brahma*(*n*) which is in neuter gender, *Brahman* signifies knowledge itself. The word *veda* also signifies knowledge. But *veda* is not ordinary knowledge; likewise, *Brahman* is not ordinary knowledge. The word *Brahman* is derived from the root *bṛṁh*, meaning that which grows constantly. So knowledge which keeps on geowing with the new challenges, it is not static — it is dynamic knowledge which evolves as per existing or emerging challenges. When the new challenges come, it refreshes itself. It takes a new form and that knowledge is known as *Brahma*(*n*). In this verse of the Veda, *Brahman* (knowledge) is not for individual concern, this is for universal well-being because it is ever-growing, ever-evolving knowledge — this is for the whole of humanity. We should cultivate such knowledge in these times when the world is facing this greatest challenge in the form of the pandemic corona. Everybody is joining hands to have some escape from the dreaded disease; the vaccine is being developed in some countries and the trial is being done; after this trial, everybody will be having a privilege to use it. So, this knowledge is not for a particular section of humanity or a particular section of land; this is universal knowledge which is known as *Brahma*(*n*).

vi. Finally, the concept of *yajña*. By the word *yajña*, we usually understand that this is a religious ritual. But, actually, this is not just a ritual. *Yajña* is the most important clue, the key concept of Vedic philosophy for sustaining the environment, for maintaining ecological balance. The *yajña* is in fact the idea of offering oneself for collective good. The word is derived from a root *yaj*, which connotes three meanings:

- The first is *deva-pujā* (propitiating the divine natural forces); that is one aspect of it and that may be taken to be a religious rite, but there is much more implied in it.
- Next meaning of the root *yaj* is *saṅgatīkaraṇa*, it is a communitarian concept which means meeting and sharing ideas, that is also *yajña* suggested by *saṅgatīkaraṇa.* Right now, we are holding this academic session which is also *saṅgatīkaraṇa.* We are here, we have joined here to collectively think of some ways and means for solving the problems that we have been facing over the years. That is *saṅgatīkaraṇa.* This is also *yajña.* Anything which is not concerned with an individual alone, and where benefit of others is also taken into consideration, that is *yajña.*
- The third meaning of *yajña* is *dāna. Dāna* means sharing of resources. If a particular individual or a country has some resources, it cannot contain all the resources for itself. It has to share with others, so this sharing, this giving away, that is known as *dāna*. Therefore, *yajña* has many broad ideas connected with this. *Yajña* is not just the ritual; from ritual, we have to transcend up to the spiritual and this has been stated in the Veda itself:

  ayaṁ yajño bhuvanasya nābhiḥ । — *YV*, 23.62

  Yajña is the genesis, this is the centre point of the universe.

Besides this basic concept of *yajña*, we also have the five types of *yajña* which have been assigned and prescribed for every householder. Let us just have a look at these five types of *yajña*:

- The first is *brahma-yajña,* which means reading and reflecting upon ever growing knowledge for the welfare of everyone, that is what is *brahma-yajña.* Anything when we read, when we contemplate, when we meditate and when we think of others, that is *brahma-yajña.* If a scientist is working in a lab, he is doing *brahma-yajña* because he is searching the stock of knowledge for the benefit of humanity.
- The second is *deva-yajña* by what we usually understand the ritual, but that is in fact *agnihotra,* offering something into fire for the sake of divine forces. Although that also has a significance, yet it is not just a mechanical act, it has some inherent aspect as well.
- Then the third is *pitṛ-yajña*, which signifies respecting and taking care of the elders in the family and society. In ancient Indian tradition, there was the system of joint family; each family had some elderly people and they were duly respected and taken care of. The elders deserve reverence, respect, affection and care; so every householder is obliged to do this *pitṛ-yajña* in his/her home everyday.
- The fourth one is *atithi-yajña.* It means that whenever somebody, a guest, comes to our home unannounced, we have to respect him/her, we have to offer him/her water, food with respect and seek his/her blessings.
- The fifth and the last one is *bhūta-yajña* which is for the other beings: for the birds, for the insects, for the animals; before we start eating, we are obliged to offer food for all these forms of life. If we go back to our past three generations, in our kitchens, our grandmothers used to first cook a small *roṭī* for offering to the cow. People used to give some grains for the birds and insects. So this is known as *bhūta-yajña.*

The above are five aspects of *yajña,* all these acts are inherently related; in our ancient tradition they were connected to religious routine with a specific motive because if one connects these ideas with religion, then people follow them with a feeling of devotion; there were, and still are, lots of people who are used to offer water to *tulasī* plant as a daily religious practice. It means that even if one does not understand the significance or logic behind it; at least one is taking care of nature. Thus, in Vedas we have plenty of prayers where the welfare of birds and animals is sought, and a lot of animals are described there, the whole biodiversity has been enumerated and many researches have been done about this aspect, but here we are mainly discussing about the concept of *yajña*. So it would be worthwhile to note that many scientific experiments have also been going on around the world for examining the positive effect of this principle of *yajña*.

There are a number of places where investigation about *yajña*s is going on:

a. In the year 2006-07, at the School of Environmental Sciences, in Jawaharlal Nehru University, a lecture by two German scholars was organised and they demonstrated the positive effects of homatherapy on agriculture. They had an inverted copper pyramid which is known as *havana-kuṇḍa*. Several scientific evidences have been documented that when fire is ignited in an inverted copper pyramid which has certain specifications — when one puts some cow-dung cakes into it at the time of sunset and sunrise, and recites some *mantra*s after igniting fire into that copper pyramid, there are some scientific changes in the air and in the environment around. They are still pursuing the research and anybody can find further details on the website www.homatherapie.de
b. Here in India also we have the Yajñopathy lab at Brahmavarchas Shodha Sansthana in Shantikunj, Haridwar, where the integrated science of *yajña* and its effects are being studied.
c. In the Jawaharlal Nehru Medical College at Ajmer, Dr Vijay Lata Rastogi in the microbiology department conducted a

research on Homatherapy in 2011 and obtained some positive results.

d. Homatherapy in India was propounded by Shree Vasant Paranjpe in the year 1973. He established the first fire temple in Madison, Virginia. He is the disciple of Shri Gajanan Maharaj of Akkalkot in India. Shree Paranjpe pioneered the use of Homatherapy in agriculture, psychotherapy, alternative medicine, self-development and healing the environment. He has also authored a book titled *Homatherapy: Our Last Chance* (2020).

e. We all know of the Bhopal gas tragedy and there is a documented evidence in the newspaper *Hindu* of 19 May 1985 Delhi Edition that two families (of Mr Kushwaha and Mr Rathore) were saved from the side effects of gas tragedy because they were regularly performing *homa* in their houses before the tragedy took place.

What follows from the above is that *yajña* is an important Vedic clue for saving the environment. This is not just ecology or deep ecology, this is in fact the deepest ecology that India has developed and needs to be practised and propagated. As already stated, corona has crossed all the boundaries and we have to have a broader outlook and bring these valuable ideas into practice; these ideas are not just theoretical, but they are the tested and tried practices of our tradition for centuries.

Obviously, *yajña* is the most important clue for meeting the challenge of environmental pollution. Even if we do not believe in the religiosity of the act, this needs to be practised simply for the sake of the environment.

Just like *yajña*, the idea of *yoga* is thousands of years old. In India it was always a practice, but it has caught the attention of the world after Shri Narendra Modi ji, honourable Prime Minister of India, propagated it not only as a theory but through his own personal example. Now people across the world have started practising and benefitting from it.

Recently, the whole world saw that when the French President and the German Chancellor met, they greeted each other with *namaste* posture (greeting with folded hands) and not with hands-shake due to ill effects of corona. *Namaste* is the Indian way of greeting which is practised for thousands of years but now with the onslaught of this pandemic, people are motivated to use this hand-posture as a safe and hygeinic way of greeting each other.

Coming back to the above six Vedic ideas from the Pr̥thvī Sūkta of the *Atharvaveda* it must be mentioned that there are thousands of more such ideas. Many researches have been done and many more are still being conducted which can take us to the new frontiers of knowledge. It is our duty and obligation not only for ourselves but for the welfare of humanity that we think seriously about these traditions. Now the time has gone when anything Indian and anything ancient was looked up and looked down; the perception has changed. Now anything Indian and anything ancient is seen with respect. So we have to move away from sheer consumerism, from overindulgence. We have to come to the philosophy of restraint which our prime minister very rightly quoted recently in one of his lectures as *saṁyama*; the word *saṅyama* had been lost somewhere, *saṅyama* is the idea of enjoying with restraint as quoted above from the *Yajurveda*:

tena tyaktena bhunjīthāḥ

first *tyāga* and then *bhoga.*

Another verse of the *Yajurveda* says that one should aspire to be engaged in action through out life:

kurvanneveha karmāṇi jijīviśecchataṁ samāḥ ॥ — *YV*, 40.2

It means that we have to be proactive for hundreds of years; we have to live, but not in an idle manner; we have to be active throughout our lives. These days, we have the *I Phone* and *Youtube*

— *I* and *U*. This "I" and "you" have been explained by our greatest traditional scholar Śrī Śaṅkarācārya when he wrote his commentary on the *Vedāntasūtra*. He began his commentary of the *Brahmasūtra* with the idea of *asmat* and *yuṣmat* — *asmat* means "I" and *yuṣmat* means "you", which encompasses the whole world. But now this "I" and "you" have just become very limited, a technical notion has overpowered the broad essence of these terms. The inherent interpersonal human concern has been lost, that has to be brought in again and we have to cross over; not just pray for ourselves — we have to pray for others around us as well. That is the basic idea that we have to practise again which our forefathers were practising. Let us conclude with a prayer for universal peace from the *Yajurveda* —

> *oṁ dyauḥ śāntirantarikṣaṁ śāntiḥ pr̥thivī śāntirāpaḥ śāntiroṣadhayaḥ śāntiḥ vanaspatayaḥ śāntirviśvedevāḥ śantirbrahma śāntiḥ sarvaṁ śāntiḥ śāntireva śāntiḥ sā mā śāntiredhi* । *oṁ śāntiḥ śāntiḥ śāntiḥ* । — *YV*, 36.17

> The earth is peaceful, the mid-space is peaceful, the trees are peaceful, forests are peaceful, may the sky be peaceful, may the earth be peaceful, may the waters be peaceful, may the plants be peaceful, may the forests be peaceful, may all the bounties of nature be peaceful, may the knowledge be peaceful, may all the things be peaceful, may there be peace and peace. May that peace come to me.

This means that everywhere there is peace and the same peace which prevails everywhere around should come to us.

Obviously, the problem is that everywhere around, there is peace but there is no peace within one's own being. If there is peace within oneself, then everything will be peaceful; with this *mantra* of *śānti-pāṭha* we not only pray for peace, we also act for peace; we just arise and awake for bringing peace on earth. The current talk of the scientific wisdom is worthwhile but it is only the mechanical aspect which needs to be coupled with the spiritual outlook that the Vedic philosophy provides; this blend of both these aspects which the *Īśopaniṣad* very beautifully enunciates in the terms of *vidyā* and *avidyā*, *sambhūti* and *asambhūti* — this joining of the twins, complementarity of binary aspects is missing, we have to bring it back. May God give us capacity to actualize our good intentions so that we perform good actions and may our good actions accomplish these goals that we are desiring and aspiring.

Question and Answer Session

SPEAKER: Let me mention that I got an advance question from Col. Pradeep Gautam for today's talk and I do share his concern and his sentiments towards this polluted environment, his question is: Why is it that our ancient wisdom on ecology in Vedas is not visible at the practical level? Is it due to economic version and corporate greed that we conveniently call Western? So, where do we place and locate the *dharma* and *karma* of intellectual academics and scholars? In this regard, are these just theoretical ideas?

This is his question and as an answer to this question, I would say that as academicians and intellectuals, it is our duty to explore and expound such ideas and then propagate them among masses, among such platforms where some policymaking can be influenced. We as academicians have no direct control over policymaking, But, we have to bring in these ideas — I do not think these ideas are very well known to our society or in our academic circles as these ideas are not taught beyond the departments of Sanskrit across the country. But these ideas are quite valuable, they need to be projected and propagated so that we can do our bit towards the society and world at large

AMB. SATISH CHANDRA: Thank you ShashiPrabha ji for enumerating your excellent exposition. The point that I wanted you to discuss is natural that personally many of my generation may be aware of these ideas, to be conscious of the need to be careful about the environment and to use only what is essential of the environment. Most of us have been aware of it not because we learnt in books but we learnt from our elders. The problem that arises internationally is that now-a-days there is very little awareness of this. It has come about under the pressure of climate change to some extent. But in practice it is being done in our own country. Of course, the way out perhaps for us in India is more education and more classes on this issue but on the wider domain you mentioned that we should not be wasteful about the resources and we have consumeristic society world over which is terribly wasteful about all that. Now I do not know as to what is the best way to go about. But I believe we need to constantly think about it and one of the ways of course is what the director has said about the greater knowledge in this respect could be imparted in schools and colleges, and in national and international community. But I think we all need to contemplate as to how and what is the best way of going about that.

Q — Somebody asked Swami Vivekananda used to say it is in the practice of *pañca-mahāyajñas,* from the practice it will revitalize. ... So how to do this?

SPEAKER: First of all, I thank Shri Satish Chandra ji. Actually, it was his question last month which propelled me to think of this topic although I had planned another topic for my second lecture under the series and according to the structure that was prepared earlier. But I thought I would begin with this very important topic which is also related to the current situation. Sir, your question was how to implement Vedic ideas. If I understood it well, then it is only possible through our own individual effort, if we keep on waiting for the government or for the policy makers, that will take time; the only thing that we can do is that wherever we are stationed, in whatever position we are, we should start practicing these ideas. For example, we at Bharatiya Vidya Bhavan are also performing the *agnihotra* first Wednesday of every month and we are also teaching our students to perform it and they are enjoying learning it. For my own individual self, I can say that since the day this lockdown started I have been performing *homa* daily not for my personal well-being but for everyone around me; I think each one of us can begin at his or her own level; that is the most possible, most efficient and most easy solution for this problem. If once you start doing it, then it goes on from one to ten, ten to hundred and like that. Somewhere we have to make the beginning and the beginning is possible at the earliest and the shortest time; it is within our own hands.

The second question was about the *pañca-mahāyajña*, I did not go in detail but Swami Vivekananda has rightly said that these practices can revitalize our society because these are meant not for just one individual or one family but for the whole extended family across the world. *Brahma-yajña* is for our own progress and enhancement of colletive wisdom. *Deva-yajña* is for nurturing the nature. *Pitr̥-yajña* is for the well-being of the elders in every family. *Atithi-yajña* is for the well-being of the society and *bhūta-yajña* is for other living beings that exist around us. In short, this is just one idea, we have many such ideas in our tradition.

Another idea is of *r̥ṇa-traya*. It means that according to Vedic philosophy each one of us is born with three debts: *r̥ṇa-traya* (three obligations) — first is the *deva-r̥ṇa*, we are born with *deva-r̥ṇa*, a debt on us all and that debt is towards the *devas* (divine forces), so we are obliged to take care of nature because we are indebted to nature. After *deva-r̥ṇa* comes *r̥ṣi-r̥ṇa*. *R̥ṣis* are the ancient seers and preceptors and we are indebted to them because it is their knowledge that we are inheriting and enriching ourselves with and transmitting to the next generation. Therefore, we are obliged to our ancestors, to the seers and preceptors. The third one is *pitr̥-r̥ṇa*, we are indebted to our parents because they are the ones who brought us into the world and gave us life with all the required lessons.

Along with the three *r̥ṇas* and *pañca-mahāyajñas* we have the idea of *puruṣārtha-catuṣṭaya* (four pursuits of human beings), they are: *dharma, artha, kāma* and *mokṣa*. Somebody might say these are only individual pursuits but even if these are individual pursuits and if everybody pursues his or her own duty seriously, there is no doubt that everybody will benefit from it and there will be less of clash, less of conflict in society. If we are conscious of our own duties, then others' rights will automatically be protected. From this point of view, Vedic philosophy is so rich, so deep and so subtle that it cannot be encompassed in a limited lecture or write up but at least it gives us a glimpse into the worthy ideas which are available. These ideas are universal, there is no distinction based on any caste, colour, creed, clime or time. These are the ideas which can be practised by anyone and anywhere. As mentioned by Dr Gupta, the idea of *yoga* has been adopted by the world, the idea of *namaste* is gaining ground but now the idea of *yajña* needs to be propagated, not only in the ritual sense but also in its deeper spiritual sense. We have to propagate it because this is also very typical Vedic idea which is there in our tradition, the four Vedas begin with the invocation to fire. The first verse of each of the Vedas is related to *agni* (fire) and *yajña*.

One more thing needs to be noted here is that in the Vedic tradition we find the very first dictionary of Vedas known as *Nighaṇṭu;* this is created and authored by a *ṛṣi* called Yāska, his time may be around 700 BCE (approx). Yāska's *Nighaṇṭu* is a Vedic dictionary, dictionary of synonymous terms which have been used in Vedas. You will be amazed to know that for the connotation of earth there are twenty-one names, there are one hundred and one names for water; it indicates that these people must have been very close to nature. Their observations for water are in different shapes, different shades and different aspects — one hundred and one names for water; sixteen names for the mid-space; thirty names for the cloud, thirty-seven names for the river; sixteen names for the dawn (Uṣā); fifteen names for the rays of sun; twenty-four names for the sky and earth; the dual deity called *dyāvāpṛthvī* and last, but not the least, there are fifteen names of *yajña*. *Yajña* is also known as *adhvara*, i.e. where there is no violence, where there is no negativity. That is what *adhvara* is. So a linguistic study or philological study of these terms must also be undertaken. Many of these ideas have already been analysed but much more needs to be done in the philosophy of Vedas relating with the current context. That is what needs to be done. Dr Gupta, you have very rightly suggested that we can collect various *śānti-pāṭhas* from Vedas. We can bring out at least one hundred *śānti-mantras*. There is a whole chapter on *śānti* where the word *śanno (-śaṁ+no)* is repeatedly used: *śaṁ* means peace and *no* means for all of us. Nowhere it is said 'just for me only'. In many of the *śānti-pāṭhas* it is prayed as follows:

> *śanno dvipade śaṁ catuṣpade.*
>
> May there be peace for the bipeds and quadrupeds ... may there be peace for humans and the animals.

It means that peace was aspired for everybody, the rivers, the mountains, for every aspect of nature. In brief, this is so rich and elevating philosophy that it can inspire many of us in this doomsday, in this very difficult and desperate situation that we are placed in today. Thank you.

SHRI BASANT GUPTA: My question was with regard to the moving away from greed and focusing on human need because if I recall correctly, the *Hitopadeśa* says you can offer a river of gold to humans and they will never be satiated. So my question is: how do we work on people that they can act with the sense of detachment, *tyāga* and renunciation, and move away from this greed? Thank you.

SPEAKER: Thank you Shri Basant Gupta ji. This is an eternal question which has been bothering humanity, not only in modern times but also from ancient times. The idea which you talked of is also found in the *Kaṭhopaniṣad* in different words as a statement of Naciketā. Naciketā is the young boy to whom Lord Yama lures that I will give you so much of gold, so many pleasures to enjoy but do not ask me the question regarding life after death. However Naciketā stays firm and says:

> *na vittena tarpaṇīyo manuṣyaḥ* । — *Kaṭha Upaniṣad* 1.27
>
> No human being can ever be satiated with wealth or money.

If we ask the richest person in the world today whether he is satisfied, he will say he does not know, because actually he is not satisfied even today. Nobody will ever be satisfied with whatever amount of money he or she has. This truth had been visualized by Naciketā, a young boy of 12-13 years, in ancient times. Today the West is teaching us how they have brought us to this mindset of "dominion over nature", which they have practised for the past 2,000 years only but long before that we had been living in "communion with nature"; today we are very wise and very well read but what are the consequences of our consumeristic attitude. We can choose whether we want to have a "dominion over nature" or we should live in "communion with nature". As far as this question of people and teaching them, weaning them away from greed and leading them to satisfaction, it is an open ended question in front of everybody – whether we need satisfaction or whether we need dissatisfaction. In fact, these were the basic values which were being taught to our generation by our earlier generations from the childhood itself. But today nobody listens to the older generation. Everybody wants to learn it from his or her own experience. Therefore we see that the corporate professionals are fed up of this excessive race after money at a very young age of 45-50. Hence, this idea of restraint has to be brought in by the philosophical attitude as nothing else can help. As stated earlier the idea of *aparigraha* is there in Yoga philosophy, it is there in Jaina philosophy and it is there in Buddhism as well. In Indian thought it is permeated everywhere that money is not the only pursuit. Out of the four pursuits in Hindu philosophy: *dharma* is the first, *artha* is the second but *artha* is not independent, only *artha* cannot lead you to prosperity nor to peace, none of these will come with money alone. *Artha* needs to be regulated by *dharma* and pursued for *mokṣa*; only then it will be satisfying. These ideas need to be taught to the younger generation but before we teach them to younger people we have to practise ourselves, if we practise, it does make a powerful influence. If Gandhi ji did not practise *aparigraha* himself, then he could not have talked of it; he was practising it with very few possessions and he was living in a satisfied manner. These days each one of us knows that in this lockdown period we can lead our life peacefully with very limited resources and actually there are only limited requirements. In fact, very little is needed for a happy and contented life. If we go on running after this race for money, then there is no end. ... We have to realize it, we have to absorb it and then we have to get it imbibed by our family members and then from one family it goes on to other families. Even in our surroundings, we can see, we get inspired from such noble persons who have so much of wealth but they do not show, they do not run after money; they want to live a peaceful life. Unfortunately, we have come from need to greed, now we have to take a U-turn from greed to need, that is the minimum we all have to do.

Vedic Feminism

WHEN we say "Vedic Feminism", it should be clear that Vedic feminism is much beyond the concerns of what we understand by feminism these days in other parts of the world. "Vedic Feminism" is in sharp contrast with the current manifestation of the aggressive movement which was originated in the West for activity on behalf of women's right to equality. Vedic view is basically characterized by an inherent spiritual outlook which projects a perfect parity between women and men in every sphere of life and existence as we shall see. It is neither exclusive nor radical in its approach; rather, it reflects a positive and participatory, constructive and complementary, healthy and holistic viewpoint for the needs and aspirations of a gender-just egalitarian society.

> *tvaṁ strī tvaṁ pumānasi* । — *AV* 10.8.27
>
> Oh God! you are a female and a male as well.

So says the Veda. On the spiritual level, there is no difference between women and men according to Vedic view, both are said to be born as two equal parts of the same substance:

> *tasmāt ardhaṁ vr̥galam iva svaḥ* । — *Br̥Up* 1.4.3
>
> Therefore, both of us are like half of the sprouted seed.

Just as one seed of a cereal sprouts into two equal halves, similarly woman and man are born as two equal halves of the Supreme Being. There is no better half or worse half, just two equal halves. From this point of view, equality between both the sexes is an inherent feature of Vedic philosophy. This metaphysical presupposition is very well reflected in the later conceptions of *prakr̥ti* and *puruṣa* in the realm of Sāṁkhya philosophy while the idea of Ardhanārīśvara in the field of Hindu mythology does not envisage any distinction between woman and man. It is a relation of total identity or inseparability because none can do without the other.

But even if we come down from the spiritual realm to the empirical realm, the concept of complementarity between both the sexes is the core of Vedic philosophy, which is deeply rooted in the Vedic idea of duality or bipolarity. Accordingly, Agni and Soma are said to be two constituents of the world, it is said:

agnīṣomātmakam viśvam । — *Bṛhajjābālopaniṣad* I.4

This world is constituted of twin principles: Agni and Soma.

The same is also manifested as *rayi* and *prāṇa* in Vedic view, they are seemingly opposite, but they represent the matter and energy matrix for creation; and both of them are required as essential for creation. No creation can take place from one element. The fact is very well expressed at the worldly level through the Vedic ritual of marriage, i.e. *saptapadī* ritual which is still in practice in Hindu marriages. Vedic marriage ceremony not only signifies equal status of husband and wife but also solicits benign friendship between both of them. The last and the most important step in this *saptapadī* is:

sakhe saptapadī bhava । — *Pāraskara Gṛhyasūtra* 1.8

Oh wife! come and take the seventh step; let us be friends.

There is another statement in the Brāhmaṇa text:

ehi jāye svarārohava । — *Śatapatha Brāhmaṇa* 5.2.1.10

Oh wife! come, both of us ascend to heaven, the abode of joy.

Obviously, the husband does not even think of ascending to heaven alone, there also he invites his wife and the address that he is making to his wife is *jāyā*. In fact, three terms are used in Vedas for a wife: *jāyā*, *jani* and *patnī*. *Jāyā* is the lady who gives birth to his progeny. *Jani* is a mother, but *patnī* is very important because the word *patnī* is preceded by *dharma* in Vedic view, *dharmapatnī* is not an ordinary partner in life, but she is the legally wed wife of a man. In the *Atharvaveda*, the *mantra* says:

> *patnī tvamasi dharmaṇā ahaṁ gr̥hapatistava* । — *AV* 14.1.51
>
> I am (just) the master of the house, but you are my partner in all the religious duties.

In Vedic tradition, no religious action can be performed by a husband without his wife sitting by his side. As we know very well, in the *Vālmīki Rāmāyaṇa*, Rāma could not perform the Aśvamedha Yajña without Sītā, his wife sitting beside him. Actually he had to have a golden statue of Sītā so that he could perform the religious rite. On the other hand, women can perform specific rites alone. So, women are privileged in Vedic view as we shall see further. The one single term that is used for husband and wife in Vedic philosophy is *dampatī* with the prolonged "Ī". It is not the small "I" but the prolonged "Ī"- since dual number is intended here and it denotes that both of them — husband and wife — are the owners, joint owners of the house. No one is the owner alone. Both of them are owners of the house. Another address of the bridegroom to the bride in the *Atharvaveda* has been used in the later Vedic literature as a sacred formula for lifting the biology of human reproduction to a spiritual plane:

> *amo'hamasmi sā tvaṁ, sāmāhamasmi r̥k tvam* ।
> *dyaurahṁ pr̥thivī tvam* ।
> *Tāviha saṁ bhavāva prajāmājanayāvahai* ॥ — AV 14.2.71
>
> I am song, thou are verse; I am heaven, thou are earth; we two shall live together here becoming the parents of our children.

Vedic feminism is quite distinct in the sense that women are portrayed in the most distinguished and dignified manner in Vedas. They are unparalleled in the world literature in this respect. The women are also seers of *mantras* in Vedas. They have realized the *mantras*, they are the *r̥ṣikās*. There are more than twenty-eight female seers of Vedic hymns such as Sūryā, Apālā, Viśvavārā, Śacī/ Indrāṇī and also several female deities like Sarasvatī, Uṣā, Svāhā and Aditi besides Kuhū, Rākā, etc. Various forms of feminine roles of respect are enunciated in the epithets used as adjectives to denote a woman as follows: *syonā, subhagā, sumaṅgalī, suśevā, śivā, suvarcā, subudhā, candrā, suyamā, śivatamā,* etc. Such respectful and dignified depictions have been made of women; in one of the Vedic verses it is said:

> *śuddhā pūtā yoṣito yajñiyā imāḥ* । — *AV* 11.1.17
>
> These women are *śuddhā*, they are pure, *pūtā* — they are auspicious and they are religiously accomplished.

At one stage, the creative force in women has been extolled as Brahmā:

> *strī hi brahmā babhuvitha* । — *R̥V* 8.33.19
>
> Invariably, woman has been the creator.

She has been given the position of Brahmā because she is the creator. The root verb *br̥ṁh* means to expand, to grow. Just like Brahmā, the creator, a woman is also ever-growing, ever-expanding, giving birth to her progeny. Therefore, she is the Brahmā. She has been depicted in various other ways.[1] Her physical charm and grace is not neglected; rather, it is extolled in the form of the divine dawn (Uṣā):

> *eṣā divo duhitā pratyadarśi jyotirvasānā samanā purastāt* ।
> *r̥tasya panthāmanveti sādhu prajānatīva na diśo mināti* ॥
> — *R̥V* I.124.3
>
> Clad in effulgence, this daughter of heaven has appeared in the east as on days before; like one who knows well the regions, she goes along the path of the sun, faithfully following the quarters of horizon.

Another term used for depicting Uṣā is worth consideration. *Purāṇī yuvatī*, she is *purāṇī* (old one) as well as *yuvatī* (ever new, ever

1 Shashi Prabha Kumar, 2009, "Persona of Women in the Vedas", in *Women in Ancient and Medieval India*, PHISPC, vol. IX, part 2, ed. Bhuvan Chandel, pp. 31-42, New Delhi: Munshiram Manoharlal.

young). Uṣā comes everyday since eternal time, so she is *purāṇī*, but everyday she looks fresh. So she is *yuvatī* also.

Besides, a woman is not only confined to the home and hearth. She was supposed to go and participate in the intellectual discussions in committees and assemblies. The woman is entitled to go to the *sabhā* and participate in the discussions:

yoṣā sabhāvatī । — *Ṛ̥V* I.167.3

She is the intellectually accomplished participant in discussions.

Therefore, she speaks eloquently at congregations:

vaśinī tvaṁ vidathamāvadāsi । — *AV* 14.1.20

Oh lady! you will address and command the assembly.

In the Vedic view, *sabhā* and *samiti* are two committees of different types. *Vidatha* is an assembly or the group of people gathered at the site of the *yajña*. So when the woman comes to her new home after marriage, she is not only entitled to participate in the *yajña* (religious rituals), but she is also enabled to address the gathering and explain the Vedic narrative to them, i.e. *vidatha* and *sabhā*. Besides, the moral strength of a woman is praised through Śacī, the wife of Indra. She proclaims:

avīrāmiva māmayaṁ śarārurabhi manyate ।
utāhamasmi vīriṇīndrapatnī marutsakhā ॥ — *Ṛ̥V* X.86.9

This devil thinks that I am weak but I am very brave. I am the wife of Indra and a friend of Maruts.

It follows from the above that it is the later part of our literature Which portrays women as weak (*abalā*). Vedas have never mentioned woman as *abalā*, rather the woman is depicted here as saying that the devil thinks she is *avīrā*, while she is very brave.

Yāska defines the Vedic deity Aditi as an independent woman:

aditiradīnā devamātā । — *Nirukta* 4.22

Aditi is the independent mother of divine forces.

By definition and by etymology, the term Aditi means independent: *aditiradīnā*. So, when we are invoking the deity called Aditi, it means that a woman in the form of an independent person is being invoked. At one place in the *Ṛgveda*, it is said that a woman is religiously better accomplished than a man:

> *uta tvā strī śaśīyasī puṁso bhavati vasyasī* । — *Ṛ*V V.61.6
>
> A woman is better than the man who does not perform religious rites and who does not give away in charity.

These are just a few statements from Vedas, but actually in the comprehensive Vedic view, we can see that there is a totally complimentary pattern which has been projected and propagated.

In the Vedic society, young women had a freedom to choose their husbands:

> *brahmacaryeṇa kanyā yuvānaṁ vindate patim ...* । — *AV* 11.5.18
>
> A young girl chooses her husband as she likes, when she observes *brahmacarya*.[2]

Now-a-days we are talking of ecofeminism and visionary feminism; even the Western feminists have realized that this kind of aggressive and exclusive feminism is not going to help humanity. They are thinking of different and broad paradigms. But if we compare Vedic feminism with these types of models that have been projected, then I would like to make a few points in which it is different from the Western feminism. By feminism, we usually understand an aspiration that women should be given equal opportunity and equal rights. But the question arises as to when we talk of women, are we talking of women as spiritual beings or just as bodies? When we see the current Western model of feminism, it is only talking of women as bodies or just at the physical level while the Vedic

---

[2] The term does not only indicate celebacy in Vedic view; it has broader connotation which means indulging in the pursuit of knowledge.

feminism talks of women at the spiritual level as well as at the empirical, social and familial levels. Vedic view venerates women not only from the spiritual point, but also in the familial gatherings and the social groups while the Western model objectifies women in the consumeristic model of living that we are in today. It objectifies women to such an extent that it has become impossible to look and talk of dignified persona of women as narrated in Vedas. In other words, Vedic view is inclusive and holistic while the modern view is exclusive and fragmented.

The Vedic view inherently motivates complementarity and coordination while the current notion of feminism is aggressive and it puts women on an antagonistic platform. Vedic view is family-oriented while the current view of feminism is individualistic. Vedic view is duty-centric while the modern notion of feminism or any "ism" for that matter is rights-centric. This is the most basic distinction that we should understand. In Vedas, duties of different persons, different roles and different groups are described but there is not the specific mention of rights. If and when everybody performs his or her duty in his own way, then the rights of others are automatically protected. On the other hand, the model of feminism that is being projected today, it is exclusive and talks of empowerment of women; now suppose we empower women only, then we are bound to have the notion of disempowerment for the other section of humanity. We have numerous examples of empowered women today, in fact, very empowered women, but then if you empower one section of the society, the other section naturally gets disempowered. Vedas do not talk of such a model, they talk of equality for all the beings — not only men and women, but all beings of the world; they should be treated equally and at par.

Moreover, in the Vedic notion, women are born equal while in the current Western notion women are not held to be born equal. So, we should realize that this notion of feminism which is aggressive and exclusive, is in fact originated from the basic idea that women are not born equal. We should not draw inspiration from such alien models. We should rather go back to our own sources and look for such elevating and ennobling ideas. Constitutionally we know that women have been given complete equality of status but there are several contradictions visible in our society also at the empirical level. We know that these days on the one hand, we worship the female power as divinity but at the practical level there are such instances which are very shameful and degrading not only for women but also for men. Obviously these contradictions cannot be resolved only by the constitutional framework. The mindset has to change, the mindset of not only women but the mindset of men, the mindset of every social being has to change and that is when the idea of equality can actually be accomplished.

It will be appropriate to quote one of the contemporary feminists and her definition of feminism. Recently, a prominent lady judge in the US Supreme Court, who successfully fought for gender equality and women's rights, late Ruth Bader Ginsburg held that feminism is not talking of empowerment of women. It is not only women's liberation. It is the liberation of men and women both. She said:

> I don't say women's rights — I say the constitutional principle of the equal citizenship stature of men and women.

In this regard, the following statement of the Mother of Pondicherry in India is very inspiring and needs to be quoted. She says:

> No law can liberate women unless they liberate themselves. What makes them slaves is:
>
> • Attraction towards the male and his strength,
> • desire for home life and its security, and
> • attachment to motherhood.
>
> If they get free from these three slaveries, they will truly be the equal of men.
>
> Men also have three slaveries:
>
> • Spirit of possession, attachment to power and domination,

- desire for sexual relation with women, and
- attachment to the small comforts of married life.

> If they get rid of these three slaveries, they can truly become the equal of women. — 1 August 1951

The sum of above statement is that women and men are not born identical, they are born equal: two equal parts of the Supreme Being but there are biological differences, there are psychological differences too and these differences are the design of nature. They should be respected and they should be accepted rather than being rejected or castigated. So we have to respect the basic biological differences and not want to crush these basic natural differences.

It means that if women become like men and men become like women, then again the problem will be there, because the conflict will be there, the confrontation will be there. So we have to accept both of them as they are because nature has created them for different purposes, for creating a world full of harmony, complementarity and coordination.

Interestingly, several other Western feminists themselves talk of equality like this:

G.D. Anderson (an Australian feminist) says:

> Feminism isn't about making women stronger, women are already strong. It's about changing the way the world perceives that strength.

Mary Shelley (an English novelist, author of Frankenstein) says:

> I do not wish them (women) to have power over men, but over themselves.

No doubt, there are basic and natural distinctions between both the sexes. Women have their strong points, men have their strong points. The essence is that they are complementary. So whether we focus on this complementarity model or we focus on the confrontation model — that makes all the difference; if we adopt the so called feminism, which focuses on conflict and confrontation, then we have problems as we are having today. If women are perceived only as objects and if they are perceived as bodies only, then the problems that we are having today will persist, these will never be solved. If we have to solve these problems, then we have to change our perception. We must realize that women may be physically vulnerable, but they are morally strong, they are spiritually strong; they have to perceive themselves strong, they have to project themselves as moral and spiritual beings rather than just the physical objects — that is where the crux of Vedic feminism lies and that is where we have to bring about change. The core Vedic view depicting the creative force of women (*mātṛ-śakti*) has to be re-awakened and that has been there in Indian society for centuries, this idea of mother worship is deeply inherent in Indian culture. Unfortunately, this inherent value of respecting woman as a mother has started eroding from our society.

Earlier in an Indian village or in society, one's daughter was considered to be the daughter of everybody; if there was a community the daughter of the group was held to be a daughter for everyone, but these days the relations of daughter, mother and sister, they have no meaning at all, because women are seen only as the objects of pleasure. So, this objectification has to stop somewhere. We have to change the mindset; attitude of women must also change, women also have started thinking of themselves as bodies and have a physical approach, therefore a paradigm shift is needed. As mentioned earlier, one section should not aim at disempowering the other, rather both should grow together; they should both enrich each other and strengthen each other. If each section of the society starts fighting for its rights, then there will be no peace and harmony, therefore, each one of us has to care for others' rights and focus more on the duties assigned to one and all.

Vedic view is distinct in this manner. In Western culture, as we know, women are standing on a pedestal of conflict and confrontation. There is the model of constant competition. If we promote and project this competition in an unlimited manner, then it will be the end of the family and society. If we have to build an amicable world, which is full of peace and harmony, this should begin from the family. Vedic feminism stems from this family. We must narrate happy pictures of family that are portrayed in the Vedas. These pictures define that women were given the prime status in the family and the role of woman as wife was very important. Here, wife is called the *dharmapatnī*, not just the better half or the weaker sex, as we say these days — either she is weaker sex, or she is better half or she is narrated as *abalā* in our later literature. There is another word *bhāryā*, it means that she has to be provided for. Man became *bhartā,* the provider and woman became the *bhāryā,* she needs to be provided and man will be her provider. These words are not available in Vedas — neither *bhāryā* not *bhartā*. There are other words like *jāyā*, *jani*, *patnī* and *yoṣā*; *menā* is also used for women in Vedas, *menā* means that women need to be respected: *mānayanti enā iti menāḥ.*[3] *Menā* is the woman who should be respected. By birth she is to be respected, by design of nature she needs to be respected because she is the creative force as she gives birth to humanity. She gives birth to the future generations. She not only gives birth, she in fact nurtures and nourishes humanity.

It is worth mentioning here that the ecofeminists are also saying this today. Ecofeminism is an idea that woman is like nature and in our tradition of philosophy, we have that model of *prakṛti* and *puruṣa*, the balance between both of these is projected; unless they both join, creation cannot take place, but when they join they have to perform their own basic duties, they have their opposite qualities, but these opposite qualities need to be complemented for a happy world. If both of them are not different, if both of them are not endowed with their basic attributes, then this world will not be as beautiful as it looks today. Therefore, we have to think of other ways. In today's time we know that this pandemic (Covid 19) has hurt humanity at its worst. Humanity is passing through the most turbulent times, the tiny virus of corona, the invisible virus,

---

3 *Nirukta*, 3.4

has threatened our existence; but as in all calamities, natural or man-made, the onus of suffering falls upon the so-called "weaker sex" of society who has to bear the brunt of physical and emotional torture. It is not without reason that during the last six months or so, during the period of this pandemic, cases of domestic violence have substantially increased with a horrifying surge. To quote the view of UN Secretary General, who says that cases of domestic violence have increased in this period from 32 to 70 per cent, which is an evident pointer to the fact of prevailing inequalities between both the sexes in modern times. We cannot deny this. Only recently (two days ago) the *Times of India* carried an article regarding unequal pay to female professors of Princeton University in the United States, where women were given voting rights only in the twentieth century. So equality was not there in the Western society till the recent past while in Indian society right from the Vedic period there was not only equal but special status of women. In fact Vedic period was the best period. If you study the basic sources, you will realize that women were venerated, this was the culture of reverence for women; the most dignified and distinguished portrayals of women are available in Vedas.

Drawing from the cultural tradition of India and from the philosophy of Vedas, one would say that the objective of achieving gender equality is already given to us, it is there in our sourobooks. It only needs to be unveiled and re-invented. This is because now-a-days we are not made aware of these ideas. Nobody reads these texts, nobody knows these original sources — we only begin from the medieval period of Dharmaśāstras. Dharmaśāstra is only a part of *smr̥ti* while the Veda is *śruti* and as per Indian tradition, whenever there is a contradiction between *śruti* and *smr̥ti*, *śruti* will prevail. It is a well known maxim of Indian tradition:

> *śrutismr̥tivirodhe tu śrutireva garīyasī* ।
> — Commentany of Kullukabhaṭṭa on *Manusmr̥ti* (2.3)
> If there is a contradiction between the *śruti* and *smr̥ti*, then *śruti* will always be more powerful.

But who reads the *śruti*, who knows that the *śruti* has such beautiful pictures, adorable glimpses of wife, of mother, of daughter, of sister, of all the family members. There are pictures of working women as well. If one tries to prepare a list of what were the professions in which women were engaged in Vedic societly then he/she will come to know their professions according to Vedas. Like today, women were labourers, but women were also scholars (*ācāryas*). Women were teachers, women were physicians (*bhiṣaks*), women were *vīrāṅganās* (brave fighters) like Śacī/Indrāṇī as already quoted above. There is another statement by Indrāṇī who says:

> *ahaṁ keturahaṁ mūrdha aham ugrā vivācanī* । — ṚV X.159.2
>
> I am the flag of the society, I am the forehead of my community,
> I am very fierce and I can be a good orator.

Women were the ritual priestesses also as they were given the right of participating and performing the Vedic rites.

We are worshipping Goddess Durgā in the form of a *brahmacāriṇī* even today. But that is only symbolic while in Vedas we have the real *brahmacāriṇī*s present in the *gurukulas*; they were the *ṛṣikās*, the seers who visualized the Vedic *mantras.* The Vedic *mantras* are not just seen by male seers. Significantly, Vedas were not thought to be created. They are held to be divine knowledge, but transmitted to men and women both — women seers were there and of course various feminine deities are there in Vedas, who are invoked, who are venerated and who are worshipped. There were women who nurtured and nourished the animal kingdom: *paśu-poṣikā* or *go-sevikā* epithets are available. Women were not only taking care of the family, they were also taking care of the animals. They were taking care of the environment and they were taking care of the whole society. Not only that, a very important point explained by Ms Nivedita Bhide (2022) is that of *saṁskāra*s or values. *Saṁskāra*s were transmitted from one generation to another by women only, because women are the first teachers of human beings. When the child is born, mother is the first teacher of the child. So mother in the form of a teacher is transmitting the *saṁskāras* of one generation to the other; and mother, in the form of a very strict disciplinarian, builds the personality of her progeny; mother in the form of a *vaidya* or *bhiṣak* takes care of everyone in the family, but specially of the one who is ill, she has to be an expert in home remedy as well.

All these ideas are there which have been mentioned by scholars in the interpretations of the Vedic *mantras*. So all these different roles for women have been enunciated in our source books but the overall picture that emerges from this depiction is that women were not denied any right; they were not deprived of any opportunity. They were not only equal but they were rather more privileged than men because they were said to be the empresses (*samrājñī*) of the house. When the bride enters the house of her husband after the wedding ceremony, she receives lots of blessings. If one reads the Sūrya Sūkta, which is found in the *Ṛgveda* as well as in the *Atharvaveda*, he/she will realize that the same hymn is recited in our Vedic marriage ceremony, even today. Most of the *mantras* that are recited in the Vedic wedding ceremony, they are from Sūrya Sūkta and Sūryā is the *ṛṣikā* of these *mantras*. These marriage *mantras* are seen by a female seer named Sūryā Sāvitrī (daughter of sage Savitā).

Significantly, Vedic marriage is not a compromise or a contract, it is a sacrament. It is one of the sixteen *saṁskāras* — *vivāha saṁskāra* leads the couple to *gṛhastha āśrama.* It is not just for enjoying physical pleasures that one marries but one marries for being a householder, entering into *gṛhastha āśrama. Āśrama* (*ā+śrama)* means hard work from all sides, hard work being performed by men and women by all means because they have to take care of everyone — all the other three *āśramas*. The *brahmacārīs* are looked after by *gṛhasthas*, the *vānaprasthas* and the *saṁnyāsīs* are fed by the *gṛhastha* men and women (*pati* and *patnī* or *dampatī),* so to say; they have to take care of three-fourth of the society, twenty-five per cent of the society has to take care of seventy-five per cent of the population. These seventy-five per cent persons do not earn money; the money, food and shelter are provided to them by *gṛhasthas*. So *gṛhastha* is the most important *āśrama* and in an *āśrama* they do not just indulge in physical pleasures, but they work really hard because they are the builders of society. They are the builders of the community. They are the builders of posterity. This is the original Vedic view and this duty, this burden, this load of *saṁskāras* has to be borne, mainly by women. Women are held to be more privileged and more responsible. That is why they are called *dharmapatnī*. *Dharma* is carried forward by women and therefore when women perform so many roles, when they enter the house, they are addressed as *samrājñī:*

> *samrājñī śvaśure bhava, samrājñī śvaśravāṁ bhava* ।
>
> — *ṚV* X.85.46

> You are the empress of the house, you have to rule over the family (of your husband).

Obviously, when a person is given so many rights and so many obligations, then she or he will perform to the best of her/his capacity. Benign blessings are showered on the bride in Sūrya Sūkta which is a beautiful hymn that needs to be read by everyone. On the other hand, when the wedding ceremony takes place today, then all the paraphernalia, all the other celebrations are held in great detail. Seven days programme is set, there are many types of parties too. But when the actual marriage ceremony takes place, nobody bothers as to what is going on. The priest (*paṇḍita*) also does not know what he is going to do. He just recites a few *mantras*, whereas he is asked to speed up. Significantly, these are not ordinary activities, they are *saṁskāras*, and *vivāha* is the most important *saṁskāra*. After *vivāha saṁskāra,* there are only three more left: *vānaprastha*, *saṁnyāsa* and *antyeṣṭi* — all these *saṁskāras* are meant for refining human nature; the formulation of human personality is complete after a man or a woman enters into the family system. So this family system needs to be strengthened; the ritual of marriage, the *mantras* of marriage need to be interpreted and explained in such a way that everyone understands them. Then only we will be able to build a harmonious society. We will build a peaceful group and community and will understand that women are in no way less powerful than men. They are rather more powerful. They are more responsible and more respectable in Vedic view.

With these words, I would like to conclude by saying that Vedic feminism is such an elevating and ennobling concept that we should go and find for ourselves what is available there. We do not need to be feminists, we are feminists from the core of its foundation. If we look at the Vedic depictions, then we will realize that women were given all the rights possible in this world. And if they are so powerful, why are we making them weak by following the Western and alien models of competing and conflicting with others? If we keep on confronting, we will not be able to accomplish the goal, which is set for the *gr̥hastha āśrama* in our culture.

Question and Answer Session

DR ARVIND GUPTA: Thank you very much Dr ShashiPrabha ji for this beautiful lecture and what struck me was that we enter into these debates on feminism, women empowerment, etc. without being fully aware of what has already been discussed and even practised. I think that is a tragedy because neither do we know enough about Eastern systems nor Western systems and we join these debates and form our views. But the very fact is as you have indicated that there was a very evolved system in the ancient times which gives equal treatment to men and women, and it was the harmony and coordination that were emphasized and the interest was that of the whole family, society and nation. So I think first we should study these issues with an open mind; all that is being said on either side and then join the debate.

Even about Western feminism, I mean what we read in the headlines and what we know in slogans there may be one point or two about which we do not know how to articulate. Maybe even some similarities are there. But what you have just said clearly shows that the subject requires a much wider treatment. There is much more that was said in Vedic feminism than in the Western feminism. Western feminism in some sense is very limited, that is the point that has come out very clearly. So there are now a number of comments and questions.

Let me just review some long comments also but we will first invite Mr Ajay Mohan Goyal.

MR AJAY MOHAN GOYAL: I am also a professor in a university and I happen to be immediate neighbour of Ma'am, just say to each other. So we are just sitting probably ten metres apart. My point of view is — we need to teach and inform our students about the nature of males and females in the Vedic view, what have our ancient sages said about it, which is still applicable and it is not about dominance of one over the other and also what does this whole institution called marriage mean, what is its purpose? Because when young people marry, I am clicking back on my own marriage, there is nothing which we had to fall back; the only thing one could fall back upon is that how our parents treated each other, how my grandparents treated each other. So the three pairs which are available to you — maternal grandparents, paternal grandparents and your own parents. Okay, and each one of them has their own weaknesses and issues. So probably a very systemic way is to look at the issue and provide that education to young children, especially at the university level. The only thing is: when we get into this whole business of secularism, one does not know actually what happens. How do we bring it into education system? So, that is probably one question I have.

MS AMRUTA: Thank you so much and thank you ma'am for a very enlightening lecture. I just had two comments ma'am: one that as you said about Western feminism, it does not believe in equality since birth and how that is responsible for justification. I would disagree to that because there is nothing like that in Western feminism. But to say that you are not born equal, despite that old essence, the fact that you are equal to men and objectification and commodification of women have come. It is a part of patriarchy, it is nothing to do with Western feminism per se and my question would be that what led to the loss of women's status in Indian society? When and what led to it like if there was any specific period. Thank you.

SPEAKER: As regards equality of women at the time of birth, my intention was to say that the Western model of thinking or Western philosophy is based on this idea. Maybe I have said Western feminism, but that was not my specific intention. I mean to say that in Indian or Vedic view, women were held to be born as equal halves of the Supreme Reality. while in the Western (Biblical) notion, they were not born equal. They were not given equal rights; only in the last century they got their voting rights; even today the Princeton University is not paying equal emoluments to the female professors. At least in India we, as professors, are getting equal pay. I retired from a university, we were never treated as unequal. There is inequality of payment in India also among various areas where women are working. But at least in the university system to which I belong to, there was no disparity. Regarding your second question, I may say that it is out of the purview of today's talk because there is not one single reason which I can cite, not one definite year that I can quote and say this is the time and this is the reason why women's role and status began to deteriorate in Indian society. That needs a separate discussion and for that different scholars need to sit together — the historian, the political scientist and the Sanskritist, then only we can discuss reasons behind it. Thank you.

DR ARPITA MITRA: I read out my question. Now in the Vedic view which enumerates so many qualities about women. My only question was rather than looking at these qualities as inherent in women, should we not look at them as one set of women are especially capable of cultivating. For example, we cannot say about modern women that they are more religious but one can accept that when women are spiritual they have the capacity to surpass men in that quality. In other words, no quality can remain unless it is cultivated. So that was the first point and second question is that most of our problems regarding this inequality and a lot of other things, do not they disappear when both women and men realize that they are not bodies, but *ātmans* — that is also the way of the ancient *ṛṣikās* and the *brahmavādinīs*.

SPEAKER: Yeah, if I understood your first question properly, I said that women are religiously more accomplished and in Vedic narrative they were given all the religious rites and the onus of fulfilling those religious rites was put on the wife in a household. She was responsible for maintaining and holding all the religious rites.

According to Vedic view, a wife is the *dharmapatnī* but by temperament also women are more religious, that we can see even today. But, yes, you are right in saying that they are not awakened if they are not educated. They are not made aware of different reasons, different backgrounds and different rituals. That is a separate issue. But being more emotional they are more prone to religious activities. That is what I meant to say.

AMB. SATISH CHANDRA: Dr ShashiPrabha ji, first, many thanks for the wonderful and very educative talk.

I have a comment and question. I would agree with Professor Goyal that really India needs to make this knowledge available that men and women are equal and that it was so in Vedic times. We need to publicize this much more and make it known. I think most people really come into the world with the mindset that they are taught at home. I was privileged in this context because in my home, women and men were always treated equal. In some respects women had a privilege but the specific query I had from you was look this was so in Vedic time and it was wonderful at that point in time over the centuries, you said. But as we all know women are also exploited, to a number of them, terrible things have happened in the present-day India, as you say.

What caused these changes, why did this actually happen? Because our past was glorious and everything was good but why did this degeneration happen and then of course how it did happen. Thank you.

SPEAKER: Thank you, Mr Chandra. That is the question that keeps bothering every educated person because when we read the comments and the quotations that are being flung these days, they are only of those types which denigrate women but as we know the original form of our culture and the original source of our literature — Vedas — do not have a single idea where women are denigrated. But why, when and how did this happen? This question bothers me as well, but I think that this may be due to the invasions, the foreign invasions or maybe I do not know, but I can say for myself that because my family as you said in your family, you never saw this inequality. Similarly, I never experienced any form of inequality in my family. I had three brothers. I was the only sister, so I had a more privileged position, but I know of many instances around me and my family in the ancient times and also in current times. I know of many women who are suffering this pang of inequality. They have to suffer oppression, subjugation and exploitation of various kinds. So I think this is basically a psychological problem more than a physical problem. And that is why I said that the mindset needs to be changed. If we have a positive mindset, if we know what our culture teaches and imparts, if we go to our traditions, our roots, I think this will help us in changing our mindset. That mindset was moulded in a special way by the grandmothers we had in our family because for the equations between the boys and girls they would always tell the boys you have to do this for your sister; a sister was always given a privileged position in the family, but now-a-days ever since a child is born, this competition, confrontation and fighting starts taking place. I do not know how to change this situation, but we must change the situation. Otherwise, it is going to be even more difficult. So, I think we all should evolve the ways and means to change the mindset of our boys, of our family members, of boys and girls both actually. Both have to be taught just like the religious equality, we have to teach them this gender equality. These days we have the Women Studies Centres in many academic institutions, but we talk of more exclusion rather than of inclusion.

By the way, for preparing this lecture, I also happened to get an idea of visionary feminism which is propounded by an African-American writer named Bell Hooks. It is very fascinating and it seems that it is like going back to our own ancient tradition. She says:

> This visionary feminism is a wise and loving politics. It is rooted in love of female, and female being the soul of feminist politics is the commitment to ending domination of women and men, girls and boys. Love cannot exist in any relationship that is based on domination, in coercion. Males cannot love themselves in patriarchal culture of their very self-definition. Self-definition relies on submission to patriarchal rules, then men embrace feminist thinking and practice which emphasizes the value of mutual growth and self-actualization of all relationships, their emotional well-being will be enhanced. I think men need more to be feminists and if men are feminists, then this purpose of mutual love and understanding will grow and get strengthened. So a genuine feminist politics brings us from bondage to freedom, from lovelessness to loving.

Significantly, this is the type of feminism, visionary feminism, which is saying what was there in our original Indian tradition and this is where we are going in a circle after experiencing all sorts of models. We are going back to our roots — that much I can say. Thank you.

DR ARVIND GUPTA: I think one reason why this degradation happened as you said; of course, there could be many reasons. One is that the way of our economic systems and social systems developed. Men spend more time outside and women spend more time at home; someday that happened because responsibilities, duties and so on and that led to the certain power asymmetry and probably led to patriarchy. So the reason and source of trouble is this extreme patriarchy. I think that is probably what led to get degradations of these. There are many people here, many women in this audience. Anybody would like to ask a question because she has given this very enlightening talk and I am sure there must be many questions. We have a few minutes.

MS SOUMYA AWASTHI: Good evening Madam. I may not be able to phrase this question properly. But kindly understand what I am trying to say. Basically I am talking about women's own rights to decide about their body, like the body politics which is involved with the women. So if a woman wants to decide and take the call whether she wants to get pregnant or not and it should not be the society's call that so and so is married and now they must have a child.

SPEAKER: It was women's own prerogative even in ancient times. We had women who did not marry, who did not bear children. We had two kinds of women up to the period of Upaniṣads: *sadyovadhū* and *brahmavādinī*, for example, we see Sage Yājñavalkya, he is said to have two wives — one was the *sadyovadhū, sādhāraṇa strīprajñā* her name was Kātyāyanī and the other wife was Maitreyī who was *brahmavādinī*, although married. So women were free to choose their own path. They were married or not married, this was their own prerogative. I think in the Vedic feminism, there was no denial but in modern times if you see the other side of the picture, now that women have been given all the legal rights — when very strong laws are in place, women also have started exploiting in certain ways. I may be excused to say so. But there is disempowerment on one side and the empowerment on other side. Therefore, a balance has to be maintained, nobody should dictate the other but each should respect the others' idea, the others' view and the others' personality — that much is required for a happy living. Whether we marry or we do not marry, we have to stay together. We have to live together. We have to work together, we have to exist together. So we have to have a meeting point where we can respect each other up to a minimum level. That is what I think is optimum and that is what we should achieve. It can be achieved with a little effort.

DR ARPITA MITRA: It also depends on the reason for not wanting to marry or not wanting to have a child, because different people have different reasons. I mean so far as I have understood, Vedas recognized only two parts: one was either you dedicate your life to the question of *Brahman* or you take the life of a householder, which means basically taking up the life of serving society. Now in modern time, circumstances are different. We do have a lot of options like one may not become a *saṁnyāsī* and may not marry but lead a life which is for the service of society. We have that option also, but it really depends on why one chose a particular path and why not, because the main point is that we should, I mean if it is a question of just pursuing self-interest, then it is a different thing. But if it is a question of pursuing a higher goal, whether it is service of society or whether it is the quest of Ultimate Reality because both of these are higher goals. So these are two separate issues and self-interest is a separate issue.

SPEAKER: Actually that brings us to the idea of individual and society. You see modern society is individualistic while Vedic philosophy is not individualistic, although it talks of individuals and their rights. But individuals are parts of a group, of a family, of a society, so, the part and the whole are not separate. They are integrated. The health of an individual will determine the health of the bigger group. So we cannot only think of an individual, if somebody does not care, if there were no reasons mentioned — women were free to marry or not to marry, to give birth to children or not to give birth to children, the society was different but values that Vedas propound are more holistic and more integral rather than the current individual rights. There was no self-interest as such, everybody is a part of a group and that group may be a family, that group may be a society, that society will constitute a bigger group that is the country or the nation. So, we have to be adjusted in a setting. Nobody can stay discrete or disconnected in his or her own way. Nobody can exist like that. Even if I choose to pursue my own path, even if I decide to follow my own interest, I will need the help of others in some way or the other, so we have to be mutually helping each other, mutually caring for each other; we may have our own goals, may be some higher goal. The Vedic view inherently talks of higher goals. Not only for women, also for men, each human being has to elevate oneself from where he is positioned. It is not that where you are put up, you just stick to that, you have to elevate yourself everyday, every moment in every possible manner. So that is the basic idea of Vedic philosophy which has to be kept in view. Thank you.

DR ARPITA MITRA: Just one last word, basically according to Vedas, if people marry because they feel a sense of incompleteness, both men and women, we do feel a sense of incompleteness without the other but if there is a man or a woman who feels complete in himself or herself without the need for marriage or progeny, then that person is already half free.

SPEAKER: Yeah, but I think that may be your personal view. As far as the Vedic view is concerned, I would like to mention a narrative from the Upaniṣads where it is said that even the Supreme Being Brahman does not think he is complete without the other and so he divided himself into two: male and the female. It means that the idea of equality and mutual complimentarity is inherent in the Vedic view.

> *sa vai naiva reme tasmādekākī na ramate; ātmānaṁ dvedhā apātayattat patiśca patnī cābhavatāṁ ...*
>
> — *Bṛhadāraṇyaka Upaniṣad* 1.4.3

> It (*Brahman*) did not enjoy being alone, so none enjoys being alone. It divided itself into two: One became *pati* and the other became *patnī*;

Obviously it means that even the Supreme Being who is full, who is complete, who is *pūrṇa*; It did not enjoy being alone. In brief, man and woman are made to be together, to enrich each other, to complement each other and to live with each other. But there are exceptions and there can always be exceptions.

MS SREE LAKSHMI: I will just read out. I was just looking at the situation how it is regarding abortion and surrogacy in the present Indian condition, whereas we Indians are spiritually motivated having such an ancient civilizational legacy. How well that we have accepted surrogacy and abortion in a pragmatic way like that is in America. We still need to address the bone of contention and how this is quite a perplexing social situation. Can you throw some light on this?

SPEAKER: Actually in the Vedic view or say the classical Indian view, which runs up to Kālidāsa, I can say up to first century BCE (Kālidāsa is placed at first century BCE), marriage was meant for procreating. That was the aim of marriage. It was not just for marrying and being together; enjoying physical pleasures was never the aim of marriage in Indian system of values. Kālidāsa talks of *Raghuvaṁśa* (1st canto), the clan of Raghu and Rāma and he says that the ancestors of Raghu and Rāma used to marry for their *santāna*, for *prajā*:

> *prajāyai gr̥hamedhinām* । — *Raghuvaṁśa* I.7
>
> They used to marry for getting progeny.

In other words, *santāna* or *prajā* is the aim of marriage, because in the form of *santāna* one gets extended oneself. One seeks immortality, the mortal being seeks immortality and through *santāna* or *prajā*, he/she gets that immortality up to a certain extent. I may die, but my son will live after me. This is the sense of fulfilment towards the goal of immortality. So in that system, in that frame of mind, marriage was actually for getting progeny.

As regards the talk of abortion and surrogacy, we do not find such specific instances because Vedas are not the descriptive literature that we find in ordinary parlance. There are only suggestions and there are brief narratives in general, not the specific ones. So I could not find any such particular instance of surrogacy in the Vedas, but the description of Niyoga is there in the *Mahābhārata*. Then there are instances and statements in the *Atharvaveda* which refer to avoid abortion, to sustain the embryo that is there within the womb of the pregnant woman. There are many medicines and herbs mentioned about how to strengthen that embryo in the womb, we can find such types of instances. It means the progeny, the *santāna* or the *prajā*, was very significant for the *gṛhastha*. So, they actually wanted to have *prajā* and benign blessings were given to the newly-wed bride for getting *santāna: putravatī bhava, or saubhāgyavatī bhava* — that was there: It must be clarified that *putra* here denotes both the boy and the girl because there are references for the birth of a daughter also in the *Bṛhadāraṇyaka Upaniṣad*. In *Ṛgveda* also Indrāṇī says:

> *mama putrāḥ śatruhaṇo atho me duhitā virāṭ* ।. — *Ṛ*V X.159.3
>
> My sons are brave and my daughter is illustrious. She is *tejasvinī* or *virāṭ*.

We find many words in the Vedas for the daughter, *duhitā* is one of them: *kanyā, kanā, kanīnikā,* these are all different epithets for a daughter and denote her loving role in the family.

So *putra* and *putrī, prajā* for that matter, were very important to the family and the family members adored their children. They wanted to nourish them, to nurture them, to enable them, for the welfare of society and their community.

Okay, I think there are no further questions.

Thank you ShashiPrabha ji.

Introduction to Vedic Literature

Veda is the earliest available sourcebook of knowledge. The word *veda* itself is derived from the root *vid* which means "to know"; this is the primary meaning of this root but there are other meanings as well and it signifies universal knowledge. Accordingly, Veda is the storehouse of knowledge, valuable for an integral vision which can perennially guide humanity towards its journey to perfection. Each syllable of the Vedic verses is profoundly significant in appeal and abundantly rich in content. The same has been percolating in Indian mind through the ages.

Vedic knowledge is, in fact, a vast ocean of nectar. It exhorts all beings of the whole universe as progeny of the immortal and calls upon them to be humane as also to procreate divine progeny:

śr̥ṇvantu viśve amr̥tasya putrāḥ ... । — R̥V X.13.1

***

manurbhava janayā daivyaṁ janam ... ॥ — R̥V X.53.6

It is therefore that Vedic message of eternal peace and cosmic harmony is not for any particular country, caste, creed or clime; it is universal. Anyone who has had the opportunity to glance through the Vedic verses is bound to feel the elevating spirit and ennobling substance of these impersonal (*apauruṣeya*) utterances quite understandably. This is the underlying reason for the sanctity of Vedic statements. It is not only the Indians who hold Vedas in the highest esteem but there are many great scholars of the world who have uttered such inspiring words about Vedas. It will be appropriate to quote Max Müller, who says:

> The Veda has a twofold interest: it belongs to the history of the world and to the history of India. In the history of the world the Veda fills a gap which no literary work in any other language could fill. It carries us back to times of which we have no records anywhere.
>
> As long as man continues to take an interest in the history of his race and as long as we collect in libraries and museums the relics of former ages, the first place in that long row of books which contain the records of the Aryan branch of mankind, will belong forever to the *R̥gveda*.
>
> — *History of Ancient Sanskrit Literature*, p. 63

In the words of Sri Aurobindo:

> The language of Veda itself is a *śruti*, a rhythm not composed by the intellect but heard; a divine word that came vibrating out of infinite to the inner audience of the man who had previously made himself fit for the impersonal knowledge.
>
> — *Secret of the Veda*, chap. II, p. 10

The last words are very important that the Vedic knowledge is not personal knowledge; it is impersonal knowledge.

As we all know, recently United Nations has accepted the *R̥gveda* to be the earliest available literary document of humankind. It is not only about antiquity of Veda but also the significance of Veda in Indian tradition that it is held to be the supreme authority. According to Vedic view, when all the other evidences fail, then the Veda is held to be the supreme authority. Sāyaṇa, the great commentator of Vedas, says:

pratyakṣeṇānumityā vā yastūpāyo na vidyate ।
etaṁ vidanti vedena tasmād vedasya vedatā ॥
— Intro. to *Taittirīyasaṁhitā-Bhāṣya*

> Whatever cannot be known through perception or inference is made known by the Veda, this is the significance of The Veda.

What is so distinct about the Veda? Why do we Indians hold Vedas in such a high esteem? Sāyana gives the answer that where perception fails, where no reasoning can work, then whatever remains as the means of knowing; that ultimate means of knowing is the Veda and when the Veda says something, then there should be no doubt, no question should arise — that is the sanctity of the Veda in Indian tradition, but as per the statement of Max Müller cited above, Veda is not only for India but for the humankind also because the Vedic message is universal. We shall seed that it is not limited or restricted to any country, any race, any caste or any creed.

The next unique feature about Vedic literature is that this tradition is an oral tradition. Therefore, another term for the Veda is *śruti*; originally it was not written or published, it was orally transmitted from one generation to other for thousands of years and that too without any change in a single syllable of the text. To quote Swami Satya Prakash Sarasvati:

> In the British Museum there may be seen a written Bible of third and fourth centuries CE; The Holy Quran of 1,300 years ago, both beautifully scribed but one would rarely find the script of the Veda of such an ancient date. Such an amazing phenomenon of preserving the most ancient texts of 20,000 verses through all the years of history could not have occured in any other land. The credit goes to the traditional brahmanas of India who against all hazards of human history could keep the texts so well preserved, with the right phonetic exchange and accuracy to this day,
>
> — pp. 11-12

> The Vedas constitute the backbone of our entire culture and development through the millennia not only in India but also abroad. For most of us, they constitute the first literature that dawned on us at the earliest time of man's appearance on this globe. In India, we regard them as the revealed knowledge.
>
> — Introduction to *The Holy Vedas*, pp. 11-12

The Veda is also known as *āmnāya,* compilation of the verses or invocations. It is also known as a *saṁhitā* — the collection of verses and there are as many as thousands of verses in the four Vedas. There are almost 20,000 and above verses in all the four Vedas.

But before coming to the content of Vedas, let us first acquaint ourselves with the structure or the outline as also the enormity of Vedic literature. The first point to note in this regard is that there are four portions, four parts of the ancient Vedic corpus — the first are the four Vedic Saṁhitās, *saṁhitā* means compilation, collection or anthology; the four Vedic Saṁhitās which we know as the *Ṛgveda*, *Yajurveda*, *Sāmaveda* and *Atharvaveda*. These are the four popular Saṁhitās but they are not only four — there were many more branches of them; more than 1,100 branches of all the four Vedas have been mentioned but much of these have been lost.

The *Ṛgveda* is divided into ten *maṇḍalas*, 1,017 *sūktas* and 10,552 *mantras* — *sūkta* is a hymn, a collection of verses termed as *mantras* — there are three sections. The first section is that *mantras* are divided into *maṇḍalas*, then the *sūktas* and then the *mantras*; for example, first *maṇḍala*, first *sūkta* of the *Ṛgveda* is Agni Sūkta. *Sūkta* means a hymn and *mantra* means the verse; the first *mantra* of the *Ṛgveda*; when we have to quote this *mantra*, we shall write I.1.1, i.e. first *maṇḍala*, first *sūkta* and first *mantra*.

The *Yajurveda* is divided into *adhayāyas* and *mantras*; there are no *sūktas* in the *Yajurveda*. There are forty *adhyāyas* (chapters) and 1,900 *mantras* in the *Yajurveda*, so if we have to quote from the *Yajurveda* we shall only write twentieth chapter, first *mantra* or simply 20.1.

Then comes the *Sāmaveda*. The *Sāmaveda* is divided into two portions — *pūrvārcika* and *uttarārcika*; the first section and the second section; and then there are *mantras*; no *sūktas* in the *Sāmaveda* also. There are only two *ārcikas* and 1,875 *mantras* in the *Sāmaveda*.

Last, but not the least, the *Atharvaveda* is divided into three parts. First is *kāṇḍa*, then we have the *sūktas* like the *Ṛgveda* and then *mantras*. Twenty *kāṇḍas*, 731 *sūktas* and 5,977 *mantras* are there in the *Atharvaveda*.

Obviously, *Ṛgveda* is the biggest compilation, the biggest *saṁhitā* and it is the most ancient and the most significant for understanding the philosophy of Vedas, the culture in the Vedic period and also the main aspects of Vedic tradition. Precisely, there are total 20,304 *mantras* in all the four Vedas. Saṁhitās are held to be the earliest portion of Vedic corpus and then there were different branches which can just be mentioned by name today. The *Ṛgveda* had many branches, their names are available as Sākala Śākhā, Bāṣkala Śākhā, Āśvalāyana Śākhā, Śāṅkhāyana Śākhā and Māṇḍūkāyana Śākhā — these five names are prevalent but nowadays there are only three available *śākhās* (branches): Śākala Śākhā, Bāṣkala Śākhā and Āśvālāyana Śākhā.

The *Yajurveda* is divided into two types: *Śukla Yajurveda* and *Kṛṣṇa Yajurveda. Śukla* means that it is white and pure since it is only in verse form. *Kṛṣṇa* means that there is a mixture of prose in it. The *Kṛṣṇa Yajurveda* is popular in the south of India while *Śukla Yajurveda* is popular in the north of India. *Śukla Yajurveda* has two branches again — Mādhyandina or Vājasaneyī and the Kāṇva Śākhā. The *Kṛṣṇa Yajurveda* has four *śākhās* — Taittirīya, Maitrāyāṇī, Kaṭha and Kapiṣṭhala. The *Yajurveda* had 100 branches, so says Jaimini. But now-a-days *Śukla Yajurveda* has only two and *Kṛṣṇa Yajurveda* has just four branches.

The *Sāmaveda* has three branches now but there were many more branches of it in ancient times. The *Sāmaveda* has Kauthuma Śākhā, Rāṇayanīya Śākhā and Jaiminīya Śākhā.

The *Atharvaveda* also has many branches like Paippalāda, Śaunakīya, Tauda and Mauda.

It needs to be reiterated that — not a single syllable of these Vedic *mantras* has changed over thousands of years due to its orality. Today we have all the advanced techniques of printing and publishing, and even after so many levels of proofreading, many printing mistakes occur in the printed books, but there was a technique of Vedic recitation which we call *vikṛti pāṭha*: *saṁhitā-pāṭha* is the popular way in which we recite Vedic invocation now-a-days. Just like we have *saragama*, (gamut) in music, only seven *svaras* are there: *sā re gā mā pā dhā ni*, but there are mutations and permutations of these seven *svaras* and thus different *rāgas* emerge; similarly Vedas were preserved through a technique which is known as *vikr̥ti-pāṭha*; eight types of *vikr̥tis* are mentioned in Vedic texts. These are known as different types of recitation. But the unfortunate fact is that we do not have really-trained people, those know how to apply these techniques, are getting extinct. So those many recordings are being done by several institutions. These eight *pāṭhas* are enumerated as *vikr̥ti-pāṭhas*. They are: *jaṭā-pāṭha, mālā-pāṭha, śikhā-pāṭha, rekhā-pāṭha, dhvajā-pāṭha, daṇḍa-pāṭha, ratha-pāṭha* and *ghana-pāṭha*. From *saṁhitā-pāṭha*, we go to *pada-pāṭha* where we segregate each of the terms cited in the *mantra-pāṭha*. So, these are known as the three *Prakr̥ti-pāṭhas*: *Samihita-pāṭha, pada-pāṭha* and *krama-pāṭha*; And if one listens to these different types of recitations by Vedic scholars one will be mesmerized; very few scholars are available in south of India who know these techniques today because these are not being taught in the universities. There are no capable teachers who can teach these, but these were the traits and techniques which kept Vedas and the Vedic sourcetexts intact for thousands of years. Although there was some difference in the pronunciation of different regions as is very normal, even today when we speak Hindi or English in Delhi we speak in a different manner, if we go to Haryana the pronunciation will be different; if we go to Lucknow, it will be different; in Maharashtra, it will be different. Similarly these different branches (*śākhās*) of Vedic recitation evolved.

Vedas were so valuable that the scholars and the *paṇḍitas* toiled hard and took so much of care to preserve them through these oral techniques. After the four Vedic Saṁhitās, which are mostly in poetic style and which are held to be the most original, most pious and most valuable, we come to the interpretation part of the four Vedic Saṁhitās. But the next level of texts is Brāhmaṇa texts, which are in prose style; Brāhmaṇa is not a *jāti* here. Brāhmaṇa is a type of text which is again a very huge corpus of exegetical texts of the four Vedas. Every Veda has one or more Brāhmaṇas of its own, which explains each verse in a specific context with the ritualistic aspect because the verses were meant to be recited at the ritual. There are two sides of Vedic literature: one is the ritual side and other is the spiritual side. So the Brāhmaṇa texts mainly deal with the ritualistic aspect and they explain as to where this verse is to be employed and where this is to be recited, how an offering is to be made in the sacrifice. To quote names of the Brāhmaṇas of the four Vedas:

There are two Brāhmaṇas of *Ṛgveda*: The *Aitareya Brāhmaṇa* and *Śāṅkhāyana Brāhmaṇa.*

The *Śukla Yajurveda* has two Brāhmaṇas, the *Śatapatha Brāhmaṇa* pertaining to Mādhyandina Śākhā and the *Kāṇva Śatapatha Brāhmaṇa*. The title *Śatapatha Brāhmaṇa* indicates hundred ways (*śatapatha*). Evidently the name itself suggests that this is a very vast text — the *Śatapatha Brāhmaṇa* is a very voluminous text and it is available for both the Mādhayndina and Kāṇva branches of the *Śukla Yajurveda*. The *Kṛṣṇa Yajurveda* has its own Brāhmaṇas: The *Taittirīya Brāhmaṇa*, *Maitrāyaṇī Brāhmaṇa*, *Kaṭha Brāhmaṇa* and *Kapiṣṭhala Brāhmaṇa.*

The *Sāmaveda* has its own Brāhmaṇas: The *Pūrva Brāhmaṇa* or *Pañcaviṁśa Brāhmaṇa*, *Ṣaḍviṁśa Brāhmaṇa*, *Sāmavidhāna Brāhmaṇa*, *Ārṣeya Brāhmaṇa*, *Devatādhyāya Brāhmaṇa*, *Mantra Brāhmaṇa*, *Saṁhitā Brāhmaṇa*, *Vaṁśa Brāhmaṇa*, *Jaiminīya* or *Talavakāra Brāhmaṇa*, etc.

The *Atharvaveda* has only one Brāhmaṇa and that is known as the *Gopatha Brāhmaṇa.*

Very few of these texts are taught as part of the curriculum these days, especially in the universities. In the traditional system of *gurukulas* portions of these texts are being taught but this is only an outline — if one goes deeper into these texts, the translations are needed, the interpretations are needed; their relevance in present society is to be explained — a huge work is awaiting in this field.

Now we come to the Āraṇyakas. The first level of Vedic literature is Saṁhitās, second level is Brāhmaṇas or the ritualistic aspect of the Vedic literature and the third level of Vedic texts are the Āraṇyakas which are the beginning of contemplation as the name *āraṇyaka* (pertaining to the forests) itself suggests.

First, let us understand the word *Brahman*. Brāhmaṇa is derived from the word *Brahman*. *Brahman* has many meanings in Sanskrit but here the meaning of *Brahman* is "Veda", *Brahman* is also *yajña* (ritual) because the Brāhmaṇas deal with the ritual; therefore, they are known as Brāhmaṇa text. Because they are connected directly with the Veda, Brāhmaṇa is also *yajña*, Brāhmaṇa is also the Supreme Self, which is explained in the Upaniṣads. But here it does not denote the Supreme Self, it signifies only the Veda and *yajña*. In short the Brāhmaṇa texts deal with these two aspects while the Āraṇyaka texts are the beginnings of contemplation. Since *araṇya* means forest, hence after the rituals became too complicated for the common people and they were fed up of all these complexities, then the scholars, intellectuals, i.e. intelligentsia of the society, turned towards the forests for contemplation on the Supreme Self or *Brahman*, which is conveyed as the Ultimate Reality and explained in the Upaniṣads.

The *Ṛgveda* has two Āraṇyakas: the *Aitareya Āraṇyaka* and *Śāṅkhāyanā Āraṇyaka*. The *Yajurveda* has two Āraṇyakas: the *Bṛhadāraṇyaka* which is also an Upaniṣad. We know it more as *Bṛhadāraṇyaka Upaniṣad* but the name itself suggests *Bṛhad-āraṇyaka- Upaniṣad*. This is a unique text which is a mixture of Āraṇyaka as well as Upaniṣad, *bṛhat* means it is very big and voluminous. It is big in form and it is also Āraṇyaka and Upaniṣad both because there is contemplation and there is also the culmination of Vedic knowledge as available in Upaniṣads. The *Sāmaveda* has two Āraṇyakas, the *Talavakāra Āraṇyaka* or *Jaiminīya Āraṇyaka* and *Chāndogya Āraṇyaka*. For the *Atharvaveda*, i.e. the fourth Saṁhitā; no Āraṇyaka connected with it is available.

Now, we come to the very important, rather the most important and the last portion of Vedic literature. According to its four parts — Saṁhitā, Brāhmaṇa, Āraṇyaka and+Upaniṣad — Upaniṣads are the culminating part or the concluding portion of Vedic literature. The Upaniṣads are also known as Vedānta: *Veda* + *anta*; here *anta* means two things: first is the conclusion it indicates that this is the last portion of Vedic literture; *anta* also means the essence or the gist. Upaniṣads are the gist of Vedic knowledge, so also they are known as Vedānta and they are the most popular form of Vedic literature because they do not deal with the ritual aspect, they focus only on the spiritual aspect of Vedic knowledge. In other words, the Vedic literature is a journey from ritual to spiritual, but if you read the Veda-Samhitā in itself, there are not many details of the ritual. There are mostly invocations to the natural forces like Agni and Vāyu. Pajanya means all forms of water or clouds. There are birds, there are animals. There are invocations to all of them, but these invocations were employed in the rituals according to the Brāhmaṇa texts and their available interpretations up to seventeenth or eighteenth centuries. Sāyaṇa is the most important commentator of Vedas, he has mainly focused on the ritualistic aspect of the Veda and that is why the Veda was thought to be the type of literature which is not connected with the day-to-day life of people in current situation of contemporary society.

Upaniṣads are close to everyone across the world because they deal with the questions of Ultimate Reality, life and death, and how to know oneself. These are the questions that confront every human being, wherever one is placed or in whatever society or time one is living. The very term *upaniṣad* consists of three syllables: *upa*, *ni* and *ṣad*; *upa* means near, in proximity with the teacher. There is a seer, the teacher or the preceptor and there is a seeker. Upaniṣad is not the type of knowledge, which can be imparted to anyone and everyone. We make our curricula these days and there is a right to education, so anybody and everybody is entitled to basic education but Upaniṣad is not such ordinary knowledge, it cannot be taught to anyone and everyone, one has to prepare oneself, prepare for having patience and perseverance doing hard work, for having humility towards the teacher — these are some of the traits that are mentioned in Upaniṣads that only such type of people should be given this knowledge which is secret. More significantly, these are not restrictions based on caste or heirarchy; rather it is a question of aptitude, eligibility of the seeker; it means that one should be able to receive whatever is being imparted. You see the syllabus of MA class cannot be taught to a student of class four, one has to enable himself up to that level.

So this is what is meant by the term *upaniṣad* and the eligible seeker is the one who is termed as *adhikārī*. The knowledge of Upaniṣads can only be imparted to an *adhikārī*. *Adhikārī* here does not mean an officer; *adhikārī* is the *pātra* (eligible person), *pātra* also means a pot. But if you put milk in a dirty pot, milk will get dirty. Therefore the word *pātra* suggests that one's mind has to be clean. It has to be pure to absorb the pristine knowledge that is being imparted by the preceptor, there are two parameters of Upaniṣadic discourse, one is the seer, other is the seeker. The seer has to be a realized soul and not necessarily a very well-read person. He should not be a degree holder; he has to be a *ṛṣi*. *Ṛṣi* is one who has experienced the reality and the seeker or the student has to be a person who has the quest for this knowledge, who can go to any extent, who can tolerate any difficulty to acquire this knowledge. Before we discuss the philosophy of Upaniṣads through parables and narratives in Upaniṣads; it is important to know how the *guru* or the *ṛṣi* would test his disciple. He will not give knowledge just as somebody comes and tells him that please teach me this subject. First the teacher will test how much patience one has. How much preparation the aspirant has made? Only then this knowledge of the highest level can be imparted. Coming back to the derivation of the term *upaniṣad* — *upa* means near, in proximity. For Upaniṣadic knowledge one has to live in proximity with the seer and learn through observance of his lifestyle and conduct. The seer and the seeker, they had to be in close contact. Why? Because the seer would not deliver long lectures, mostly he would speak very little but the seeker would watch him, observe him and learn many things from his character, from his way of life. Hence, this closeness, this proximity between the teacher and the disciple is a precondition of Upaniṣadic knowledge. *Ni* means near, it is not that just proximity is required but humanity is also a pre-requisite; *ni* means sitting near and down, both the proximity and humility have to be combined. Teacher should always sit higher than the disciple or the disciple should always make himself seated below the teacher. The aspirant should always think, even though he/she might be knowing many more things in other respects, but when one comes to learn something, one has to be humble towards the teacher. Only then he can learn something from him. So *ni* means humility — it has to be there in the seeker, and the root *ṣad* means sitting. It means that the student should sit near the teacher and he should sit down, that is why the word "sit down", we never say sit up, we always say "sit down". A student is always supposed to sit down and the teacher is held in high esteem. This much about the nomenclature of the term *upaniṣad*.

Here the question arises as to how many Upaniṣads are there exactly? In fact, Upaniṣads have become so popular that there is even a mention of more than two hundred Upaniṣads. This is because people began composing Upaniṣads after the very term *upaniṣad* started signifying something very serious, very important. Just like the name of poet Kālidāsa in Sanskrit, when Kālidāsa became famous, people started writing poetry and ascribed it to the name of Kālidāsa; likewise the appellation Śaṅkarācārya. When Ādi Śaṅkarācārya became popular, then we find hundreds of texts in the name of Śaṅkara. Now, it is difficult to decide whether they are by the original Śaṅkara, the Ādi Śaṅkarācārya or the later Śaṅkarācāryas — when it became a title, an *upādhi*. Similarly, the term *upaniṣad* became so popular that people started writing Upaniṣads in the later period but the principal Upaniṣads or the authentic Upaniṣads are held to be only ten or eleven.

In the above background, why and how do we decide the authenticity or validity of these texts? It is only through the commentaries because Vedic tradition, or Indian tradition for that matter, has been a tradition of commentaries and interpretations. Commentaries are very important in the development of Vedic thought. Vedic Saṁhitās were transmitted to humanity thousands of years ago, but the first Vedic commentary available in Sanskrit is by Sāyaṇa in the fourteenth century. This was a teamwork entrusted by the kings of Vijayanagara dynasty, they appointed Sāyaṇa as the chief editor of this project and he wrote commentaries on the four Vedic Saṁhitās as well as Brāhmaṇas. Similarly, Upaniṣads have been commented upon by various scholars but the most significant commentator of these is Ādi-Śaṅkarācārya. He wrote commentaries on all the ten major Upaniṣads although it is debatable whether he wrote a commentary on the eleventh, i.e. the *Śvetāśvatara Upaniṣad*. It is confirmed that he wrote commentaries on the main ten Upaniṣads. We have eleven principal Upaniṣads, namely *Īśopaniṣad*, *Kena Upaniṣad*, *Kaṭha Upaniṣad*, *Praśna Upaniṣad*, *Muṇḍaka Upaniṣad*, *Māṇḍūkya Upaniṣad*, *Aitareya Upaniṣad*, *Taittirīya Upaniṣad*, *Chāndogya Upaniṣad*, *Bṛhadāraṇyaka Upaniṣad* and *Śvetāśvatara Upaniṣad*. We will also discuss as to which Upaniṣad is connected to which Vedic Saṁhitā. After the four Vedic Saṁhitās, no text is held to be independent in Vedic tradition. Vedas are the foundation and everything that comes in the tradition is always connected to one of the four Vedic Saṁhitās — like Brāhmaṇas and like Āraṇyakas, Upaniṣads are also connected to the four Vedic Saṁhitās.

The *Ṛgveda* has three major Upaniṣads: the *Aitareya Upaniṣad*, *Kauṣītaki Upaniṣad* and *Maitrī Upaniṣad*. Out of these *Maitrī*, *Kauṣītaki* and *Bāṣkala* are known as minor Upaniṣads of the *Ṛgveda*. Ādi Śaṅkara has not commented on *Maitrī*, *Kauṣītaki* and *Bāṣkala*. He has commented on *Aitareya* only. Then the *Yajurveda* has six Upaniṣads: the *Īśāvāsya Upaniṣad*, *Bṛhadāraṇyaka Upaniṣad*, *Kaṭha Upaniṣad*, *Maitrāyaṇī Upaniṣad*, *Taittirīya Upaniṣad* and *Śvetāśvatara Upaniṣad*. Out of these, the *Maitrāyaṇī Upaniṣad* again is not commented by Śaṅkara, it belongs to the *Maitrāyaṇī Saṁhitā* of the *Kṛṣṇa Yajurveda*. *Sāmaveda* has two Upaniṣads: the *Kena* or *Talavakāra Upaniṣad* or

Jaminīya Upaniṣad and *Chāndogya Upaniṣad*. The *Atharvaveda* has three Upaniṣads, viz. The *Praśna Upaniṣad*, *Muṇḍaka Upaniṣad* and *Māṇḍūkyopaniṣad*. The *Kena Upaniṣad* is very popular. It is the same as the *Talavakāra Upaniṣad* or *Jaiminīya Upaniṣad*. It is a part of the *Jaiminīya Brāhmaṇa* itself. So, these eleven are known as principal Upaniṣads or major Upaniṣads.

As regards the commentators of Vedas and Upaniṣads, there is a whole list of ancient Sanskrit commentators and then there are several scholars as translators in the Western tradition too. We have a whole list of these as well. There are twenty ancient commentators of Vedas who have commented in the Sanskrit language: Skanda Swāmī, Nārāyaṇa, Udgītha, Hastāmalaka, Veṅkaṭamādhava, Lakṣmaṇācārya, Dhanuṣkayajvā, Ānandatīrtha, Ātmānandatīrtha, Sāyaṇācārya, Rāvaṇa, Mudgalācārya, Devala Swāmī, Caturvedīya Swāmī, Bhaṭṭa Swāmī, Bhaṭṭa Bhāskara, Guhadeva, Durgācārya, Uvvaṭa and Mahīdhara.[1] Besides, we also have many modern Indian commentators out of which Swami Dayananda Saraswati is the first who came in early nineteenth century, he commented on the complete *Vājasaneyī Saṁhitā* of the Śukla *Yajurveda* branch and also up to the sixth *maṇḍala* of the *Ṛgveda*, he could not complete his commentary on the *Ṛgveda*, but he was the first exponent of modern India who commented on the Vedas in Sanskrit and his was the first Hindi translation; his Sanskrit commentary was published with Hindi translation for the first time in the vernacular and he was the one who not only championed the cause of the Veda but also proclaimed that the Vedas should be read by everyone. Till now, the traditional *paṇḍitas* did not agree that the Veda should be read by each and everyone just like other books are read, but now-a-days, thanks to the efforts of Swami Dayananda Saraswati, anybody can read Upaniṣads and anybody can read the original Vedas. Swami Dayananda Saraswati also opened the doors of Vedic studies for women and stated that women can also read Vedas;

---

1 Vide Dwijendra Nath Shastri, 1956, *Sanskrit Sāhitya Vimarśaḥ*, pp. 83-86, Meerut: Bharati Pratisthana.

they can also become the priestesses. Evidently, this was his major contribution, his commentary was first published from Nirṇaya Sagar Press, Mumbai, which is a very significant publication house in Sanskrit tradition and has published many important texts of Vedic literature. Unfortunately, Dayananda's commentary could not be completed. He only wrote a commentary in Sanskrit on the *Śukla Yajurveda Mādhyandina Saṁhitā* and on the *Ṛgveda* only up to sixth *maṇḍala*. Thereafter Sri Vinayak Damodar Satavalekar commented in Hindi on all the four Vedas and his commentary is also quite lucid as the name of his commentary Subodha Bhāṣya suggests.

Later on we have Śaṅkara Pāṇḍuraṅga Paṇḍit who commented on the sovereignty of the *Atharvaveda* in the last part of the nineteenth century. Subsequently, Lakshman Sarup from Lahore, Ram Gopal Shastri from Lahore, Samba Shiva Shastri from Trivandrum, Sri Kunhan Raja from Trivandrum; and Acharya Vishva Bandhu from Hoshiarpur, Punjab published their interpretations of the Vedas. As stated above Vinayak Damodar Satavalekar commented in Hindi on all the four Vedas and published it from Swadhyaya Mandala, Pardi, Maharashtra.

In addition to the above, we have the Western scholars as editors and translators of Vedas who have contributed a lot and many of these are European/German scholars. We should acknowledge their contribution because they edited a few texts which have not yet been re-edited by any of the Indian scholars. Out of these, the first name is that of Friedrich Rosen. He was a German scholar but he studied in Paris, France. Max Müller also studied in Paris. Eugene Burnouf, professor of Rosen was the one who taught both F. Rosen and Max Müller, and Rosen was the first who published a few hymns of the *Ṛgveda* for the first time in modern times, in 1830, with Latin translation of the first chapter. Thereafter Max Müller, Aufrecht, Stevenson, Benfrey, etc. published different Saṁhitās; Stevenson edited the *Sāmaveda* with English translation; Benfrey translated the *Sāmaveda* into German. Then Kalin translated the Jaiminīya branch of the *Atharvaveda*. R. Roth translated the *Atharvaveda* and so did Whitney. We have R. Garbe and M. Bloomfield who edited and published the Paippalāda branch of the *Atharvaveda* in Śāradā script. They found the manuscript from Kashmir and published it in Śāradā script. E. Roer published the *Yajurveda* from 1852 to 1859. He also published the *Śatapatha Brāhmaṇa*, *Kātyāyana Śrautasūtra*, *Taittirīya Saṁhitā*, with *Mādhava Bhāṣya*. Shroeder published the *Maitrāyaṇī Saṁhitā* and *Kāṭhaka Saṁhitā*. Aufrecht published the *Aitareya Brāhmaṇa* with Sāyaṇa *Bhāṣya*. The list is a very lengthy one. You can go on and on. Those interested, can refer to *The Vedic Bibliography* by R.N. Dandekar published in five volumes from Bhandarkar Oriental Research Institute, Pune.

But before we conclude the outline of Vedic literature, one more very important portion of Vedic literature is still remaining which needs to be noted. In this list there must be added the six Vedāṅgas — *aṅgas* or subsidiaries of the Veda. It means that for reading the Veda, you cannot just pick up a book and read it like a popular novel. You have to take help from other secondary sources, which explain the techniques and the technical terms — how you should read and how you should interpret Vedas. These six Vedāṅgas are connected with the *aṅgī* or the primary, i.e. four Vedic Saṁhitās and these six are said to be subsidiaries (*aṅgas*) to them. Their names and details are as follows:

Śikṣā is the phonetic science of ancient Hindus and it describes how to recite a particular verse as per particular branch of the Veda because the Veda is an oral tradition, therefore study of phonetics is very important for recitation. Even a small variation in the tone can change the meaning of the Vedic verse. Therefore, these Śikṣā texts were composed; these are also known as Prātiśākhya texts. Śikṣā here does not mean education. Śikṣā in the Vedic parlance means the science of recitation. It is defined as:

svaravarṇādyuccāraṇa-prakāro śikṣyete yayā sā śikṣā ।

— Sāyaṇa in his *Ṛgveda — bhāṣya-bhumika*, p. 49
quoted in Upadhyaya, *Vaidika Sāhitya* p. 285

> Śikṣā is that technique which teaches one to recite the vowels and the consonants with their (*mātrā*) incantations in a proper manner.

To put it more precisely, Vedic Śikṣā signifies the Prātiśākhya texts. Hundreds of Prātiśākhya texts were there. The *Ṛgveda* has different Prātiśākhyas, the *Yajurveda* has different Prātiśākhyas. It is a pity that much work has not been done pertaining to these texts, only one or two studies have been done all over India in all these years. Not many scholars are available today who can teach these Prātiśākhya texts because most of the modern scholars are not trained to recite Vedic verses in traditional manner.

Vyākaraṇa is the next Vedāṅga. Vyākaraṇa is the discipline of grammar. The Vedic language is also Sanskrit language, but it is different from the classical Sanskrit. Classical Sanskrit grammar was written by Pāṇini. But Vedic grammar is different, it is quite ancient than the classical Sanskrit. So Vyākaraṇa is the next Vedāṅga.

Third one is **Jyotiṣa** (science of astronomy), it is not astrology. It is the science of astronomy because there is mention of *nakṣatras* (planets) in Vedas. Therefore Jyotiṣa is important for understanding Vedas and Lokamanya Tilak has written a book titled *Orion* (1893) in which he has tried to estimate the timings of Vedic Saṁhitās with the help of Jyotiṣa. In fact, Jyotiṣa is an essential part of Vedic literature. One must have a basic knowledge of Jyotiṣa, only then he/she can interpret the Veda properly.

Next is **Chanda** (science of prosody). Prosody is also important because the Vedic *mantras* are all encapsuled in metres (*chandas*). Vedic metres are also different from the classical metres. In classical poetry, the *Vālmīki Rāmāyaṇa* is written in Anuṣṭup Chanda, we usually call it *śloka*. But Vedic *mantras* are different from the classical *ślokas*, because a *śloka* is a Laukika *chanda*. In Vedas also, we have Anuṣṭup *chanda* but it is different; we have *chandas* like Gāyatrī,Triṣṭup, we have Jagatī; like that there are more than twenty *chandas* which have been used in Vedas.

Next is **Nirukta** which is also very important, *Nirukta* is the science of etymology. As already mentioned, the Vedic language is not classical or ordinary Sanskrit, it is derivative in nature. Every term can be derived from several roots and the meaning would change accordingly. Therefore, it is very flexible, elasticity of meanings is there in the language of Vedas, one can interpret the same words of a Vedic verse in various ways with the help of this science of *Nirukta*. *Nirukta* was written by Maharṣi Yāska around seventh century BCE. This was a commentary on the Vedic dictionary of synonymns - *Nighaṇṭu*. Several of such dictionaries and indices were also composed in Vedic tradition. There was a research methodology before these Vedic scholars too, so they made their own indices and dictionaries. When the European scholars came, they made their own indices. Like we have the Sanskrit-German *Wörterbuch* by Bothlink and Roth and Monier-Williams Sanskrit-*English-Dictionary*. We have The *Vedic Index* by A.A. Macdonell and *A Vedic Concordance* by Mourice Bloomfield. Modern European scholars prepared their own dictionaries while the Vedic scholars had their own and, as mentioned above, *Nighaṇṭu* is the first Vedic dictionary of synonymns. Only one *Nighaṇṭu* is available now — The *Nighaṇṭu* by Yāska. Yāska compiled those words in the *Nighaṇṭu* and explained them in the *Nirukta*. Without the help of the *Nirukta*, if somebody tries to read and interpret Vedas it will not be correct. Therefore the *Nirukta* is very important among the six Vedāṅgas.

The last one of the Vedāṅgas is **Kalpa**, this is the sixth Vedāṅga. Śikṣā, Vyākaraṇa, Jyotiṣa, Chanda, Nirukta and Kalpa. Kalpa is also known as the *Kalpasūtra*. This is a type of literature from which Sūtra tradition started and continued through the later texts. *Kalpasūtra* is again of four types: Śrautasūtras, Śulbasūtras, Dharmasūtras and Gr̥hyasūtras. All the systems of philosophy in India were composed in the form of *sūtras*, like we have the formulae in chemistry today.

Out of these four types of Sūtras, Śrautasūtras were the ones which were directly related to the *śruti* (Veda). Dharmasūtras are the legal texts of that period and Śulbasūtras pertain to the technique of measurement for preparing the altar (*vedī*). These are known as the most ancient source of geometry. Last, but not the least, Gṛhyasūtras pertain to the domestic rituals, which were ordained for the householders. Whatever needs to be done in the household, which sacrifices are to be held, how the offering is to be made — all that is enjoined in Gṛhyasūtras. This is the last leg of Vedic literature where the *aṅgas* (subsidiaries) of Vedas are mentioned. There is a corpus of Vedāṅga texts and a huge number of books are available in this tradition too. Jyotiṣa itself has thousands of books; Vyākaraṇa is said to be of many types and fourteen or eighteen *niruktas* have been mentioned in the *Nirukta* by Yāska.

All of these texts are not available now, but since Yāska has mentioned them, it proves that at his time there were eighteen scholars who had prepared their own Nighaṇṭus and Niruktas. Similarly, Chandaśāstra; now-a-days, we have only one Chandaśāstra by Piṅgala, but there were many traditions of *chanda* and for understanding Vedas we have to understand the science of prosody (*chanda*) because *chanda* is the form of the Veda. *Chanda* means *chādana,* like a shawl, which covers one. *Chanda* means that which covers the Vedic words. So *chandas* are like the robes of Vedic knowledge. The Vedic verses are encapsuled in these *chandas*. Besides, there is a *ṛṣi* the seer and there is a *devatā* who is being invoked. Significantly, *devatā* is not just a deity to be worshipped; *devatā* means the content of the Vedic verses:

> *yā tenocyate sā devatā* । — *Sarvānukramaṇī* of Kātyāyana 2.5
>
> Whatever is being mentioned in that verse, that theme is *devatā*.

To put it in simpler terms the theme of the Vedic verses is the *devatā*. *Ṛṣi* is the seer, if you open the book of the Veda there are three things mentioned on the top of every *sūkta*: *ṛṣi*, *devatā* and *chanda*; for example, Viśvāmitra is the *ṛṣi*, Gāyatrī is the *chanda* and Savita is *devatā*. So *devatā* means the theme of the *sūkta*. *Ṛṣi* means the realized one who got revelation of that particular *sūkta* and *chanda* is the metre of that particular *sūkta*. For a proper Vedic study, all these three have to be taken into account. Actually we have to build a museum where we can showcase each of these texts or the representative texts of these types. These days we are discussing the National Education Policy (NEP) where it is mentioned that we should have museums for introducing our ancient heritage to the youngsters — the vast storehouse where everything is stored but only as the text and not in a visual manner. This is despite the fact that thousands and thousands of books had been burnt, even then we have lakhs of these books in manuscript form which are waiting for scholars, who would come and explore, edit and interpret these texts.

Question and Answer Session

SPEAKER: I have taught for more than forty-five years in two of the premier Indian universities. I have found that not many scholars are interested in these manuscripts. These are not easily available and we have to do something not only to preserve our heritage but also project and promote it in a proper manner. Now is the time. We should be proud of this rich heritage. This legacy has been transmitted to us and we have an obligation to transmit it to the next generation.

ANURAG SHARMA: *Namaste* Ma'am. Thank you for this insightful talk on Vedic literature. My point is that how the Veda has defined the phenomenon of *Parama-Brahman* because as to my limited knowledge, the *Parama-Brahman* comprises of three Lords like Viṣṇu, Maheśa and Brahmā, and how the feminine power out of which these three *Parama-Brahman*s were born. Śiva and Viṣṇu, which is Ādi-Śakti and Yogamāyā respectively born out of the same *Parama-Brahman* as defined in our Vedic literature. May I request to be excused for asking this question which has arisen out of the curiosity and limited knowledge on the subject. Thank you, ma'am.

SPEAKER: Welcome Anurag. First thing is that the question you have asked pertains to Hindu mythology and not the philosophy of

Vedas because as already mentioned Vedic knowledge is impersonal knowledge. When we come to the conception of God, we will discuss that Vedas do not depict a personal God like Viṣṇu, Maheśa or Brahmā. The God depicted and invoked here is impersonal God, manifested in various forms of nature and these have been invoked as divine forces. So trinity of deities that you are mentioning is described much later in the Purāṇas.

Devī and the feminine form of the deity come even later in the Tantras, while we are discussing now the most original and the most ancient texts, the Vedas and the subsequent Vedic literature, where these forms are not mentioned at all. *Parama-Brahman* is mentioned only in the Upaniṣads. In Vedas, we do not find details of *Parama-Brahman* as such although we find the term *brahman*. But as I said that the term *brahman* in Vedas means two things: first is *veda* (knowledge) and the second is *yajña* (ritual). So up to the Vedic tradition or in the Vedic literature the idea of *Brahman* in this sense was not there. It is true that the concepts of *Parama-Brahman* (Ultimate Reality) and the Supreme Self are described in Upaniṣads and we will discuss about it in the next lecture.

SHRI PRAKASH SINGH: As you talk about the New Education Policy, government plans to establish museums where our ancient heritage is preserved. I think two things are beyond the museum: how to inculcate the teaching of Upaniṣads and considering that they have a universal message and that they do not talk of Hindu religion as such, but they talk of impersonal God. They talk of the Ultimate Reality. They discuss questions of life and death, would it be wrong or would it be treated as insecular, if I am accurate in putting it that way that Upaniṣads' teachings become part of our curriculum.

SPEAKER: Thank you for your remarks Prakash Singh ji. Upaniṣads are very much a part of our curriculum and a very popular part. It is about the earlier literature of Vedas — Brāhmaṇas, Āraṇyakas or Vedāṅgas that they are not part of the curriculum. But Upaniṣads are very popular and the whole of Vedic literature except the ritual part of it, which is very technical and very restricted in that sense, the four Veda Saṁhitās and the Upaniṣads, they are totally secular, as I said in the beginning and I keep repeating this. As regards the museum, at least we can showcase that there are so many types of Vedic texts, if not their hidden content.

Dr Gupta rightly said that people do not even know that much about Vedic literature, many people know about Upaniṣads, because the Westerners translated them in English and other languages. A whole lot of Upaniṣads have been translated into English and other European languages. Vedas were also translated. Out of the Vedic literature many texts were translated into the European languages, but they are not very popular. So teaching in the curriculum is one thing but while teaching we should also let them know that these are the types of literature that were composed in our tradition. These are available, these are not available. Many of us who read Vedas, even we do not know details about Chandaśāstra or Nirukta. We read Vedas, we read Upaniṣads. Jyotiṣa, we only know the astrology part of it while the Vedic subsidiary Śāstra is the astronomy (Jyotiṣaśāstra). That is the science of calculation. Then we have Sūtra literature. There was geometry, complete exact geometry. How to lay the altar, there were different types of altars: *śyena citi* ... in the form of birds; each brick was counted, its size was given; these were known as Śulva or Śulba, Śulbasutras. Most of the students do not know about this type of literature. I think that the very idea to have some museums must be appreciated to showcase our heritage to them. There are students who are reading a few of these texts as part of their curriculum, but there are people in the public who just do not get an opportunity to read them, therefore all of us should at least be aware of these types of literature. I think that is a welcome idea. Upaniṣads are being taught, they are being worked upon for the research degrees also because they are philosophical texts, although not restricted to philosophy only. In short, the Upaniṣads are very popular in the philosophy and the Sanskrit departments.

DR ARVIND GUPTA: Let me begin. I have a couple of questions. एक तो ये था कि आपने बताया दयानन्द सरस्वतीजी ने उन्नीसवीं शताब्दी में पहले वेद और वैदिक साहित्य को आगे बढ़ाया। That means people were constantly thinking about writing on Vedic literature. So in the twentieth and twenty-first century in India, have there been commentaries on these texts, and second, आपने जो कहा ब्राह्मण, आरण्यक ये सारे मुख्यतः उपनिषदों से पहले लिखे गए। Is it possible to write now? Something which can be called Upaniṣad or kind of addition to the Vedic literature. Why should it stop at a certain point of time? And why is it that because knowledge is growing, our understanding of the world is growing and new questions are coming up. So, is Vedic literature stagnant or can something be added to it? But something can be counted as good as the commentary type that you mentioned. That is my one question.

The second question is: what is the state of knowledge and education or curriculum on these subjects in the country? You mentioned that they are the part of philosophy and Sanskrit departments etc. But supposing someone wants to complete five years in pursuing Vedic literature course — now are such degrees available, that means after school you can join and do it and not necessarily in English. Also, for instance, somebody wants to study and know. Whether that kind of flexibility is there in our curriculum, so these are my two questions.

SPEAKER: Thank you, Dr Gupta. Yes, in twentieth century numerous translations have been done and commentaries have been written on Vedas in Sanskrit, Hindi and many other languages; Vedas have been translated into Bangla, Malayalam — not complete but portions of them. Dayananda Saraswati was the champion of Vedic knowledge in nineteenth century and whatever little of the Veda I have read, it is because of him and his Arya Samaj principles which my family was following. In the twentieth century, translations were being written, commentaries were also being written; many commentaries have been written. In Rajasthan, Paṇḍit Madhusūdan Ojhā has written his commentary titled as *Vijñāna-Bhāṣya* on Vedas and Upaniṣads, very scholarly commentary. They have formed an institution and they are trying to interpret his commentary and propagate the message that he has given. Similarly, in Maharashtra, we have many scholars who have written commentaries on Vedas and Vedic literature.

As regards your second question, can Upaniṣads be written nowadays, my answer is, yes, why not, people are still writing. Recently I am told that an *Allopaniṣad* has been authored. Number of Upaniṣads is increasing and people have also started writing new Smr̥tis, one of my colleagues at JNU had started to write a new *smr̥ti*. *Smr̥ti* is a Dharmaśāstra. So one can also write the Upaniṣad if it is focusing on the topic of self and its knowledge. Nevertheless, even though one can write and add to the stock of knowledge, the undeniable fact is that these ancient texts were realized by the *r̥ṣi*s, I mean the principal Upaniṣads. Vedas were not composed by any human being; they contain the impersonal knowledge transmitted to the seers (*r̥ṣi*s). But the Upaniṣads were also revealed to, or realized by the *r̥ṣi*s. Suppose I write a new one today, it will not have the same stature or same authenticity because there are two types of texts: *ārṣa* and *anārṣa*. *Ārṣa* is that which is composed or authored by a *r̥ṣi* and *anārṣa* is that which is composed by any other scholar/human being who is not a *r̥ṣi*. Today's scholar is not a *r̥ṣi*. Of course there are scientists who are purely and totally engrossed in their research, those who are searching for the vaccine of corona today; they are no less than the *r̥ṣi* because they have devoted themselves and they are able to realize whatever is the truth in that particular area. But the one who has directly realized the Ultimate Truth he is known as *r̥ṣi*. The sanctity that these texts enjoy in our tradition, Vedas, Brāhmaṇas, Āraṇyakas and the major Upaniṣads, that sanctity will take hundreds of years because these texts are thousands of years old. They have been tested on the time scale. So, it will take some time when a new book is published, although these days we get an ISBN and ISSN assigned but that is only a number for identification, it does not talk about its authenticity, it only provides an identity to a book and does not present its validity. Validity has to be tested.

Regarding the Vedic studies, yes, there are *gurukula*s where these Vedic texts and Vedic subjects are being taught; if somebody is not just after a vocational degree, but he or she wants to learn these techniques or to study the Vedic literature. He or she can go to any of the *gurukulas*. Recently I came to know that there is a *gurukula* of Devdutt Patil Guruji in Goa. In fact there are hundreds of *gurukula*s being run by Arya Samaj and by many other institutions, I am also associated with a few of them. We have a Rashtriya Veda Vidya Pratisthan set up by the Government of India, which is functioning from its headquarters in Ujjain. It runs many formal and non-formal courses in Vedas. Anyone interested from general public can contact the Veda Vidya Pratisthan and the Pratisthan helps people in studing, popularizing and propagating the Vedic message. The online classes "Veda Classes for All" which we are running at Bharatiya Vidya Bhavan on every Saturday for the last two years — these are supported by the Maharshi Sandipani Rashtriya Veda Vidya Pratisthan, Ujjain. But now with the New Education Policy, I think such types of institutions, such types of *gurukula*s and such types of learnings will get more validity. New Education Policy envisages to merge the non-formal with the formal, so I think that is a great idea if it is handled properly and implemented in the true spirit in which it is envisioned. Thank you.

GENERAL RAVI SAWHNEY: Thank you so much. I think it is absolutely amazing to know about such a depth of knowledge. Well, I think as Mr Prakash Singh has said that whatever you have brought about Vedic traditions, they are not narrow in their prospects. I mean, there is nothing as people's knowledge and secular as I call it in a way where there is no orthodoxy at all. And that is the beauty of this particular philosophy. If they are not trying to tell you that there is only one way that they talk to you about the philosophy, then how you can broaden your horizon. And there is such a huge depth of knowledge in a very sophisticated language. I think Sanskrit is the mother language of all and is the beautiful language. We should bring these particular projects to light. These rituals came later. These are writings beyond ritual. They actually brought in the sense why anybody reads Vedic literature in the true sense. I think the whole process points to the fact that if this type of value is to be brought then you start by Vedas. This should be propagated.

SPEAKER: Thank you very much sir. You have in fact presented the gist of Vedic vision and it is true that the Vedic philosophy does not restrict itself to one or the other aspect. In the Veda itself, we find that very popular maxim, which says:

> *ekaṁ sadviprā bahudhā vadanti* । — *R̥V* I.164.46
>
> Reality is one but wise persons narrate it in many ways.

It means that the narration may be different, but reality or truth is one and you are right and I agree with you that this vision of an intrinsic and universal vision of Vedas needs to be propagated because this is the need of the time as there is no sectarian division in Vedic literature. It is a very inclusive vision which incorporates every aspect of the cosmos, every section of the society and it also connects the *piṇḍa* (microcosm) with the *brahmāṇḍa* (macrocosm). Also, there is a synthesis between opposites. There is no contradiction. Whatever apparent contradictions are there, they can be resolved through the message of these Vedic teachings and these teachings should be made known to everybody. In fact this is the essence of Indian tradition, which we have lost. I think we need to read and revive and then propagate this corpus of knowledge. Thank you so much for what you have said. Thank you.

DR ARVIND GUPTA: I think we have now come to the end of the session. So, one of the reasons, why we are discussing this at the VIF, which is really focusing on foreign policy, defence security and those kinds of issues. We have not quite taken up with one question, which is building a narrative for India or the modern world. If India is to rise, we have to come up with our own ideas, our own narrative, our own views, etc. And one way to do this is to really look for ideas and draw inspiration from our ancient thinking and Vedic texts, etc. So this is the reason why and, of course in the process, you have been very kind to give us four, five talks already, maybe a few more. So this will be very useful like you mentioned about Vedic vision. General Sawhney and Mr Prakash Singh also talked about it. I think it would be very useful to collate some of the key themes which can be accepted by other countries, people were coming from different civilizations and cultures and yet we touched their hearts. So it is a collection of a few such themes which we can then propagate while we talk to other think-tanks or when our leaders meet other leaders. It is not just that these ideas should be taught only amongst that type of audience. But they should have tactical value. So I think it would be useful to collect, collate and discuss some of these eight or ten main schools, which can provide the path to the multilateralism which is already there you know, the old ideas about multilateralism in the Western civilizations and cultures gave and which had led us into environmental degradation; more war, more conflict, more identity crisis — I think these broader ideas which are acceptable not only to us but also to the others. So we must always be on the lookout for this one reason why we are engaging. You can help us in identifying some of these broad themes. So a collation of maxims, like the one you quoted just now — *ekaṁ sat* — which is very popular and many people know about it. The prime minister himself has spoken about it. We should collate, then our scholars and strategists, those who are researching on strategies, policies and policy discourse; they should comment. Otherwise, it will remain in the *gurukula*s, Sanskrit departments and the philosophy departments, and they cater to only a certain section of people. So, in this, I think you can help us. So, thank you very much for taking time for this very well-researched talk. Thank you.

Philosophy of Upaniṣads

According to the Indian philosophical tradition, there are eleven principal Upaniṣads: *Īśa, Kena, Kaṭha, Praśna, Muṇḍaka, Māṇḍūkya, Aitareya, Taittirīya, Chāndogya, Bṛhadāraṇyaka* and *Śvetāśvatara*. Out of these, *Īśa, Kaṭha* and *Bṛhadāraṇyaka* are connected with the *Śukla Yajurveda; Taittirīya* and *Śvetāśvatara* are connected with the *Kṛṣṇa Yajurveda*. The *Kena* and *Chāndogya* are connected with the *Sāmaveda*. The *Muṇḍaka, Māṇḍūkya* and *Praśna* are related to the *Atharvaveda* and the *Aitareya Upaniṣad* is related with the *Ṛgveda*.

As explained earlier, the derivation of the term *upaniṣad* is (as we split it) *upa, ni* and *ṣad* — *upa* means near, *ni* means down and *ṣad* signifies sitting. In other words, *upa* means proximity with the teacher, *ni* denotes humility towards the teacher and *ṣad* means consistency in study. Significantly this is not an ordinary teaching which is being started. There is a seer who has realized the truth and there is a seeker who is very focussed on comprehending the essence of reality. Both the seer and the seeker, they mostly talk between them; this is a dialogue question-answer method; sometimes there are other methods also, but mostly they are dialogues or question-answers. Naturally, the question arises as to what should be the attributes of a seeker? Because, as stated already, this is not an ordinary knowledge, this is known as *ātma-vidyā* (knowledge about the self); *brahma-vidyā* (knowledge about *Brahman*, the Supreme Reality); "*adhyātma-vidyā vidyānām*", so says Śrī Kṛṣṇa in the *Bhagavadgītā*. Upaniṣads are known as *ātma-vidyā, brahma-vidyā, adhyātma-vidyā* or *sarva-vidyā-pratiṣṭhā*. This is the ultimate of all knowledge and wisdom that one can think of. Other names used for it are *tattva-vidyā* and *guhya-vidyā*. Since ordinary persons are not interested in such deep knowledge, hence they are also not eligible to receive such knowledge and the teacher too is not an ordinary teacher like us, who can only speak about it, but the extraordinary one who has directly realized it.

For denoting eligibility of the seeker, we have several attributes mentioned in Upaniṣads. But the most significant attribute of a seeker is patience; only a patient person is qualified to receive this type of knowledge. He has to be very humble. He has to be committed to the knowledge that he is trying to attain. He should be very peaceful within himself and with others. He should be devoted to his teacher and he should be patient (*dhīra*). In fact, this term has been repeated many times in the *Kaṭhopaniṣad* by Yamācārya when he talks to Naciketā and says that many persons have questioned about this topic of life after death, but you are the real *dhīra*, a patient seeker, who does not lose heart howsoever hard test you may have to undergo on the instruction of the preceptor.

Then what type of a seer or the teacher can teach this *vidyā*? There is a mention of two types of teachers in the *Muṇḍaka Upaniṣad*: one is *śrotriya* and the other is *brahmaniṣṭha*. *Śrotriya*, as the name suggests, is one who has read a lot, who has listened to many speakers, because our tradition is basically Śruti tradition and not a printed book tradition; knowledge was mostly acquired through listening directly from the teacher. So the first type of teacher, who is a *śrotriya*, is like the professors of today who are very well read, they have lots of information but there are a few chosen ones who are *brahmaniṣṭha* and have realized the truth themselves. We have a long series of such sages or realized souls in our tradition. They were the *brahmaniṣṭha* seers like Kabīr, Nānak, Ramakrishna and Ramaṇa Maharṣi; they did not get a formal education; they were not very well read. But they were the realized souls. They were the *ṛṣis* — the sages or the seers. Who is a *ṛṣi*? *Ṛṣi* is he who has seen the truth, who has had the perception of the Ultimate Reality — *ṛṣirdarśanāt* (*Nirukta* of Yāska 2.3).

Before we discuss the philosophy of Upaniṣads it must be mentioned that these days we teach philosophy under three broad heads: metaphysics, epistemology and ethics. Although Upaniṣads do not divide their content into these three heads because Indian knowledge systems are basically inclusive and holistic. They do not segregate the themes like today but they always try to incorporate everything or all the aspects of reality and knowledge within their purview. Accordingly, metaphysics deals with the nature of Ultimate Reality; many Upaniṣads begin with a question by the seeker as to what is it by knowing which everything else is known.

kasminnu bhagavo vijñāte sarvamidaṁ vijñātaṁ bhavati ।

— *Muṇḍaka Upaniṣad* 1.1.3

Oh the revered one! What is that by knowing which everything else will be known.

The rest is not said, but it is implied that there must be a knowledge system like today in which one knows a lot but does not have the satisfaction since he or she has not had one's own realization. The education system of today is such in which one has information about many things, but does not know the essence or purpose of one's own being. Hence, even by knowing so much we crave for the essence of knowledge.

Upaniṣads guide us to the other direction where by knowing ourselves we can realize the essence or the ultimate aspect of things and beings around us. From this point of view metaphysics basically covers the content or the theme of Upaniṣads — that is *ātman* and *Brahman*. They are not two separate entities as mentioned earlier. They are one and the same; one aspect of the same reality is known as *ātman* and other as *Brahman*. In Upaniṣads, there is no division or separation between *ātman* and *Brahman*.

Coming to epistemology, or the second part of philosophy, it deals with the means of knowing. We want to know about the *ātman* or the *Brahman* but what are the means available to us? Ordinarily, we have means of knowing such as our sense organs or the faculties of knowing like smelling, tasting, touching and seeing. But all these means of knowing fail as far as the content of Upaniṣads is concerned. We all can realize and experience *ātman* or our own self but we also know that it cannot be touched because it has no form. It cannot be tasted because it does not have any attributes like that. It cannot be heard because whatever can be heard will be gross and corporeal while *ātman* is beyond these names and forms. We have these faculties of knowing but these are not able to catch and convey the reality of the self. In one of the Upaniṣads this question has been asked by the student very beautifully; he asks the teacher:

> *keneṣitaṁ patati preṣitaṁ manaḥ ...* ।
> *keneṣitāṁ vācamimāṁ vadanti ...* ॥ — *Kena Upaniṣad* 1.1.1
>
> Who is that who motivates our mind and sense organs; by whom is our speech impelled to speak?

Do we ever go deeper and think? No, never. In fact we keep on listening, we keep on looking at things, we keep on eating, touching but we never pause and ponder as to who is motivating and moving all these organs to their desired objects. There is definitely some power because when it stops, everything stops functioning and when we are alive, we are healthy, we do not realize the value of these activities going on in our life. But when we want to know the ultimate truth behind all these — like the current of electricity; we see all these forms and shapes of electrical fittings; they are shining, fans are moving, air conditioners are on but there is something which is not visible, which is not to be touched but we know that there is something which is making all these electrical fittings function as per our choice. That is the force of electricity which is behind all these. Like this electric current there is something behind all these apparent activities being performed by us, that is what Upaniṣads are trying to convey and communicate in a language that fails to describe it:

> *yato vāco nivartante* । *aprāpya manasā saha* ।
> — *Taittirīya Upaniṣad* 2.9.1

> Speech returns (fails) from describing it (the reality) along with the mind.

The mind also cannot reach there. The speech cannot describe it, why? Because speech itself is speaking due to that power. How can it speak about the power which is enabling it speak? That is the problem. Therefore epistemology of Upaniṣads for knowing the self (*Brahman*) has to be very unique. What is that epistemology? There are just three steps of realizing that Ultimate Reality: *śravaṇa* (listening) — the first step is listening to various people who have realized this truth, this is *śravaṇa*, but only *śravaṇa* cannot lead us there. Hence, *manana* (contemplation) and then *nididhyāsana* (concentration) need to be practised. As the Upaniṣad says:

> *nāyamātmā pravacanena labhyo na medhayā na bahunā śrutena* ।
> —*Kaṭhopaniṣad* 1.2.23

> This *ātman* cannot be understood just by attending to the discourses nor by intelligence; not even by listening a lot (many people keep on listening to the *gurus* throughout their lives, but they do not understand the reality).

After *śravaṇa*, comes *manana* (thinking, pondering, considering, meditating) and the last or third step is *nididhyāsana*. *Nididhyāsana* is concentration on that very point which we have been hearing, which we have been pondering upon, which we have been meditating. Now we have to concentrate on that particular point and we have to be steadfast. This is called *dhyāna*:

> *tatra pratyayaikatānatā dhyānam* । — *Yogasūtra* 3.2

> *Dhyāna* pertains to concentrate continuously on the reality.

In short, these three are the steps to realization. But they are not exactly the means which can lead us to the object that we want to know. It is so because in the worldly or practical matters the subject is different and the object is something else. One wants to know this pen; pen is a visible object. A person who is knowing, thinking or listening is the subject. Somebody is explaining about the pen. Someone else is looking at a particular pen, so they are the subject and object respectively. What are the means of knowing this pen, first the light has to be there, only then one can see this pen; it can also be touched. There has to be the material from which this pen has been made of, but in the case of the *ātman* (*Brahman*), there is no possibility of subject — object division. *Ātman* is the subject; *ātman* is the object; *ātman* itself is the means of knowing — this is very enigmatic because an object itself becomes the subject. Both of them get merged into one, not only both of them — the third aspect also, that is the means of knowing which cannot be separated from the subject or the object:

> *... vijñātāramare kena vijānīyāt* ।
> — *Bṛhadāraṇyaka Upaniṣad* 2.4.14

> Who can know the subject itself because it is the knower and the knower cannot be known by any object of knowing.

Evidently, this is quite intriguing about the epistemology of Upaniṣads.

Last comes the ethics in philosophy of Upaniṣads. As mentioned above, we have metaphysics, we have epistemology and we have ethics as three different aspects of philosophy these days. Ethics indicates that the seeker has to be well equipped on the moral plane as well. He may be well-read, he is also inquisitive; he may be humble, but he should also be morally sound. He has to undergo a strict discipline under the guidance and supervision of the preceptor. It is not without reason then that the term used for the seeker in Upaniṣad is *antevāsī*, he who stays in close proximity with the *ācārya*. He doesn't have to stay in the comforts of his home. He has to stay with the mentor, observe him, learn more from his conduct than through his words. Both these *antevāsī* and *ācārya* are the two pillars of Upaniṣadic teaching. What are the moral properties that the seeker has to acquire and observe? These are *satya*, *tapa*, *śraddhā*, *dama*, *dāna*, *dayā* and *brahmacarya*.

Upaniṣads have many methods; dialogue is one of them, then there is question — answer method and also this method of narrating something in the mode of a parable or through an allegory. To illustrate, there is a story in the *Bṛhadāraṇyaka Upaniṣad,* which explains the types of seekers and the method of teaching. Once three types of disciples go to Prajāpati and ask him a question: please teach us something so that we may become morally sound. Who are these three types of seekers? They are the *devas* (divine persons, or noble persons); in between are the *mānavas* (human beings who are a mix of good and bad) and, then, *dānavas* (very bad persons or evil people). Prajāpati does not deliver a lengthy discourse he just utters only one letter and repeats it three times. He utters:

> *da, da, da.*
> Nothing more, nothing less.
> But this signifies: *Dānyata, datta, dayadhvam.*
>
> — *Bṛhadāraṇyaka Upaniṣad* 5.2.1.4

Significantly, all the three types of disciples could understand what had been communicated to them by three single letter utterances of Prajāpati.

- The *devas* knew that they are very indulgent people, they always indulge in limitless pleasures and comforts. So Prajāpati has taught them not to over indulge. *Da* in *dāmyata* signifies *damana:* restrain yourself: *dāmyata.*
- *Datta* is for the human beings and the human beings realized that we are always concerned with our own selfish gratification, we do not think about others. So Prajāpati has asked us to give away, to share our possessions with our fellow beings who are staying with us, who are living around us. So *dāmyata* for the *devas* and *datta* for the human beings.
- And the third type of persons are the *dānavas* (evil persons). Although they are bad people but even they are so much morally conscious that they could understand what they had been told by Prajāpati: to empathize, to observe compassion: we do not have to kill people, we do not have to be violent, we have to be compassionate.

In this way, *da, da, da* signifies *dāmyata, datta* and *dayadhvaṁ* respectively. This is the message of Upaniṣads conveyed through a single syllable. This is also known as an *ekākṣara upadeśa*. In Upaniṣads, we have such *ekākṣara upadeśa*. Just like we have *ekākṣara upāsanā*: *oṁ*, similarly, this is an *ekākṣara upadeśa*, only one letter *da* has been uttered but the seekers know what they have to practise. It means these are the three aspects of teaching in the philosophy of Upaniṣads, but before we go to other aspects for many more themes under these three, let us see what Arthur Schopenhauer, a German philosopher, who was so much enamoured of Upaniṣads, has said about the Upaniṣads:

> From every sentence, deep, original, and sublime thoughts arise and the whole is pervaded by a high and holy and earnest spirit. In the whole world, there is no study except that of the originals so beneficial and so elevating as that of the *Aupanekhat*. It has been the solace of my life, it will be solace of my death.
>
> — *Parerga and Paralipomena*, vol. 2, p. 422

Schopenhauer did not know Sanskrit, so he did not read the original Upaniṣads. Upaniṣads were first translated into Persian in the sixteenth century by Dara Shikoh and his team of scholars; who translated fifty Upaniṣads into Persian. This is the collection known as *Sirrey Akbar*. And this Persian translation was sent to Europe. When the East India Company came here, then one of the officers of East India Company Anquateel Duperon, who was a French scholar, was sent a copy of *Sirrey Akbar*. He translated the text from Persian into Latin and then into German. Schopenhauer got this Latin translation of Upaniṣads. This was a tertiary translation, first was the original text, the next was a Persian translation by Dara Shikoh named *Sirrey Akbar*, then the third one was Latin translation by Anquateel Duperon done in the beginning of the nineteenth century (1801-02). This reached Schopenhauer and once he read this, he was so delighted that he said I have found whatever I desired to find. It is said that he always carried with him that copy of the Latin translation titled *Aupanekhat*. Schopenhauer kept the book at his bedside and every night before going to sleep, he used to read some portions of the same. When the tertiary translation can stimulate the mind of a philosopher like Schopenhauer to such an extreme, then one can well imagine the joy of those who can read Upaniṣads in original Sanskrit. How much positive influence they would have felt! Blessed are those who can read this in original Sanskrit.

To quote Dr. S. Radhakrishnan who says:

> Anyone who reads Upaniṣads in original Sanskrit will be caught up and carried away by the elevation. The poetry, the compelling fascination of the many utterances through which they lay bare the secret and sacred relations of the human soul and Ultimate Reality. When we read them, we cannot help being impressed by the exceptional ability, earnestness and righteousness of mind of those who wrestled with these ultimate questions. These souls who tackle these problems still remain and will remain for all time in essential harmony with the highest ideals of civilization.
>
> — Preface to *The Principal Upaniṣads,* pp. 9-10

This clearly indicates the significance pertaining to the philosophy of the Upaniṣads.[1] Another very well-known Upaniṣadic dialogue is between Yama and Naciketā in the *Kaṭhopaniṣad* where Yama (Lord of Death) is the seer and Naciketā is the seeker. There is the story of a young lad Naciketā who was around 11-12 years old, but he questions about life after death: Does something remain after death, or does nothing remain? When Yama lures him with so many material possessions so as to distract him from asking questions about death and beyond, the clear response of Naciketā is as follows:

---

[1] As regards the translations of Upaniṣads, there are lots of translations available. In fact, Upaniṣads and Śrī Bhagavadgītā are the most translated texts of Sanskrit. There are many Sanskrit commentaries on Upaniṣads: by Śaṅkarācārya, Rāmānujācārya, Madhvācārya, Vidyāraṇya, etc. Persian translation by Dara Shikoh, Latin translation (from Persian) by Duperon and English translations first by Raja Rammohun Roy, E. Roer, F. Max Müller (Sacred Books of the East series), and then we have many other English translations including that of Radhakrishnan quoted above.

na vittena tarpaṇīyo manuṣyaḥ ... । — *Kaṭhopaniṣad* 1.1.27

A human being cannot be satiated with money.

Naciketā says emphatically that no amount of money can satisfy a human being, so I do not need money; I want to seek the answer of my question whether something remains after death or nothing is left. Yama, after testing the patience of Naciketā, was forced to deliver the essence of knowledge in this regard that only he could have done.

The famous Maitreyī — Yājñavalkya dialogue occurs in the *Bṛhadāraṇyaka Upaniṣad*. Maitreyī and Gārgī are two extraordinary women in our tradition, two women intellectuals from Upaniṣads. Maitreyī was the wife of Sage Yājñavalkya and Gārgī was an independent scholar, a seeker of the self and of the knowledge that Yājñavalkya professed to preach. Maitreyī asks Yājñavalkya, she confronts her husband with the question when Yājñavalkya was going to renounce. In fact he was a householder and after a certain period one has to take recourse to the *vānaprastha* as per *āśrama-vyavasthā* in ancient Indian tradition. It means that after spending twenty-five years as a householder one was allowed to renounce the world and household. He then goes to the wider society for serving the larger humanity. Yājñavalkya said: I am going to renounce. This is my wealth and I'm dividing it between two of you. There was another wife of Yājñavalkya. Her name was Kātyāyanī. But nobody knows the name of Kātyāyanī today while everyone knows Maitreyī. Kātyāyanī was an ordinary human being and she was satisfied with her share of money. She did not question. But Maitreyī was extraordinary, she questioned her husband, where are you going and why are you going? Yājñavalkya said I am going in search of something which can make me immortal. Then Maitreyī asked further:

yannu mā iyam bhagoḥ sarvā pṛthivī vittena pūrṇā syāt kathaṁ tenāmṛtā syāmiti ।

Shall I be immortal with this money that you are leaving for me?

Yājñavalkya responds:

> *amṛtatvasya tu nāśāsti vittena* ।
> — *Bṛhadāraṇyaka Upaniṣad* 2.4.2
>
> No amount of money can promise immortality.

Maitreyī says I do not want this money. I want that knowledge for which you are renouncing: I also seek *amṛtatva* (immortality).

Upaniṣads teach us the technique of attaining immortality. Mortality is given to us, this body is mortal, but in this mortal body there is a spark of immortality. Each one of us is destined to attain immortality through our own preparation, through our own persistence and through our own practices.

Upaniṣads show us the way towards immortality. Maitreyī says money cannot give me immortality, so I do not want money but want to attain immortality. Likewise, Naciketā says no amount of money can make me immortal and I seek immortality.

There are many more such stories in Upaniṣads — different types of stories, different types of narrations. We have an allegory of a chariot, a beautiful allegory in the *Kaṭha Upaniṣad*. It says:

> *ātmānaṁ rathinaṁ viddhi śarīraṁ rathameva tu* ।
> *buddhiṁ tu sārathiṁ viddhi manaḥ pragrahameva ca* ॥
> — *Kaṭhopaniṣad* 1.3.3
>
> The *Ātman* is the *rathī* or owner of the chariot and this body is the chariot, intellect is the charioteer; mind is like the *pragraha* or the rein.

Obviously, this bring us to the discourse of the *Gītā* which is delivered by Kṛṣṇa sitting in a chariot. Arjuna was standing while Kṛṣṇa is sitting in the chariot. Chariot is a spiritually symbolic metaphor in our knowledge tradition. Chariot signifies the body and owner of the chariot is the *ātman* (self). Kṛṣṇa became the charioteer or *sārathī* of Arjuna in the battle of Mahābhārata. *Sārathī* is also very significant because *sārathī* symbolizes *buddhi* (intellect). It is the intellect which guides us which way to go. ... In modern days one can explain this through the example of a car where mind is the steering wheel, which controls the vehicle. *Ātman* is the owner, body is the chariot or the vehicle, *buddhi* is the driver and steering wheel is the mind, mind can move towards the wrong direction also. It is *buddhi* which can control it. Sense organs are like the horses in it. In a chariot we have the horses and the horses are always tempted towards their food, the grass. In the above narrative, the objects of our sense organs are like the food for horses. We have to control and discipline each of these six aspects right from the food for our sense organs which we are providing constanly. Here it is imperative to understand the food and its significance in our tradition. The theory of *pañcakośa* is well-known in Upaniṣads. This is available in the *Taittirīya Upaniṣad*. According to it, there are five sheaths of human personality and *anna* (food) is one of them. Food is the first sheath. As already mentioned in the beginning, it is a holistic philosophy. It begins from the body. Body is a vehicle in which we have to move and we have to reach our destination. If this vehicle or the chariot is taken care of, if it is kept in proper manner, then only we shall be able to reach our destination that we want to reach. So *anna* is very important. Whatever we eat, it affects our mind. We have heard our ancestors saying: जैसा खाओगे अन्न वैसा बनेगा मन।

That is exactly what is stated in the Upaniṣad:
annamayaṁ hi somya manaḥ ... — *Chāndogya Upaniṣad* 6.6.5

Manas is dependent on the food you eat.

We get Upaniṣadic instructions about growing plenty of food:

annaṁ bahu kurvīta । — *Taittirīya Upaniṣad* 3.9.1

One must grow the food in plenty.

One should never neglect the food. Food is like a divine gift, so we should respect and value it.

At the beginning of our journey to the spiritual end, we have to begin from the material. *Anna* is the most gross material that we have to eat for the sustenance of our life. So beginning is to be made from *anna*, *anna* is verily *Brahman*:

> *annaṁ brahma* । — *Taittirīya Upaniṣad* 3.2.1
>
> *Anna* itself is *Brahman*.

When we eat food, it should be felt that this is the ultimate real because the life and health of our body is dependent on this, not only our gross body, whatever we eat determines our thoughts or the subtle body. So *anna* will take us to the mind. *Annamaya kośa* is the outer sheath, it is the physical level and from it we go to the mental level — *manomaya kośa*. From *manomaya* we go to *prāṇamaya*, the vital level or the vital sheath, the *prāṇa*. These days, we are facing this crisis of *prāṇa* (oxygen) due to corona; *prāṇa* (balance of oxygen within the body) is maintained by *anna*. Drawing upon *anna*, our mind becomes healthy. If we eat good food, our *prāṇa* is vital and healthy. Good food means *sāttvika* food or *sāttvika anna*. So, the teacher tells about the second sheath:

> *mano brahma* । — *Taittirīya Upaniṣad* 3.4.1
>
> *Manas* (mind) is *Brahman*.

Thereafter the seeker practises restraint, controls his mind and comes again. Then the teacher tells him the significance of *prāṇa* as *prāṇa* is subtler than the mind. Mind is subtler than food and *prāṇa* is subtler than the mind. So *anna*, *mana*, *prāṇa* and at fourth level comes the *vijñāna* (intellect). As already explained above, *buddhi* is *sārathī*, so *buddhi* (intellect) comes at the fourth level, this is also dependent on the *anna* we are eating. Food is determining the type of intellect that we will develop within us. These are all given to us, but we are the shapers of these aspects of our own personality. So, from *anna* to *mana* and from *mana* to *prāṇa*, from *prāṇa* to *vijñāna* and last, what are we all searching for? What are we all pursuing? We have everything that is required for making a decent living. We have food, we have house, we have vehicle, we have good health, but still something is missing. What is that? We are all in pursuit of happiness and that happiness is not dependent on the objects we have accumulated. When we start our journey of life, we think that these acquisitions will make us happy. If we have a dwelling of our own we will be happy, if we have a flat, we will be happy. We have a flat, and now if we have a bigger house, we will be happy. We have a big house, if we have a car we will be happy, if we have a bigger car, we will be happy. Everything we aspire we get, and still happiness is eluding us. What is that which will bring us happiness; when we realize that core of our life, i.e. the essence of Upaniṣads, and the ultimate level or the fifth sheath of human personality — that *pañcama kośa* is *ānandamaya kośa:*

> *ānando brahmeti vyajānāt* । — *Taittirīya Upaniṣad* 3.6.1
>
> Then he came to know that bliss is *Brahman.*

We begin from *anna*, but we have to reach up to the level of *annāda* (one who eats food). In fact there is a chapter in the *Taittirīya Upaniṣad* titled Brahmānandavallī. Significantly, nowhere in the world do we find *ānanda-mīmāṁsā* (quantification of happiness) like that has been done in the *Taittirīya Upaniṣad*, Bhṛguvallī; it tells us how to derive true happiness. Happiness is also of several levels. You can get little of happiness from various material objects. Your grandson is born, hence you are happy. That is another level of happiness, but is that the ultimate happiness? Is this the happiness that will always be like that; no, tomorrow there will be some other kind of happiness. Therefore the epithet used for quantifying happiness in the *Chāndogya Upaniṣad* is *bhūmā* (abundant): There is no real *ānanda* in the small amount of acquisitions.

> *yo vai bhūmā tatsukham* ।
> *nālpe sukham ...* ॥ — *Chāndogya Upaniṣad* 7.23.1
>
> That, which is abundant, is real bliss. There is no joy in the small things.

Alpa and *bhūmā*, *alpa* is small while *bhūmā* means abundant — it signifies so much of happiness that nothing else remains, one does not think of anything else. One is so happy, in such a state of bliss, enjoying the level of ecstasy that is *bhūmā ānanda*. So, we have to move on from *anna* to *ānanda*, we all have the capacity to reach that *ānanda*, but most of us are stuck at the *anna*, may be some of us are at the level of *manas*, some people are practising *prāṇāyāma*. They have control over their *prāṇa* and they are doing *yoga*. So their *prāṇamaya kośa* is strong. There are people like scientists and doctors who are serving humanity. They have controlled their *vijñāna* (their intellect), they are doing whatever is right for them at this critical time, this is *vijñānamaya*, but the level of *ānandamaya* is very rare, very difficult to achieve. Upaniṣads take us to the inner cave of life where we can only see darkness, but within this darkness the spark of happiness shines forth and that is *ānandamaya kośa*: *anna*, *annāda* and *ānanda*, *annāda* means the one who eats, i.e. the subject or the self, *anna* is that object which is to be eaten. *Annāda* is the subject who eats and *ānanda* is the goal. You see the English spelling of these three terms, *anna*, *annāda* and *ānanda*; they are in juxtaposition of one or two letters from *anna* to *ānanda* but the *annāda* in between is the agent of eating, he who eats.

Moreover, it is beautifully mentioned in Upaniṣads that whatever food we eat, it is of three types:

> *annam aśitaṁ tredhā bhavati ...* ।
> The food eaten is of three types.
>
> *tasya yaḥ sthaviṣṭho dhātustat purīṣaṁ bhavati* ।
> The grossest form of food eaten is excreted.
>
> *... yo madhyamastanmāṁsam ...*
> The medium type of *anna* that we eat becomes the muscles.
>
> *yo 'ṇiṣṭhaṁ tanmanaḥ* ॥
> But the subtlest form of food that we eat becomes our mind.
>
> — *Chāndogya Upaniṣad* 6.5.1

Evidently, it means that whatever is the most subtle aspect of food, that becomes our *manas* (mind). If we have to control our mind, we just do not have to meditate, we have to eat such food, which is prepared by a calm person. If it is cooked by a violent person and an angry person and we think that we will be able to meditate, no, we will not be, because the type of food, the type of person who is cooking the food and with the mentality that he or she is preparing the food — all that determine our mental modes. If we have to control our mind, we have to begin from the grossest form, i.e. the *anna*. So in our tradition *anna* was also given the status of *Brahman* (Ultimate Reality) for beginners. We have to ascend from one level to the other. It is a dynamic, ascent-oriented philosophy; it is not static that wherever we are, we should stay there. Everyday, every moment, we have to grow and rise.

Swami Vivekananda gave a clarion call which is from the Upaniṣad.

> *uttiṣṭhata jāgrata prāpya varānnibodhata* ।
> — *Kaṭhopaniṣad* 1.3.14

> Arise, awake and make everybody awake who is around you, so that you can get the divine boons, the finest boons of immortality and abundant happiness.

Besides, one of the beautiful prayers from the Upaniṣad is well known, which is as follows:

> *asato mā sadgamaya, tamaso mā jyotirgamaya, mṛtyor mā amṛtam gamaya* ।
> — *Bṛhadāraṇyaka Upaniṣad* 1.3.28

> (O Lord!) Lead me from untruth to truth; from darkness to light; from mortality to immortality.

। *oṁ śāntiḥ śāntiḥ śāntiḥ* ।

Question and Answer Session

DR ARVIND GUPTA: Thank you Dr ShashiPrabaha ji, as usual, you have presented a very brief lecture encapsulating the main points of Upaniṣadic knowledge.

MS ANUSKHA: I had a question for Ma'am.

First of all, I thank you very much for this excellent lecture. My question is that you mentioned about the symbolic and spiritual significance of *sārathī* (charioteer). Lord Kṛṣṇa in the *Bhagavadgītā* has also talked of the charioteer (*sārathī* and *rathī*); these two sit on the chariot and they win when they act together. So my question is that is this relationship only confined to the battlefield like in the *Mahābhārata* or it is also applicable to life, between parents and children, and husband and wife or the teacher and the students. So I just want to know whether it is applicable to different relationships? Thank you Ma'am.

SPEAKER: Very brilliant question Anushka, actually the *Bhagavadgītā* or *Mahābhārata* for that matter, they are all representing a philosophy of life. They are not just simple narrations meant only for the battlefield. Viewed form this angle, the beauty of Indian knowledge systems is that anything which is said is applicable to real life and it was not just a view of life, it was practised as a way of life. So it is relevant to the family, to relations or in the battlefield or in each one's case; you see not only in *brahmāṇḍa*, but also in the *piṇḍa*. In our own individual case our body is the chariot and intellect is the *sārathi* (chaioteer) who leads our life. In fact these are symbolic narrations, which can be applied to any relationship. *Sārathī*, *rathī* or *mahārathī* are graded like the gradual degrees. Who is a very great warrior? He is *mahārathī*; but *rathī* and *sārathī*, they are closely connected. *Rathī* is the owner and *sārathī* is the one who is moving the vehicle. An owner is concerned about the way because he has to reach his destination, and for that choice of *sārathī* is very important because it is he who will take the *rathī* to his destination; if he goes astray, the destination will never be reached. The *rathī* is sitting behind with the faith and trust that *sārathī* will take him/her to the destination. But if the *sārathī* (driver) does not know the way or if he loses the way then the journey will never be successful. It is, therefore, that *sārathī* is very important. That is why Arjuna chose Śrī Kr̥ṣṇa only and not his army, he chose Śrī Kr̥ṣṇa as his *sārathī*. If Kr̥ṣṇa was not the *sārathī* of Arjuna, the victory would not have been possible as you all know. Thank you.

SHRI ANURAG SHARMA: Thank you Ma'am for this brilliant lecture. Maam my question is why; क्या उपनिषद् में यह सुख बताया गया है कि जो पाप-कर्म

हमारी इन्द्रियों के द्वारा किए जाते हैं; वे सुख वाले कार्य होते हैं; क्या उनके सन्दर्भ में उपनिषद् में पाप का कोई उल्लेख है? मतलब सुख अगर है तो वह क्या है?

SPEAKER: बहुत अच्छा प्रश्न है अनुराग। पाप की चर्चा है उपनिषदों में, पाप और पुण्य दोनों की, लेकिन वहाँ पर इसका निषेध नहीं है, वहाँ मना नहीं किया गया कि सुख नहीं लेना या भोग नहीं करना है; सुख और आनन्द में अन्तर है, सुख होता है जो इन्द्रियों से लिया जाता है। सुख — "ख" कहते हैं इन्द्रियों को और "सु" कहते हैं अच्छा, यानि जो इन्द्रियों को अच्छा लगे वह सुख है। So pleasure that is derived by sensual gratification is *sukha* and *ānanda* is bliss यानि चारों तरफ से खुशी ही खुशी — "आनन्द"। जहाँ दुःखों का नाम ही ना हो; सुख जो है वह सापेक्ष है, रिलेटिव है, जहाँ सुख होगा वहाँ दुःख भी होगा। आनन्द निरपेक्ष है, जहाँ दुःख की जरा भी सम्भावना नहीं है। उपनिषद् में भोग का या इन्द्रियों के द्वारा सुख लेने का निषेध नहीं है। न ही उसे पाप कहा गया है। *ईश उपनिषद्* में यह पहला मन्त्र है — "तेन त्यक्तेन भुञ्जीथा"। यनि भोगो लेकिन कैसे भोगो, त्यागपूर्वक भोगो। मतलब अगर आपको कोई चीज अच्छी लगे तो उसको लो, सुख भी लो, लेकिन यह सोच लो कि यह सदा रहने वाला नहीं है। यह मेरा ही नहीं है यह मुझे कहीं से मिला है, यह जा सकता है, लेकिन हम किसी चीज को लेकर उसी में आसक्त हो जाते हैं। यह बिल्कुल वही हालत हैं कि यदि हमें छत पर चढ़ना है, तो सीढ़ी लगाई गई थी छत पर पहुँचने के लिए, लेकिन हम तो सीढ़ी का पहला पाया पकड़ कर वहीं पर बैठ जाते हैं और भूल जाते हैं कि हमें आगे बढ़ना है। अत: भोग जरूरी है, इन्द्रियों के द्वारा सुख भोगना भी जरूरी है, लेकिन उसके साथ-साथ त्याग भी जरूरी है। उपनिषद् की विशेषता यही है कि यहाँ पर समन्वय है, सुख और दुःख में, सत्य और असत्य में, अन्धकार और प्रकाश में। अभी हमने प्रार्थना की —

> असतो मा सद्गमय, तमसो मा ज्योतिर्गमय, मृत्योर् मा अमृतं गमय।
>
> — *बृहदारण्यक उपनिषद्* 1.3.28

ऐसे अनेक द्वन्द्व हैं उपनिषदों में — **इसमे मृत्यु और अमृत, असत् और सत, तम और ज्योति, ये तीन युगल आये हैं,** इसके अलावा मूर्त और अमूर्त, क्षर और अक्षर, इत्यादि भी हैं। यह जो समन्वय है विलोमों में, वे दोनों विलोम जीवन का हिस्सा है। लेकिन हमको यह समझ लेना चाहिए कि कौन सा ज्यादा महत्त्वपूर्ण है। परा-विद्या–अपरा-विद्या है, विद्या–अविद्या है, सम्भूति–असम्भूति है, हर जगह पर ये द्वन्द्व हैं लेकिन जो हमारी बुद्धि है, जो हमारा विवेक है, वही बताता है कि दोनों में से हमें किसको चुनना है। नचिकेता जब यमराज से प्रश्न पूछता है तो यही कहता है –

> येयं प्रेते विचिकित्सा अस्तीत्येके नास्तीत्येके । — *कठोपनिषद्* 1.1.20

DR ARVIND GUPTA: यह जो एक शब्द आता है "सच्चिदानन्द" जरा इसके बारे में बताइए, कहाँ से इसका प्रादुर्भाव है, इसका क्या अर्थ है।

SPEAKER: जी, इसमें तीन पहलू हैं — हालांकि प्रमुख उपनिषदों में "सच्चिदानन्द"[2] शब्द नहीं आया है। वहाँ यह इस रूप में आया है —

सत्यं ज्ञानम् अनन्तं ब्रह्म। — *तैत्तिरीय उपनिषद्* 2.1.1

इसका आशय यही है कि हमारे सामने दो रास्ते खुले रहते हैं — एक श्रेय का है और दूसरा प्रेय का, जिसे हम पाप कह रहे हैं। वह पाप शब्द वहाँ नहीं है लेकिन वह रास्ता प्यारा तो लगता है, लुभाता भी है लेकिन अच्छा या श्रेयस्कर नहीं है, इसके विपरीत सुख वह है जो इन्द्रियों से नहीं मिलता है, वही श्रेय है, वही आनन्द है; जो बुद्धिमान होते हैं वे सही रास्ता चुन लेते हैं और जिनकी बुद्धि इधर-उधर भटक जाती है, जिनका सारथी योग्य नहीं होता है वे कभी अपने गन्तव्य पर पहुँचते नहीं हैं।

उक्त कथन में आनन्द शब्द नहीं आया है "अनन्त" शब्द आया है — अर्थ वही है। तीन चीजें हैं — सत्, चित् और आनन्द — सत् मतलब वह है जिसका अस्तित्व रहता है, दो चीजों की प्राय: चर्चा होती है सत् और असत्। एक वह है जो सदा रहता है वह सत् है, और जो सदा नहीं रहता, वह असत् है। शरीर असत् है और आत्मा सत् है। ब्रह्म और आत्मा एक ही हैं, इसलिए सत् है। चित् का मतलब वह सचेत है, चेतन है। वह केवल है नहीं, बल्कि उसमें चेतना भी है। शरीर असत् है और इसमें चेतना नहीं है यह असत् भी है और अचित् भी है। लेकिन अन्दर जो आत्मा है वह सत् भी है और चित् भी है। तीसरा है आनन्द — शरीर असत् है, अचित् है, और यह आनन्द भी नहीं है। लेकिन हम सारा जीवन यह सोचकर बिता देते हैं कि यही आनन्द है। हम शरीर के सुख में ही लगे रहते हैं — शरीर की सेवा में, शरीर को सजाने में, संवारने में। लेकिन जो शरीर के भीतर आत्मा है, वही सत् है, आनन्द है, वह वास्तव में तीनों कालों में रहेगी। आज भी, आने वाले कल भी, और कल जो बीत गया है उसमें भी। वह सत् है, चित् होने से सचेत है, वही चेतन है, और आनन्द भी। वही आनन्द का स्रोत है, और जो शरीर है, यह असत् है, अचित् है और यह आनन्द नहीं है।

भारतीय दर्शन में मनुष्य का जो शरीर है इसे मन्दिर के समान कहा गया है क्योंकि इसी में रहकर आनन्द को पाया जा सकता है और केवल इसी योनि में यह सम्भव है; किसी पशु या पक्षी को यह ज्ञान नहीं है कि वह अपने बारे में सोचे। यह केवल मनुष्य के शरीर में ही सम्भव है — यानी मर्त्य शरीर में अमर्त्य हो जाना। *कठोपनिषद्* में कहा गया है –

ऽअथ मर्त्योऽमृतो भवति अत्र ब्रह्म समश्नुते॥ — 2.1.4

इसी देह में रहकर जो मर्त्य है वह अमृत बन सकता है। इसी के भीतर ब्रह्म को पाया जा सकता है। इसलिए मनुष्य का शरीर बहुत दुर्लभ शरीर है। इसी में हम "सच्चिदानन्द" का साक्षात्कार कर सकते हैं। बचपन में एक भजन सुना करते थे, हमारी दादी गाती थी कि –

आनन्द स्रोत बह रहा, पर तू उदास है।

---

2 वास्तव में 'सच्चिदानंद' शब्द एक गौण उपनिषद् में मिलता है — *saccidānandaghanaṁ jyotiḥ* — Nṛsiṁhottaratāpinī *Upaniṣad* 6

अर्थात् आनन्द का स्रोत हमारे भीतर ही है, "सच्चिदानन्द" हमारे भीतर ही है। लेकिन हम सभी जगह छोटी–छोटी चीजों में उसको ढूँढ़ते रहते हैं और इसलिए निराश होते रहते हैं। एक बार अभी एक-दो दिन पहले (10 दिसम्बर 2020) *टाइम्स ऑफ़ इंण्डिया* में "स्पीकिंग ट्री" में एक लेख आया था सद्गुरू जग्गी वासुदेव जी का जिसका शीर्षक था — 'In' is the only way 'Out', यानि Turning inward is the way out, उन्होंने इसको आज के इस करोनाकाल के समय से सम्बन्धित किया "इनवार्ड" या अन्तर्मुखी हो जाने से। तो यह जो हमारे अन्दर है वही सच्चिदानन्द है।

DR ARVIND GUPTA: आपने अभी एक वाक्य बोला "तत्त्वमसि"। इसका मतलब क्या है।

SPEAKER: यह एक महावाक्य है और उपनिषद् से आया है। तत् का "अर्थ" वह या इंग्लिश में "that" है; दोनों का एक ही अर्थ है, तत् मतलब वह। त्वम् का अर्थ तू, जोकि सामने बैठा है, तत् मतलब वह जो "थर्ड पर्सन" है और त्वम् जो अंग्रेज़ी में "सेकण्ड पर्सन" है और अहम् वह है जिसे इंग्लिश में "फर्स्ट पर्सन" कहते हैं। संस्कृत में हम उसे "उत्तम पुरुष" कहते हैं। तो गुरु समझा रहा है शिष्य को कि वह जो तुम सामने देख रहे हो, दैट इज "यू" (त्वम्) — तुम ही हो। तुम में और उसमें कोई भेद नहीं है। जो जगत् की वस्तुएं हैं उनमें और तुम में कोई अन्तर नहीं है — तत् त्वम् असि। जिस दिन तुम्हें यह अनुभूति हो गई, जिस दिन तुम्हारे अन्दर यह समझ पैदा हो गई कि बाहर जो है वह मुझसे अलग नहीं है उस दिन संसार के सारे संकट दूर हो जाएंगे। इसी को दूसरी तरह से कहा है, गुरु समझा रहा है *तत् त्वम् असि* लेकिन जब शिष्य खुद समझ लेता है तब कहता है, "अहम् ब्रह्म अस्मि, अहं ब्रह्मास्मि"। मैं ही ब्रह्म हूँ, मुझसे अलग कुछ नहीं है। पहला वाक्य तो उपदेश (instruction) है "तत्त्वम् असि", और दूसरा "अहं ब्रह्मास्मि" अनुभव (realization) है। दोनों एक ही चीज़ के पहलू हैं और दोनों ही महावाक्य कह गये हैं।

DR ARVIND GUPTA: ये जो आइडियाज़ हैं क्योंकि काफी पुराने हैं क्या इनका प्रभाव पश्चिमी चिन्तन पर आता है?

SPEAKER: जी अवश्य आता है, लेकिन दिक्कत यह है कि पश्चिम में तो अलग-अलग दार्शनिक अपने-अपने व्यक्तिगत विचार देते हैं। जैसे काण्ट का है — उन्होंने कई जगह पर जो "कैटेगोरिकल इम्पिरेटिव" की बात की है, उसमें मॉरैलिटि का हाइएस्ट स्टैण्डर्ड है, इसी तरह हमारे यहाँ जो मीमांसा दर्शन में है वह "विधि" है उसी को वे कैटेगोरिकल इम्पिरेटिव कहते हैं। इसी तरह ये जो हमारा "अद्वैतवाद" है उसे आज क्वाण्टम फिज़िक्स में एप्लाई किया जा रहा है; तो मानवता में ये विचार घूमते रहते हैं और जो चेतना है वो संक्रान्त होती रहती है लेकिन इस सत्य को उपनिषदों में इतने सुन्दर शब्दों में, इतने ब्रीफ नैरेटिव में बाँधा गया है कि वह शायद और कहीं भी नहीं मिलता है, इसलिए उपनिषद् विश्व में अपनी तरह के अकेले ग्रन्थ हैं। बाद में जो व्याख्यायें लिखी गई हैं उनमें लम्बी-लम्बी चर्चायें चली हैं तो शायद असली बात उनकी जटिल शब्दावली में खो गई है। लेकिन अपने आप में उपनिषद् अदभुत हैं, जैसे *केनोपनिषद्* एक छोटा उपनिषद् है, लेकिन उसके अन्दर जीवन के जो सत्य प्रकट

हुए हैं वे इस तरह समाए हुए हैं कि आप महसूस कर सकते हैं कि ये सार्वभौम हैं। कहीं नाम नहीं है, कहीं कोई लिङ्ग नहीं है, कहीं कोई कास्ट का, नेशनलिटी का या रिलीज़न का कोई इश्यू नहीं है। यह यूनिवर्सल नॉलेज़ है — एनीबडी कैन एक्सपीरिएन्स इट एनीव्हेयर।

DR ARVIND GUPTA: यह जो मैटेरियलिज़्म है। आपने एपिस्टेमोलॉजी की बात कही। क्या ऐसे नॉलेज़ को आगे बढ़ाया जाए? क्या उसके लिए विधियां बनाई जाएं। तो इनके यहाँ मेटाफिज़िक्स और एपिस्टेमोलॉज़ी को मिलाकर इन्होंने साइंस या जो मैटिरियल वर्ल्ड है उसको जानने के लिए कुछ उपाय निकले, इंस्ट्रूमेण्ट्स बनाई, थ्योरी बनाई, एण्ड दे हैव गोन वेरी डीप इण्टू अण्डरस्टैंडिंग द नेचर। लेकिन वे वहाँ नहीं पहुँचे कि वे कॉन्शियसनैस को समझ सकें। दूसरी ओर हमारे यहाँ भी ऐसा हुआ कि हम दर्शन में ही रह गए और मैटिरियल वर्ल्ड में जो प्रोग्रेस हुई थी उस से थोड़ा विमुख हो गए थे।

SPEAKER: ऐसा नहीं है क्योंकि अभी हम बात कर रहे हैं उपनिषदों की, जिसका कन्टेण्ट है आत्मा या अल्टीमेट रिएलिटी का, लेकिन अगर हम दूसरे शास्त्र पढ़ें, जैसे हमारे यहाँ कामशास्त्र, अर्थशास्त्र, वास्तुशास्त्र, ज्योतिषशास्त्र आदि हैं; तो ऐसा नहीं है कि हमारे यहाँ मैटिरियल प्रोग्रेस नहीं है। ऐसे-ऐसे वर्णन हैं जिनसे सूचित होता है कि हमारे यहाँ पर मैटेरियल प्रोग्रेस की कोई सीमा नहीं थी, उसका वर्णन भी है लेकिन जहाँ-जहाँ पर उसका वर्णन है वहाँ-वहाँ पर भी कहीं ना कहीं हमारे मैटेरियल प्रोग्रेस के साथ-साथ स्पिरिचुअल परफेक्शन की भी बात आएगी लेकिन इसके विपरीत वेस्ट में फोकस मैटेरियल पर ही रहेगा। हमारे यहाँ पर जब हम प्रेय और श्रेय की बात करते हैं। प्रेय मैटेरियल प्रोग्रेस है और श्रेय जो है, वह स्पिरिचुअल है। लेकिन पाश्चात्य चिंतन एकांगी है। जबकि हमारे यहां सदा दोनों पक्षों की बात होगी। — स्पष्टतः उपनिषद् में वह सारी भौतिक चर्चा नहीं है लेकिन हमारे यहाँ वेद को अगर हम ले लें वहाँ कृषि विज्ञान है, जलविज्ञान है, भूविज्ञान है, एवं और भी नाना प्रकार के विज्ञान हैं। *छान्दोग्य उपनिषद्* में बत्तीस तरह की विद्याओं का वर्णन है; मधु-विद्या है, दहर-विद्या है, यह सब मैटेरियल प्रोग्रेस ही हैं। *छान्दोग्य उपनिषद् में* एक स्थान पर नारद और सनत्कुमार का संवाद आता है, जहाँ नारद गिनाते हैं कि उन्होंने उन्नीस विद्याएं पढ़ ली हैं। ये सभी विद्याएं हमारे आज के विविध विषय ही हैं। इसका मतलब यह है कि उस समय भी ये सब पढ़ाई जा रहीं थी। लेकिन नारद कहते हैं कि उन्नीस विद्याएं पढ़कर मैं विद्वान् तो बन गया हूँ लेकिन मेरे दुःख का अन्त नहीं हो रहा है। इस पर सनत्कुमार ने कहा कि दुःख का अन्त तो तभी होगा जब तुम अपने आप को जानोगे –

> तरति शोकम् आत्मवित्। — *छान्दोग्य उपनिषद्* 7.1.3

यदि दुःख का अन्त करना है तो आत्मविद्या प्राप्त करनी ही होगी। अत: भौतिक प्रगति नहीं है, यह हम नहीं कह सकते; लेकिन वही सब कुछ नहीं है, उसके परे कुछ और भी है।

MS PRERNA GANDHI: Ma'am usually it is said that we are not thoughts, we are observers of our thoughts, so the question that I want to ask is what do Upaniṣads or the ancient Indian texts say on Vedic thoughts, where do they come from?

DR SHASHIPRABHA KUMAR: Yeah, for that, you have to read the *Kena Upaniṣad*. It says that the thoughts emanate from our consciousness supported with the mind because if mind is not in between as a mediator, there will be no thoughts; so mind is the instrument or vehicle of thoughts. Therefore, so much of emphasis is laid on the control of mind. In other words, thoughts emanate from consciousness but with the instrumentality of mind; there is an observer, of course, you are right, there is an observer and that observer is the ultimate consciousness. Consciousness also has levels. There are four levels of consciouness, *jāgrat*, *svapna*, *suṣupti* and *turīya*. So that *turīya* (ultimate) is the observer but all the other three aspects are at the empirical level: *jāgrat*, *svapna* and *suṣupti, aur jo cauthā dharātala hai vo* observer *yā sākṣī caitanya hai.*

MR SANJAY BAHAL: I appreciate Dr ShashiPrabha Kumar for this very high standard lecture on Upaniṣads.

SPEAKER: Thank you Sanjay ji. The *Bhagavadgītā* is the essence of Upaniṣads. It is said:

> *sarvopaniṣado gāvo dogdhā gopālanandanaḥ* ।
> *pārtho vatsaḥ sudhīrbhoktā dugdhaṁ gītāmṛtaṁ mahat*
> (Unknown) ।।

> Upaniṣads are the cows and the *Gītā* is the milk (*dugdha*). Arjuna is like the calf who first got the taste of the milk.

Scholars or the readers of the *Bhagavadgītā*, they are like enjoyers of the milk and teaching of *Gītā* is the milk, but from where it has been drawn — Upaniṣads are like the source in the form of cows who give milk to the calf and to the seekers as well; Kṛṣṇa is like the milking man.

Thank you.

Cārvāka Philosophy

The schools of Indian philosophy have been divided mainly into two groups — *āstika* and *nāstika*. The popular notion of *āstika* is that one who believes in God is *āstika* and one who does not believe in God is *nāstika*. But there is another view also which propounds that:

> *nāstiko vedanindakaḥ* । — *Manusmr̥ti* 2.11
>
> He is an athiest who deplores the Veda.

Viewed from this angle *vedanindaka* is *nāstika*. And the third view is that the one who does not believe in the theory of rebirth is also known as *nāstika*. On all these three criteria, Cārvāka is a thorough *nāstika*. Cārvāka does not believe in God, the Cārvāka does not believe in Vedic authority or verbal testimony for that matter, which is known as *śabda-pramāṇa* in Indian philosophy. The Cārvāka does not believe in the theory of *karma* and rebirth as well. Hence, on all the three counts, Cārvāka is a thorough *nāstika*. To elaborate, I quote:

> Cārvāka is the material system of Indian philosophy. Chrono logically, its treatment must be given the first place even though the school appears as a note of discord in the symphony of Indian philosophy. On account of the tendency of this school towards gross materialism, atheism, individualistic hedonism and radical selfishness, it has become an object of ridicule. However, this fact should not prompt us to overlook the ethical contribution of the Cārvāka school to the development of Indian thought. On the contrary, this protestant ideology and radical empiricism has been responsible for strengthening the logical aspects of all other systems of Indian philosophy.
>
> — I.C. Sharma 1991: 103

The name Cārvāka can be derived from three points of view:

i. It is held that there was a *ṛṣi* named Cārvāka who is mentioned in the *Mahābhārata*. Ṛṣi Cārvāka was the propounder of this school. Therefore, the school is known as Cārvāka.

ii. Second interpretation is given that this is derived from the root √*carv* (to chew), and because the system focuses on eating, drinking and merry making, therefore, *carva* became popular as Cārvāka.

iii. The third interpretation is that, if we split the term Cārvāka, it is *cāru* + *vāk*. *Cāru vāk* means sweet talk because whatever the followers of this school talk, it appeals to the masses and, therefore, it is known as Cārvāka.

Besides, anothor aspect led to the other name of the school, that is Lokāyata: *lokeṣu āyatam mataṁ lokāyatamatam* ... because this was popular among the laymen and this can be understood by anybody and everybody, therefore, it is known as Lokāyata. We find both these names in the sources of Indian philosophy. But as far as the original sources of Cārvāka philosophy are concerned, they are largely unavailable. When we talk about Nyāya or Vaiśeṣika, Sāṁkhya or Yoga, we see that there are more than hundred books available in every school even today after a long gap of time, but for Cārvāka, we do not find any one complete original source. It is only in the *Sarvadarśanasaṁgraha* of Madhvācārya, *Sarvasiddhāntasaṁgraha* of Śaṅkarācārya, *Ṣaḍdarśanasamuccaya* of Guṇaratna Sūri and the Sanskrit drama *Prabodhacandrodaya* by Kṛṣṇa Miśra, which is a philosophical drama — that the Cārvāka view is quoted. Besides these sources, we also find Cārvāka views as *pūrva-pakṣa* or quoted as an opponent in almost all the schools of Indian philosophy. The traditional *āstika* scholars mostly begin their discussion by quoting the Cārvāka view and then after refuting it, go on to posit their own standpoints. The only text of Cārvākas that we could find and which is recently made available and has been published from Baroda is the *Tattvopaplavasiṁha* of Jayarāśi.

Chronologically Vedas are the oldest available documents in Indian philosophical tradition, then from Vedas we come to the Brāhmaṇas, Āraṇyakas and Upaniṣads. Upaniṣads propound and focus on core spiritualism. Although they talk of both matter and spirit, their focus is obviously on spiritualism. But as we shall see, Cārvāka is a rejection and repudiation of this spiritual outlook of Indian thought. This is a core materialistic and naturalistic, atheistic, individualistic, rationalistic, logical, crude humanistic and sceptic school. These are the terms used for Cārvāka by different scholars who have described its philosophy.

Philosophy of Cārvāka or of any other school for that matter can be studied in a broad canvas, but we shall try to discuss all the schools of Indian philosophy as per three broad classifications which are prevalent today and which we are all aware of. The first is metaphysics and according to Cārvāka metaphysics, matter is the only reality, and there are only four elements which the Cārvāka accepts: these are earth, water, air and fire. They do not accept *ākāśa* (ether). Why don't they accept *ākāśa*? Because it cannot be proved on the basis of their epistemology. The Cārvāka epistemology propounds that perception is the only means of knowing, while there are almost eight means of knowing which are popular in various schools of Indian philosophy. Out of these, Cārvāka accepts only one means of knowing as *pramāṇa* and that is perception; because *ākāśa* cannot be perceived through sense organs, therefore, Cārvāka does not accept *ākāśa* as an element.

Regarding the existence of *ākāśa*, the Naiyāyikas and Vaiśeṣikas had to prove through inference (*anumāna)* that *ākāśa* is the substratum of sound (*śabda-guṇa*), and they accept sound as a *guṇa*, which is given to us. We all know by perception that *śabda* is there but what is the substratum of *śabda*? According to Nyāya and Vaiśeṣika schools, it is *ākāśa*, but this cannot be proved on the basis of perception. We have to take recourse to inference and the Cārvāka does not accept *anumāna* as a means of knowing. In this respect, there is a long debate between the Cārvākas and the

Naiyāyikas, and the Cārvākas and the Buddhists. The Buddhists, the Jainas and the Vaiśeṣikas accept *anumāna,* but Cārvākas do not accept *anumāna* or inference. Why? Because the whole evidence of *anumāna* is based on invariable concomitance, i.e. *vyāpti.* For explaining *vyāpti,* a popular example is given as follows:

> *yatra yatra dhūmaḥ tatra tatra vahniḥ* ।
>
> Wherever there is smoke, there is fire.

This is the premise we have to prove on the basis of *anumāna* but the Cārvāka does not accept *vyāpti* and asks how can you prove that wherever there is smoke, there is fire. Have you seen all the places in the world where smoke is found and fire is also present there, it is humanly and physically impossible to go and see all the places. All the Naiyāyikas, and even Buddhists, are known as Naiyāyikas, because in the field of logic, there is Bauddha Nyāya, Jaina Nyāya and Hindu Nyāya — all the three accept *anumāna.* Although the Buddhists also do not accept *vyāpti* as the Nyāya of Gautama does but for repudiating Cārvāka, they are all on one side. The Cārvāka says that for proving the existence of inference you are going back to perception because *vyāpti* cannot be known through any other means except perception. So for proving perception you go to inference and for proving inference you again go to perception. This is known as *cakraka doṣa* or *anyonyāśraya doṣa*; it is a fallacy in logic. Therefore, we do not accept inference. This is one argument of the Cārvāka which is very simple, but there are many more arguments and long debates have taken place between Buddhists and Naiyāyikas both on one side and Cārvākas on the other side. So, for Cārvākas, neither inference is the means of valid knowing nor is *śabda* (verbal authority). In Indian philosophy, especially in the *āstika* schools of philosophy, *śabda* is held to be the supreme evidence; when perception fails, when inference fails, when even *upamāna* fails, then *śabda* is held as supreme. Whatever is written in the Veda, will be accepted by all the *āstika* schools, but the Cārvāka does not accept *śabda* because Cārvāka refutes Vedas. It is the only school of Indian thought which refutes Vedic authority in clear terms. The Buddhists and Jainas also do not accept the Veda, but they do not denigrate the Veda. The Cārvāka denigrates the Veda and totally rejects, whatever is written in Veda. This was in fact a strong reaction to the prevalent situation in the time of post-Upaniṣadic period.

As already stated, physical matter is the only reality for the Cārvāka and metaphysically only four elements are there: earth, water, air and fire. Epistemologically perception is the only means of knowing for them, but the basic and most important contribution of Cārvāka is to the field of ethics, the third branch of philosophy, these are the three branches or three heads under which we are studying and teaching philosophy these days. According to Cārvāka ethics, it is the pleasure or the desire, which is the ultimate goal of life. So they may be understood as hedonistic from the ethical point of view. Hedonism is the view which accepts material pleasures as the aim of life and these material pleasures can be for oneself or for everybody. On this basis, hedonism is again divided into two types — depending on an ethical viewpoint as to have pleasure for oneself or for everyone. Accordingly these are two kinds of hedonism and both these views are available among the Cārvākas. In fact there are divisions or levels among the Cārvākas such as a *dhūrta* Cārvāka or *a suśikṣita* Cārvāka. *Dhūrta* Cārvākas are those who accept that only individual or egoistic pleasure is the goal of their life, while altruistic pleasure or pleasure for all is the view of the *suśikṣita* Cārvākas, this is the universalistic ethics. In other words, there are two types of Cārvākas — laymen and the learned ones; the later are those who accept morality, who accept the goodwill for others, who care for others and society. There is no doubt about the fact that pleasure is the natural aim of all our activities. We all want pleasure and seek it as our goal. This is a psychological fact, but for Cārvākas, it ought to be, it is not just that pleasure is, but pleasure ought to be. According to them, pleasure ought to be the goal because ethics is a science or normative branch of philosophy. According to them, pleasure ought to be the goal of all our desires and actions. So, this is the principal theory of Cārvāka ethics. As per the basic assumption of Cārvāka, pleasure and the desire to be pleased are both connected with each other, so *kāma* and *artha* are the two pursuits for human life; *dharma* and *mokṣa* are not acceptable to Cārvākas. *Dharma* is the obligation or it is the injunction rooted in Vedas or Vedic scriptures; Cārvākas do not accept *dharma* as any social obligation or any moral obligation given in the scriptures. *Dharma* is outrightly rejected by them because *dharma* at that time was popular only in the form of rituals like the *yajña* or the *karma-kāṇḍa*. May be there were many distortions in the Vedic rites of *yajña*. It was not the original philosophical type of action, rather it was being practised with all sorts of distortions and superstitions. Blind faith must also have been prevalent, so Cārvākas rejected *dharma*. They do not accept *mokṣa* also because they ask as to who has seen *mokṣa*. Perception cannot prove *mokṣa*. *Mokṣa* is the ultimate goal as accepted in all the other schools of Indian philosophy, but for Cārvākas, *mokṣa* is nothing but the physical death:

> *maraṇamevāpavargaḥ* ।
> — *Bṛhaspatisūtra*, quoted in *Sarvadarśanasaṁgraha*, chap. 1

Death is annihilation of everything and when this physical body falls, that itself is liberation because after that what happens — nobody can see, what we see is that this body, this physical body has fallen — everything for this body ends then and there. And for Cārvākas this body is the *ātman*. They do not accept a conscious self or a constant *ātman*. This body itself is *ātman*, this view of Cārvāka is known as **Dehātmavāda**; *deha* is *ātman* and end of *deha* is *mokṣa*. When the body has fallen, then *mokṣa* happens. **Bhūtacaitanyavāda** is the next level of Cārvākas who accept consciousness in matter. If somebody asks Cārvāka that you do not accept conscious self, but we all see that the body moves, the body goes and the body desires, body works. So consciousness is there, we directly observe it. There are two aspects: one is matter and the other is spirit or consciousness, but you do not accept this consciousness as eternal self. The Cārvāka will say that physical body itself is the real self. We usually identify ourselves with the body, *ahaṁ kṛśo 'haṁ sthūlo 'haṁ rogī ahaṁ svastha,* etc., all these statements, they are identifying "*ahaṁ*" with the body — body is *sthūla*, body is *kṛśa*, body is *rogī* and body is *svastha* (healthy). So body itself is the self for us. Even if you accept that there is some other conscious self besides this physical body then how will you prove because Cārvākas will not accept anything else other than perception, and consciousness or self cannot be physically perceived. The Nyāya and Vaiśeṣika schools posit a conscious self and prove the existence of self based on different reasons. And these reasons are given in the form of *anumāna*. But since the Cārvāka has already refuted *anumāna* as a means of knowing, consciousness cannot be proved by reasoning.

God is also not there, according to the Cārvāka, because who has seen God? Nobody can see God. And why is God required, because usually God is held to be the creator of this world, God is the custodian of our actions, morally right or morally wrong; but for the Cārvāka, there is no theory of *karma* at play in the world. Whatever we are doing, whatever we are enjoying, it is the present moment which is important and which is real. Nobody has seen the past and nobody can see the future. So, this is the moment in which we are living and whatever we are doing, it is for the sake of our pleasure. There will be no *pāpa*, no *puṇya*, no *dharma*. Therefore, God is not required. If somebody asks them who will be managing the world, then they will say that king is the God because he is responsible for society and its well-being.

Cārvākas do not accept the theory of causation also, while all other schools of Indian philosophy believe that whatever happens, happens due to a cause; cause and effect relationship is a knot which all of them have tried to untie. Somebody says that cause and effect are inherently related, they are identical. Somebody will say that they are not identical but they are inseparably related. For the Buddhists, it is *pratītya-samutpāda;* for the Nyāya –Vaiśeṣika, this is the theory of Asatkāryavāda; for the Sāṁkhya and Yoga, it is the Satkāryavāda; for the Vedānta it is Vivartavāda. These are the different theories of causation explained in Indian philosophy. But for Cārvākas, there is no relation between cause and effect, nothing happens due to a definite cause. Naturally, the question arises as to how does this world work according to them? They will answer: everything works because this is the nature of things. How does consciousness arise out of matter? To answer this question they give an example of a green beetle leaf, an areca nut, brown catechu and white lime powder — when all these four items combine, a new colour red is produced afresh, similarly, when four material elements combine, consciousness is created.

Cārvākas believe that whatever happens, it happens by nature or just by chance. So the theory of Cārvāka may be known as Svabhāvavāda: Fire is hot, water is cold, earth and the air are neither hot nor cold. Who has made the fire hot, water cold, earth and air neither hot nor cold? This is all due to *svabhāva*, it is naturalism. It is the nature of things — it is the nature of fire to be hot, nature of water to be cold and nature of earth and air to be neither hot nor cold. Significantly in the *Śvetāśvatara Upaniṣad (SU)* towards the beginning of the text, there is a discussion about different causes of the universe. There, it is mentioned as follows:

> *kālaḥ svabhāvo niyatiryadṛcchā bhūtani yoniḥ puruṣa iti cintyam* ।
> — *SU* 1.2

In fact, six views are mentioned in this statement. The *Śvetāśvatara Upaniṣad* is one of the later Upaniṣads and following six theories are mentioned in it:

1. Kālavāda, that everything happens in its time, at an opportune time or at the destined time.
2. Svabhāvavāda is whatever the Cārvākas are propounding, that everything takes place naturally, it is Svabhāvavāda.
3. Niyativāda, everything is predestined, predetermined; predeterminism is Niyativāda.

4. Yadṛcchāvāda means that everything occurs by chance or incidentally. It is just a pure coincidence that somebody is born, somebody is dying, somebody is happy and somebody is sorry. So *yadṛcchā* is a step ahead of *svabhāva*. *Svabhāva* is nature but *yadṛcchā* is coincidence. It is a coincidence that this happens in the world. Nothing is a cause of any particular incident.
5. Bhūtavāda propounds that there are five *mahābhūtas*, viz. earth, water, fire, air and sky as causes of the universe.
6. Puruṣavāda: Last, but not the least, it is *puruṣa* or *ātman* who is held to be the original cause of creation.

Svabhāvavāda is the most popular theory of Cārvāka. Accordingly, it is the nature of things and we should not worry about their origin, their causes, the relation between cause and effect — because all this will not lead to the pleasure we are seeking. We are born and we start seeking pleasure. Now this pleasure can also be of various types. Is it mere physical pleasure or is it mental pleasure or it is intellectual pleasure? There can be several levels of pleasure. Again the *dhūrta* Cārvāka or the very first level of Cārvāka will say that physical pleasure is the ultimate goal. Sage Vātsyāyana in his *Kāmasūtra* also talks of the Lokāyatas (Cārvākas) and says that Cārvākas are not just pursuing pure physical pleasure. They also dwell upon these arts and art forms. He has enumerated sixty-four types of art forms and he says that humans should indulge in all such art forms. These are also types of pleasure. Accordingly, the Cārvāka school will differ in its viewpoint on the concept of pleasure (*sukha*). If we just break the word *sukha* — *su* means good and *kha* means the *indriya* (sense organ). Literally the term *sukha* connotes that which is giving a good feeling to one's sense organs. Whatever one sees by his eyes, if it gives him pleasure, it is *sukha*. Whenever one listens to good music, it gives pleasure to his auditory organs. Therefore, it is *sukha*; there are five *indriyas* and there are five types of objects of these *indriyas* — all these are physical pleasures, but pleasure is also above and beyond this physical pleasure and all sorts of pleasures should be incorporated in this goal of Cārvāka philosophy.

About the Veda and its authority, the Cārvāka view is quoted in the *Sarvadarśanasaṁgraha* of Mādhavācārya. As mentioned above, we do not find any original literature of Cārvāka. There are seven or eight *sūtras* which have been quoted here and they are ascribed to Bṛhaspati. So, Bṛhaspati is said to be the propounder of the Cārvāka thought and he says:

agnihotraṁ trayo vedāstridaṇḍaṁ bhasmaguṇṭhanam ।
buddhipauruṣahīnānāṁ jīvikā dhatṛnirmitā ॥
— Quoted in *Sarvadarśanasaṁgraha*, chap. 1

Performing the ritual of fire, reading of all the three Vedas and wrapping one's body with the *bhasma* — all these are activities of those who are neither intelligent nor strong enough; they derive earnings out of such activities.

Cārvāka is ridiculing or refuting the Vedic rites saying that it is all due to the vested interests of the selfish priests. They have popularized all these rites so that they can extract money from laymen, otherwise they have no religious significance; they will not lead to any *puṇya* or any good effect later on. Then what is *svarga*? And what is *parama puruṣārtha* (ultimate goal)?

aṅganādyāliṅganajanyaṁ sukhameva puruṣārthaḥ ।
— Quoted in *Sarvadarśanasaṁgraha*, chap. 1

Embracing one's beloved is the real pleasure and that is the ultimate goal of life. Then what is *naraka*?

kaṇṭakādijanyaṁ dukhameva narakaḥ ।
— Quoted in *Sarvadarśanasaṁgraha*, chap. 1

If some thorn is pricking one's skin, then that is *duḥkha* and whatever is *duḥkha*, whatever is giving pain to the sense organs, that itself is *naraka*. There is no hell beyond this physical world; there is no heaven beyond this life and body.

There is a popular statement of Cārvākas as follows:

> *yāvajjīvet sukhaṁ jīvet ṛṇaṁ kṛtvā ghṛtaṁ pibet* ।
> *bhasmībhūtasya dehasya punarāgamanaṁ kutaḥ* ॥
> — Quoted in *Sarvadarśanasaṁgraha*, chap. 1

> As long as you are alive, you should be indulging in pleasure, even if you have to borrow money from somebody, don't hesitate, borrow and drink *ghṛta* (butter oil) because this body will not come back once it is burnt to ashes.

Notably, Cārvākas were totally materialists, but they were not promoting that one should drink intoxicants or alcohol; rather, one should drink only *ghṛta* (butteroil). It means that they were health-conscious and were promoting good health because for them this body itself is all, so we have to take care of the body. We should have healthy food, because when this body is put to ashes, then who will be able to see it. Body will never come back. So enjoy to the last moment as long as this body is alive. It is for us all to see that the dead body is put to fire and it turns into ashes. Once this body is transformed into ashes, nobody will be able to bring it back. Therefore, enjoy to the last moment.

Further for Cārvākas:

> *na svargo nāpavargo vā naivātmā pāralaukikaḥ* ।
> *naiva varṇāśramādīnāṁ kriyaśca phaladāyikāḥ* ॥
> — Quoted in *Sarvadarśanasaṁgraha*, chap. 1

> There is no *svarga*, no heaven, no liberation; there is no eternal self, ... there are no restricted activities of the *varṇāśramas* which can give you good results. Nothing gives good result, nothing gives bad result because this is the only moment when you are enjoying; this present action, if it gives you pleasure, then do it.

The Cārvākas were against religious rites which were being practised without using one's own mind; like the ritual of *śrāddha*, even now-a-days people observe this *śrāddha* during the fifteen days in the *pitṛ-pakṣa*; they try to feed the priests and believe that this food which they are offering, this will reach their ancestors. But

Cārvākas do not believe in this type of rituals. They ridicule this practice and say that if food items offered to the *paṇḍits* can reach the body of your ancestors, then what is the need of a traveller carrying food along with him when he is undertaking a journey:

> *gacchatāmiha jantūnāṁ vyarthaṁ pātheyakalpanam* ।
> *gehasthakṛtaśrāddhena pathi tṛptiravāritā* ॥
> — Quoted in *Sarvadarśanasaṁgraha*, chap. 1

> The travellor takes his tiffin box with him to eat. If you can send food to heaven, you can also send food to the traveller while he is in the train or in the plane. So there is no logic behind such types of rituals. We should not observe these.

They also use all sorts of bad words for those who have authored or revealed Vedas ... if you think that there is a *paraloka*, because all the followers of the Veda believe in the doctrine of *paraloka* and *punarjanma*, then you are mistaken. When the soul goes to the other world, then it comes back according to its own actions. But Cārvākas do not believe in *paraloka* and say ... if the soul of a person can go from this body to the other world, then why does it not come back when its son or its wife, they are wailing and weeping? Why can it not come back if it can go above to the heaven or to the other world. It should also be able to come back, No rationale behind this belief that there is a *paraloka;* there is no logic. So most of the things that other schools have accepted as presuppositions, all of those are rejected by Cārvākas. As mentioned earlier, this is a philosophy for rejection of, and reaction to, the Upaniṣadic philosophy. It will be appropriate to refer to one or two statements of Cārvāka which are from the *Prabodhacandrodaya*, a Sanskrit drama. This is authored by Kṛṣṇa Miśra and the view of Cārvāka has been described here as follows:

> The *śāstra*, whose doctrines are obvious to all and which is founded on the evidence of senses alone, which admits only the elements of earth, water, fire and air, which maintains that sustenance and love are the objects of human existence, which asserts that matter possesses intelligence which denies

the existence of a separate spirit and affirms that death is blessedness, was written by Vācaspati (Bṛhaspati).

— Quoted in Radhakrishnan and Moore 1957: 247

The logical contribution of Cārvāka to the field of Indian philosophy is its scepticism and agnosticism; scepticism about the future and lack of faith and conviction in religious rites are bound to continue. The Cārvāka advocates that soul is nothing but the body characterized by attributes signified in expressions such as *ahaṁ kṛśa, ahaṁ sthūla* — I am stout, I am beautiful, I am grown up, I am old, etc. Consciousness found in the modifications of non-intelligent elements is produced in the same manner as red colour out of the combination of betel leaves, katechu, areca nut and lime.

How is consciousness produced? This question was put to Cārvākas and they answer:

kiṇvadibhyo madaśaktivatcaitanyamupajāyate ।

— Quoted in *Sarvadarśanasaṃgraha*, chap. 1

As we all see that these four elements: the betel leaves (*pāna pattā*), katechu, areca nut and lime, none of these is red. But when a green betel leaf (*pāna patta*), white limestone (*cūnā*), areca nut (wheatish *supārī*) and brown katechu (*katthā*) are combined then red colour is produced out of them. Similarly, when earth, water, air and fire — these four elements — are combined, consciousness emanates from unconscious objects; that is the logic of the Cārvākas.

Moreover, Cārvākas say that the only Supreme Being is the earthly monarch,

lokasidho rājā parameśvaraḥ ।

— Quoted in *Sarvadarśanasaṁgraha*, chap. 1

Anybody can see the king (*rājā*) whose existence is proved by all and who is controlling the world.

Hence, why do we need to infer a controller of the world whom we cannot see and feel; when the king is here to control us, to control the society and the country Besides, liberation is only the dissolution of physical body.

Cārvākas rejected all the popular notions and prevalent Vedic rites and rituals. They rejected all that was being accepted by other schools of philosophy and most of the assumptions or theories of their philosophy, because they are basically rooted in inference as everything can not be proved by perception. Perception has a very limited scope. Obviously, we have to transcend the limits of perception and we have to go beyond for reasoning or inference, for *upamāna* (similarity) and we also have to accept the verbal authority (*śabda*) but Cārvākas do not accept anything simply because others are saying; they just prompt us to think logically and believe in whatever we ourselves can see, smell, touch or hear i.e. perception, and perception alone.

If we have to do a critique of Cārvāka philosophy and want to know as to what have Cārvākas contributed to Indian philosophy; or have they actually contributed something? Then the answer would be that they have contributed a lot. The first contribution of Cārvāka is the attitude of scepticism and agnosticism as already stated above. According to them, these two are the criteria of philosophy. And even today, these two are the basic features of philosophy. Vātsyāyana (the logician — in fact there are two Vātsyāyanas — one who was the author of the *Kāmasūtra* and another is the commentator of the *Nyāyasūtra*) begins his interpretation of the *Nyāyasūtra* by explaining as to how does Nyāya begin.

About the origin of Nyāya, he says:

nānupalabdhe 'rthe nyāyaḥ pravartate na nirṇīte 'rthe kintarhi, saṁśayite 'rthe । — *Nyāyabhāṣya* on *Nyāyasūtra* 1.1.1

The philosophy of Nyāya does not take its origin from an object, which is not available. Nyāya is also not required, if a decision has been taken regarding an object, if we can see that this is a pen, then what is the need of proving it, no need. Because it is already proven. In short, neither an object, which is not available; neither an object, which is very clearly known — need any logic; we do not need Nyāya for such objects. When do we need Nyāya — *saṁśayite 'arthe* i.e. whenever there is a doubt, only then Nyāya is required. So

> *nānuplabdhe 'rthe na nirṇīte 'rthe nyāyaḥ pravartate kintarhi saṁśayite 'rthe.*

Only in a doubtful situation the need for logic and debate arises. This proves the significance of doubt in Indian logic.

Cārvākas, through their approach of scepticism and agnosticism, have put the notion of doubt in a significant position. We should not accept whatever comes to us, whatever is said to us; we should doubt why is someone saying so, is it correct? We should rationalize, so this scepticism is valid. It is a school of philosophy in Western thought also and the idea of doubt is very much there in the Veda itself:

> *yo 'syādhyakṣaḥ parame vyomantso aṅga veda yadi vā na veda* ||
>
> — *Ṛ̥V* X.129.7

> We are not sure whether He, the Lord of creation himself even knows or whether He does not, who lives in the highest region.

This tendency of doubting or the oscillating faculty, it is given to us, human beings. We human beings are rational beings, so we tend to think both ways. We should weigh the pros and cons, and then we should take a decision. This is the human faculty and this is the contribution of Cārvāka; this approach leads and restrains us from blind faith and unnecessary mechanical rites, which we practise and follow, without giving a serious thought to whatever the priest says. We just start doing this but we should think rationally — whether this will lead to what the priest is saying, whether I should practise it this way or not. So restraining from blind faith and unnecessary rituals — this is made possible due to the rationalistic approach to reality. It is not just the scriptural approach to reality, not just the inferential approach to reality; it should be a rational approach to reality as well. This is what the Cārvāka has said and historically the significance of Cārvāka is great because just after Vedas and the Upaniṣads — a critical standpoint or a different view was posited for the first time. Although all the literature they might have contributed is lost, not a single complete book of the Cārvāka school is available; even then the viewpoint of Cārvākas is quoted and refuted by all the subsequent philosophers. In fact, one of the authors of Indian philosophy has said that it is due to Cārvāka that the logicians like Gautama, the Naiyāyika and Mahāvīra and the Buddha got an occasion to preach logic; logic was preached only as a reaction to the Cārvāka. This is the single most contribution of Cārvākas. So, philosophically and historically Cārvāka has contributed a lot to Indian philosophy, although mostly they are ridiculed and their views are not taken as seriously as they should have been. But, today in this age, we know that even without teaching the tenets of Cārvāka or Lokāyata, everybody is following what the Cārvāka has said, specially those who are rationally oriented. They should read the arguments given by Cārvāka and it is as the counter argument to Cārvāka that Indian logic — whichever Nyāya, be it Hindu Nyāya, be it Buddhist Nyāya or Jaina Nyāya — has developed and flourished.

Question and Answer Session

SPEAKER: With these words, I stop here. We can discuss more during the question — answer session.

AMB. BASANT GUPTA: Thank you Dr ShashiPrabha ji. You mentioned about Cārvāka philosophy, of direct perception, it should be based on *pratyakṣa pramāṇa*. Now in the *Gītā* there is a word which comes to my mind: *rājaguhyam pavitram ...* (IX.2), king of science or king of knowledge is based on, among other things, easy-to-follow and based on direct perception and I think it is referring to the practice of *bhakti-yoga*, which is in chapters 7 to 12 and it is based on direct perception of God, so I thought there is a contradiction, that the *Gītā* directly contradicts what Cārvāka seems to be saying. I would like to have your views.

SPEAKER: Actually *pratyakṣa* is accepted as the first and the foremost *pramāṇa* by all the philosophers: be it the Veda, be it the Upaniṣads, be it the *Gītā*, because *pratyakṣa* is the first and as we say *pratyakṣaṁ kiṁ pramāṇam*? (when we have perceived something already, then what else is needed). No proof is needed beyond perception, but because perception cannot cover everything, there are many objects which we cannot perceive. Therefore, we have to take recourse to other means of knowing as well. As far as this reference to the *Gītā* is concerned, the *Gītā* is not repudiating Cārvākas.

In fact, in the above-quoted verse, there is a reference to self-realization. Even in Vedāntic discourse, *pratyakṣa* is self-realization because *pratyakṣa* can be of two types, one is the mental perception of oneself within and the other is the sense perception of objects outside. In this reference of the *Gītā*, *pratyakṣa* means self-realization and in that sense also there is no doubt that *pratyakṣa* is first and foremost, the *pradhāna pramāṇa*. So, the *Gītā* also accepts it, but it does not accept sense perception only, like the Cārvāka, because this *rāja-vidyā* is an object of self-perception or self-realization. But for Cārvākas, perception is only a sensory perception, it is limited or restricted only to the physical objects. For them, perception is not the self-perception or self-realization. This is the distinction one can draw between the two views.

DR ARVIND GUPTA: When it rejected the Veda, God, soul and everything that Hinduism stands for, then how come that this school still was not cast out as non-Hindu.

SPEAKER: No, it is not, because Hindu philosophy is inherently liberal in its outlook. As I said earlier, it is also in the Upaniṣads. We find the traces of this view in the Upaniṣad where the statement of Naciketā comes as follows:

> *astītyeke nāyamastītyeke* I — *Kaṭhopaniṣad* 1.1.20
>
> There are people who believe in the *paraloka* and there are those who do not believe in it.

Hinduism, as we all know and as we have discussed the other day also, is so inclusive and so broad in its approach that it accommodates all aspects of an object. So the view of Cārvāka is not rejected altogether, although all the schools begin with quoting and repudiating it, and they do not accept its viewpoint also. A Nyāya scholar of the tenth century, Udayanācārya, who was a logician of high order, begins his text the *Nyāya-Kusumāñjali*, to explain the evidences for proving God, with the rejection of Cārvāka argument. In fact, the viewpoint of Cārvāka is reflected in Vedas also, as was discussed in the Vedic verse quoted earlier:

> *yo 'syādhyakṣaḥ parame vyomantso aṅgā veda yadi vā na veda* ॥
>
> — *ṚV* X.129.7

> So whether He knows himself or even He does not know.

This type of scepticism was there in the Vedic view as well. This oscillating viewpoint whether this is so or whether this is not so — this is also in the Upaniṣad. In the *Śvetāśvatara Upaniṣad* in all the six points of view — Kālavāda, Svabhāvavāda, Niyativāda, bhūtavāda, puruṣavāda and Yadṛcchāvāda — are mentioned. This is the beauty of Hinduism and this is the distinctive feature of Hinduism that it incorporates and explains all the possible viewpoints, then gives you total freedom to choose any one of them, you can choose Cārvāka, you can choose Buddhism, Jainism, Hinduism, Sikhism or simply Vedānta. Even in Vedānta you can choose Advaita, Viśiṣṭādvaita, Śuddhādvaita, etc. ... there is a lot of variety; this diversity is the most beautiful feature of Indian philosophy.

DR ARVIND GUPTA: I have one more question: whether this philosophy found reflection in the ideas of politicians like that of Kauṭilya.

SPEAKER: You are right Dr Gupta. In fact, it is said that it was Bṛhaspati who wrote the *Rājanīti* or the *Arthaśāstra* which is popular in the name of Kauṭilya. Some scholars say that it was rooted in the work of Bṛhaspati. In the Vedic mythology, Bṛhaspati is known as the *guru* of the *devas*, Devaguru Bṛhaspati; but later on those students of Bṛhaspati, they also excelled in *rājanīti* and *daṇḍa*. So it is true that Cārvākas were connected with these theories of polity, because they accept *rājā* as God. The divine theory of king — that "king is divine" — is rooted in the viewpoint of Cārvāka. But this aspect needs to be studied and researched further. We do not have many researches on Cārvāka because being repudiatory it is not very respected, it is not totally rejected in our tradition but it is also not much respected in academic circles. We have a singificant and comprehensive research work on Lokāyata by D.P. Chatopadhyaya — that is the only authentic book, but there should be many more researches and as you have suggested, this should be researched more deeply. Somebody should take up this view, governance and polity with respect to the Cārvāka viewpoint.

MS PRERNA GANDHI: I would like to ask one question. How much was the emergence of Jainism and Buddhism in that historical period responsible for the decline of the Cārvāka philosophy?

SPEAKER: I cannot say instantly, but I do not think Jainism and Buddhism were the only responsible factors for the decline of the Cārvāka system. Actually, both of them accept *anumāna* (inference) as a means of knowing, so they repudiate and reject the Cārvāka theory as such but it is not that due to them the Cārvāka philosophy declined. Besides, in academic circles, the Cārvāka persence may not be very visible, but in the lives of human beings, especially in India or even across the world, this philosophy may not be the view of life, but it is very much the way of life. As Dr Gupta said, most of us are following this materialistic way of life only. We might be having views on Vedānta, we might be preaching, reading and researching on Advaita, but all of us are basically Cārvākas because we are all seeking pleasures, the only difference is in the level of pleasures. We might be finding and seeking intellectual pleasure, somebody else would be seeking pleasure in good food, in good music or in other mundane objects. So the level of pleasure may be different but everybody seeks pleasure and to that extent Cārvāka philosophy is an important segment of human existence across the world.

AMB. BASANT GUPTA: This is with regard to the fourth objective of life, i.e. *mokṣa*. I read somewhere in the *Rāmāyaṇa*, there is mention of only the first three. They emphasize on *dharma*, *artha* and *kāma*. And in later philosophy, because of the influence of Buddhism, the fourth one is added. So it became *dharma*, *artha*, *kāma* and *mokṣa* to accommodate Buddhism. Now my question is that whether *mokṣa* is other-worldly or can it be attained in this life itself.

SPEAKER: Thank you sir for this question. *Mokṣa* can be explained in both ways. It can be other-worldly, it can also be achieved during this life because as we shall see in the Sāṁkhya philosophy, they explicitly talk of *jīvan-mukti*. The *Gītā* also talks of that; Śrī Kṛṣṇa himself is a liberated person while living. He is a *jīvan-mukta*. Janakarāja Videha was a *jīvan-mukta*. It shows that one can be liberated while living. This is not just other-worldly and as far as the concept of *mokṣa* in the *Rāmāyaṇa* is concerned, maybe there is a mention of three pursuits only and the fourth one is not explicitly mentioned, but the idea was very much there in the Vedic philosophy. It is true that the word *mokṣa* does not occur in four Vedic Saṁhitās, but the concept of immortality is there and the concept of *ānanda* is there: *amṛtatva* is nothing, but the concept of liberation from mortality in an implicit manner. In the *Mahābhārata*, we find mention and also the description of all of these four ends — *dharma*, *artha*, *kāma* and *mokṣa*. In Buddhism, it is not *mokṣa*, actually it is the term *nirvāṇa:* everything calms down in *nirvāṇa*.

Buddhists also accept the idea of *punarjanma* (rebirth); and accept the theory of *karma*. Although they do not accept any eternal soul, even then the concept of liberation is acceptable to them. Actually, the concept of liberation while living and concept of liberation after life, both of them are available in Indian thought. For the Mīmāṁsakas, it is *svarga* and it is other-worldly only, but for all others it can be attained while living. For the Sāṁkhya, the idea of liberation is getting rid of all the three types of suffering for ever:

> *atha trividhaduḥkhātyantanivṛttiratyantapuruṣārthaḥ* ।
>
> — *Sāṁkhyasūtra* 1.1

> Hereafter (we explain) the ultimate end of life which is the permanent cessation of three types of suffering.

Here, *atyanta* means for ever, all the three types of *duḥkha* should be removed; not for a temporary phase, but forever. This is the ultimate goal. This can be achieved while living also. So it is both ways — other-worldly as well as in this world.

DR ARVIND GUPTA: Can Cārvāka philosophy of materialism be the view of life in modern scientific philosophy?

SPEAKER: Yes, as you have yourself mentioned in your introduction that the rationalistic approach of Cārvākas is very much akin to the scientific investigation. But here, I would add that although science is based on experimentation and observation, it also takes a lot of help from reasoning or inference. I do not think science can totally reject reasoning or inference.

DR ARVIND GUPTA: What is the difference between *sukha* and *ānanda*? This philosophy of Cārvākas talks about *sukha* as you mentioned. But there is also this other term *ānanda*, so what is the difference between *sukha* and *ānanda*?

SPEAKER: This is a very basic but foundational question raised in the Upaniṣads as well. You see *sukha* is a term, which is also available in the Upaniṣads, and *ānanda* is also there but the later term signifies Ultimate Bliss. *Sukha* is just the physical or the sensual pleasure. In the Upaniṣad it is clearly said:

> *parāñci khāni vyatr̥̄ṇat svayambhūstasmātparāṅ paśyati nāntarātman* । — *Kaṭhopaniṣad* 2.1.1

> The Lord created sense organs outwardly, therefore these look outside and not inside.

To reiterate, *sukha* is only the physical pleasure and *ānanda* is the spiritual Bliss. As already mentioned, the five layers of human personality in the Upaniṣads are explained as *annamaya, prāṇamaya, manomaya, vijñānamaya* and *ānandamaya kośa*. *Ānanda* is the ultimate level where there is no *duḥkha*. *Sukha* and *duḥkha* are relative; where there is *sukha* there will be *duḥkha* too. But *ānanda* is the absolute state where there will be no *duḥkha* at all.

Ānanda is the Ultimate Bliss. After realizing it, nothing remains to be achieved, that is *ānanda*, while *sukha* is limited and it is temporary.

DR ARVIND GUPTA: No, my question actually was this that if the Cārvāka rejects the Upaniṣads and rejects *ānanda* which is beyond *sukha*, then what is the logic about their rejection?

SPEAKER: Actually there are levels in Cārvāka philosophy as I said earlier, so there are *suśikṣita* Cārvākas (learned Cārvākas) who believe in different types of *sukha* and *ānanda*. In fact, the Cārvakas do not use the term *ānanda*, so they have not rejected *ānanda* as such. But they have rejected the self-conscious and eternal self, and because *ānanda* is to be experienced by the self, *ānanda* is to be enjoyed by oneself beyond the senses while they are only talking of this sensual pleasure. Perhaps the advanced Cārvākas who are indulging in the sixty-four types of arts and higher pursuits, they might accept the idea of higher bliss. But actually, this is not available in the literature that we find. This is because we only have the Cārvāka view in the form of *pūrva-pakṣa*.

It means that we only have Cārvāka material which has been presented to us by somebody who does not believe in its view. To elaborate further, the *Sarvadarśanasaṁgraha* is a compendium of various schools of Indian philosophy. The author himself is a Vedāntin. Similarly, the author of the *Ṣaḍdarśanasamuccaya* is a Jaina, he believes in Jainism; the *Sarvasiddhāntasaṁgraha* is of Śaṅkarācārya who is an Advaitin while he is presenting Cārvāka position, but only as a *pūrva-pakṣa* or as an opponent. The problem is that we do not have an original source or an original textbook of Cārvākas where all these details could have been authenticated. To put it more precisely, Cārvākas are not even talking of Upaniṣads, because Upaniṣads do not deal with rituals. They are talking of Vedas and Vedic rituals only and not the Vedic philosophy because the time when Cārvākas were giving their reactions was the time when rituals had been distorted and made complicated by the selfish priests. So, due to those distortions in religious rituals, they were reacting and rejecting those Vedic rituals and they also rejected Vedas. But they are not specifically talking of the Upaniṣads.

DR ARVIND GUPTA: Actually, it seems to me that this empirical method of gaining knowledge that the Cārvāka is talking about is not rejected in Vedas. The Veda seems to encompass a lot of Cārvāka philosophy also. All the arts are mentioned in Vedic literature.

SPEAKER: Yes, Dr Gupta, you are right, it is true that there is no exclusive division in ancient Indian knowledge tradition. Everything includes something of the other also, because all of them were interconnected and intertwined. All these ideas were being practised, being discussed, debated, deliberated upon and then somebody accepted one aspect, the other accepted another aspect. So it was not exclusion as such. Today, we have exclusive boundaries, segments, fragmentations; but it was not so in Indian tradition since beginning. It is a product of the later times that these diverse divisions have been erected. It was not so earlier, hence all these ideas and all these thoughts are rooted in the inclusive Vedic philosophy. They took their origin from there. They were prevailing in the same society and they were having free discussions among them. *Śāstrārtha*s were going on and there was no ill-will. When we take up any sourcebook of Indian philosophy, for that matter, say if we take the *Nyāyamañjarī* of Jayanta Bhaṭṭa, a tenth-century Kashmiri logician, his book is on Nyāya but it is such an encyclopaedic source that you will find Cārvāka, you will find Buddhism, you will find Jainism in it. Not only that, the Hindus were not only arguing with Jainas or Buddhists, Hindus were also arguing within themselves. It was a free dialogue in the form of intellectual discourse.

Nyāya was having a different viewpoint than Mīmāṁsā, Mīmāṁsā was having a different theory than Sāṁkhya and they were all giving arguments to counter the others' point of view. They were not fighting in life or in society. They were countering the ideas, the theories and that too in the textbooks. We have the record for all that. In fact, the Indian philosophy in original sources should be taught to the students as General Sawhney rightly mentioned, then they will see with their own eyes that these texts have a clear record of free debates. Otherwise, they could have just finished the Cārvāka ideas at all; Cārvāka ideology would have been finished but it is not so. It is very much there and preserved in the opponents' sourcebooks. That shows the liberal outlook and a broad viewpoint of the scholars in Indian philosophical tradition.

MS BANTI: Does Hindu philosophy regard Cārvāka as one path to attaining spiritualism among many?

SPEAKER: Yes, in a way, it does since it is included in the *Sarvadarśana-saṁgraha*. There are sixteen schools included in this book and this is one of them. It is there in all the textbooks that you see — any history of Indian philosophy. You take up any book on Indian philosophy like that of S.N. Dasgupta, S.C. Chatterjee, D.M. Dutta, S. Radhakrishnan or Baldev Upadhyaya, Arjun Sinha and Kapildev Dwivedi, Cārvāka will be there. So, it is one of the many schools, no doubt about that. But it is not a path to attaining spiritualism because the Cārvāka itself does not accept spiritualism as the goal.

MS BANTI: My question was whether the Hindu philosophy regards Cārvāka as one path towards attaining that ultimate spiritual goal.

SPEAKER: You see, Hindu philosophy does not enjoin that way, but explains that these are the sixteen schools from which you can choose any one. They have quoted their viewpoint from their own sources and any scholar or student who is anxious to study Indian philosophy can choose on his own. Anybody who deliberates and who is diligent enough to study all those, he is given a choice. First of all, he should be desirous of seeking liberation. Śaṅkarācārya rightly says:

durlabhaṁ trayamevaitaddaivānugrahahetukam ।
manuṣyatvaṁ mumukṣutvaṁ mahāpuruṣasaṁśrayaḥ ॥
— *Vivekacūḍāmaṇi* 3

> Three things are rare in this world; first is *mānuṣatvaṁ*, being born as a human; second is *mumukṣutva*: not all human beings are seeking liberation, so the second rare thing is that we are born a human being and we are also desirous of attaining liberation. And the third is *mahāpuruṣa-saṁśrayaḥ*.

Even if we are born a human being, even if we are desirous of seeking liberation, but if we do not find good people, great people who can lead us and guide us to that path, our life is futile. So, those are a very fortunate few who get all these three. ... It is only through the divine grace that one can get all these three. Blessed are the ones who seek liberation and more blessed are the ones who not only seek liberation, but they tread the path of liberation also — it is the choice of the individual. Hindu philosophy as such does not dictate, does not prescribe. It only describes and gives you options that these are the options, you can accept any one of them and you can be a stout follower as General Sawhney put it in terms of belief and non-belief. You may accept Cārvāka or you may even live life below the ideals of Cārvāka.

DR ARVIND GUPTA: Thank you Dr ShashiPrabha ji for this enlightening talk and we really enjoyed it, learned something and we will meet again after some time with another topic. Thank you so much.

Baudhha and Jaina Philosophy

JUST as Hinduism is a religion as well as a philosophy, similarly Buddhism and Jainism are also two Indian religions as well as two philosophical schools. In fact, in Indian tradition, philosophy was always closely connected with religion. Religion and philosophy were not held to be separate. Philosophy pertains to the ideas and religion pertains to the practice of those ideas. Incidentally, all the three Indian religions — Hinduism, Buddhism and Jainism — they practised what they preached. So, the philosophy behind the practices was very much known to those who preached. Unfortunately, now-a-days, those who practise, they do not know what the ideas behind these practices are. The rationale behind these religious practices and rites has been lost or one should say that Indian philosophers have also separated themselves from the religious practices on the lines of Western philosophy. It is good or bad, we can discuss both the aspects, but let us first introduce ourselves to the basic tenets of the Bauddha view first and the Jaina view later. Although chronologically Jainism is established to be prior than Buddhism and antiquity of Jainism is based on a very early date, yet we shall not go into chronological details. Let us begin with Buddhism and, as we all know, this was propounded by the Buddha who was an enlightened person. The term *buddha* signifies the one who is enlightened. He was born as a prince, married, had a son — the story is well known. He had never had an encounter with the problems of disease, decay and death. But as it was destined, just the day he had an encounter with all these three, he was detached from the world and he decided to know the real truth behind this suffering. He was very much perturbed to see that humanity suffers so much. He was enlightened at the young age of around 25 years.

I

Coming to the source literature of Buddhism, we would only refer to the earliest literature. In fact, the Buddha never wrote anything; he delivered oral discourses. Just like Hinduism, here also, we have an oral tradition, it was an oral tradition but the disciples of the Buddha compiled his teachings and the earliest literature in Buddhism is known as *Tripiṭaka* — *tri* (three), *piṭaka* (box). So there are three boxes or three collections: one is known as the *Suttapiṭaka*, which is about the theories. It contains five Nikāyas: the *Dīgha-Nikāya*, *Majjhima-Nikāya*, *Saṁyutta-Nikāya*, *Aṅguttara-Nikāya* and *Khuddaka-Nikāya*. Then we have the *Vinayapiṭaka* which deals about the ethical issues and the *Dhammapiṭaka* which talks about metaphysical questions. Besides these *tripiṭaka*s, we also have the *dhammapada* and the *jātaka* tales, which are about various incarnations of the Buddha. Later literature in Buddhism is so rich and so vast that one cannot even mention the names of all the texts. But two texts must be mentioned. One is the *Milindapañha* of Nāgasena and the other is the *Abhidharamakośa* of Vasubandhu who was from Kashmir. This is a brief description about the earliest literature of Buddhist philosophy.

As far as Buddhist epistemology is concerned, they accept two *pramāṇas* or two means of knowing just like the Vaiśeṣikas. Cārvākas accepted only perception as a means of knowing. Buddhism believes in two means of knowing: *pratyakṣa* and *anumāna*. Although their conceptions of *pratyakṣa* and *anumāna* are quite different from what the Nyāya and Vaiśeṣika or Mīmāṁsā and Sāṁkhya believe in.

Pratyakṣa for the Buddhists is only indeterminate perception. The determinate perception (*savikalpaka pratyakṣa*), as the Naiyāyika would say, is not acceptable to Buddhists; they believe in only *nirvikalpaka* (indeterminate) perception. Why so? Because the nature of reality, according to Buddhism, cannot be known in its entirety. So *pratyakṣa* is defined as *kalpanāpoḍham abhrāntam*, i.e. there are no attributes (*kalpanās*) attached to the perception and it is not. Perception is said to be of four levels: first, the sensory perception or the sense organ and object contact, then there is a psychological perception, then the consciousness itself is perceived, i.e. *sva-saṁvedana-grāhya*, and lastly the *yoga-jñāna*, that which is supernatural.

Coming to the metaphysics of the Bauddha philosophy, the Buddha himself was not interested in propounding such theories and doctrines. In fact, there are ten topics — (later on these ten topics were also increased to twenty-eight) and it is said that the Buddha maintained not to discuss such questions. What are these? To enumerate only the original ten:

- Is this world eternal?
- Is this non-eternal?
- Is this world finite?
- Or is it infinite?
- Are the soul and body different from each other?
- Or are they identical with each other?
- Is there rebirth or reincarnation after death?
- Or is there no reincarnation after death?
- Or are both of them the reincarnation as well as non-reincarnation?
- Is there any talk of reincarnation: real or unreal?

These are known as *avyaktāni. Avyākatāni* is the Pāli term for Sanskrit *avyākṛtāni*, i.e. that which we cannot explain. It is held that the Buddha always used to keep silent when such metaphysical questions were posed to him.

In later times, many more questions were added to this list. It means that the Buddha wanted to avoid such questions about whose answers we are not sure because his focus was on getting rid of suffering, he was not into philosophizing or in mere contemplation for its own sake; he only wanted that humanity should not suffer. Since he was aggrieved at the sight of an old man, of a diseased man and of a dead man, hence he wanted that humanity should get a cure from all these types of suffering. Therefore, the four noble truths that he propounded are as follows:

i. *Sarvaṁ duḥkham*: Everything in the world is suffering and this idea is not different from the Sāṁkhya school of philosophy; it also begins with the concept of *duḥkha*. There are so many types of suffering that every human being needs to get rid of. That is why we come to the domain of philosophy. We want to get rid of suffering. So *sarvaṁ duḥkham* is the first premise, the first of the Four Noble Truths. Everybody knows that there is suffering, but then what? The Buddha's viewpoint is a logical standpoint, so he says *duḥkha* is there, but nothing in this world happens without a cause. According to Cārvāka, nothing is dependent on its cause. There is no cause — effect relationship according to Cārvāka.

ii. The next noble truth in Buddhism is *duḥkha-samudaya*. The Buddha says *duḥkha* is there but every *duḥkha* is rooted in its cause. There is a cause of suffering; there is a cluster of causes for suffering and this cluster of causes we all should know — it is explained as *dvādaśa nidāna*. There are twelve factors which work like a cycle. In other words, these twelve are put into a cyclical mode and therefore it is also known as *bhava-cakra*. Out of these twelve factors, each one is dependent on the other, the second is dependent on the first, the third leads to the fourth and when we come to the twelfth, it again leads to the first, so this goes on and on; therefore suffering is never removed. These twelve factors are as follows:

    1. *avidyā* (ignorance),
    2. *saṁskāra* (impressions),
    3. *jāti* (*punarjanma*),

4. *jarā-maraṇa* (birth and death),
5. *bhava* (cycle of birth),
6. *upādāna* (taking or experiencing pain and pleasure),
7. *tṛṣṇā* (desire),
8. *vedanā* (feeling or emotions),
9. *sparśa* (contact between the sense organs and object),
10. *ṣaḍāyatana* (six sense organs (the five senses and *manas*)),
11. *nāma-rūpa* (name and form), and
12. *vijñāna* (consciousness).

Avidyā, saṁskāra, jāti, jarā-maraṇa, bhava, upādāna, tṛṣṇā, vedanā, sparśa, ṣaḍāyatana, nāma-rūpa and *vijñāna* — these are the twelve constituents of *bhava-cakra. Avidyā* is ignorance which causes *saṁskāras* (impressions). *Jāti* is birth and *jarā-maraṇa* is decay and death. *Bhava* is another life and then *upādāna is* taking anything from own experience. *Tṛṣṇā* is desire, *vedanā* is feeling or emotion and then we have *nāma-rūpa* (name and form); *ṣaḍāyatana* (six senses); *vijñāna* (consciousness) and *saṁskāra* (impressions). These twelve work in a cycle, in a *cakra,* for example; *avidyā* is the first cause or the root cause, it leads to *jāti.* Why are we born? The birth of human beings is based on their own ignorance and *avidyā* gives rise to impressions (*saṁskāras*) which in turn lead to *jāti* and *jāti* leads to *jarā-maraṇa* — decay and death — which give rise to *bhava* (next birth). One birth leads to another birth and birth leads to *upādāna,* taking or experiencing pain and pleasure and as much as we experience — the objects, *tṛṣṇā* (desire) increases and this *tṛṣṇā* leads to *vedanā* — feeling or emotions — and then *vedanā* leads to *sparśa* which is the contact between the object and the sense organ, then the six senses — the five senses of cognition and mind, these are the six senses. They lead to the cause of suffering because the senses make us experience pain and pleasure through the objects that we encounter. Then we assign *nāma-rūpa*, the name and form to the objects, and *vijñāna* is the consciousness; although the Buddhists do not accept any eternal consciousness in the form of *ātmā*, but they do accept consciousness in the form of *vijñāna*. So consciousness leads to *saṁskāra*. *Saṁskāra* is impression, when impression is left on the consciousness, then it leads to another impression. There is a chain of *saṁskāra*s known as *santāna*.

To recapitulate, out of the four noble truths, first was *sarvaṁ duḥkham* — everything is suffering. Suffering is not uncaused, every suffering has its own cause on which it is dependent. The second noble truth *duḥkha-samudaya* points to the theory of causation that Buddhist philosophy propounds and that is very important; it was really significant for the Buddha. Theory of causation in Bauddha philosophy is known as *pratītya-samutpāda* (dependent origination). This is how it is translated: *pratītya* means that which has happened, and anything that has happened gives rise to another thing; *pratītya* is the past moment and *samutpāda* is the present moment. By the time one talks of it as present, it has already become past because this has also passed. In this way, moment *A* leads to moment *B* and then *B* to moment *C*. There is not a single moment when two entities coexist. From this point of view, there are two models in philosophical arena: one model is of simultaneity and the other model is of succession. Bauddha philosophy accepts the model of succession while the other realistic schools of Indian philosophy like Nyāya and Vaiśeṣika, Sāṁkhya and Yoga — they accept the simultaneity model.

According to Buddhism, no two entities can exist in one single moment. Every entity is born in a moment and it is extinct the next moment; by the time it is extinct, next entity has already come. So there is a chain. This is known as Santānavāda. *Santāna* means continuity or extension: these days we understand progeny by the word *santāna*, but in a way that is also an extension of ourselves; *santāna* (progeny) is the extension of parents. Similarly, in Bauddha philosophy, every past entity or past moment gives rise to its next moment. And that next moment is the *santāna* of previous one. This is known as the theory of Santāna in Buddhism.

Now, even if we know that there is suffering and we have known that there is a cause to every suffering. How does it help us? Because suffering is still there. I have known that suffering has a cause, so what; therefore the third statement is even more important.

iii. The third Noble Truth is *duḥkha-nirodha*: It says that suffering can be eliminated. Not only that, the suffering can be eliminated forever, *duḥkha-nirodha* is equal to *nirvāṇa*. So, there is a possibility of *nirvāṇa*. Buddhism is usually alleged to be a pessimistic theory because it begins with an assertion that everything is *duḥkha*; but this is not correct because this third statement or the third Noble Truth gives us both hope and promise that there is a possibility for eradication of suffering.

Duḥkha-nirodha (cessation of suffering) is possible and that cessation of suffering is known as *nirvāṇa* in Buddhist terms. In fact, each school has its own technical terms which are appropriate to explain the theory of its own philosophy. So, the Buddhists talk of liberation as *nirvāṇa*, Cārvākas do not believe in any aspect of liberation, for them death itself is the release from suffering but for Buddhists, *duḥkha* can be eliminated and that is known as *nirvāṇa*. What is this term *nirvāṇa*? Literally this means putting off, just like a lamp — when it is lit, then it is *pradīpa*, but when the lamp is put off, that is known as *nirvāṇa*: *nir* + *vāta* — there is no wind, there is no light, there is no flame; that lamp has been put off on its own. It goes on burning and burning throughout the night but a moment comes — if there is no distraction, if there is no disturbance, the lamp or the flame of the lamp goes off on its own. Similarly, when we practise an ethical mode that has been prescribed for us, then this *cakra*, the *bhava-cakra* continues getting pacified on its own and a moment comes when everything is calm and quiet. That is known as *duḥkha-nirodha:* very logical sequence. There is suffering, suffering has a cause and suffering can be eliminated for ever.

iv. The fourth Noble Truth is *duḥkha-nirodhagāminī pratipat*: Naturally, the next question arises as to what is the way for elimination of suffering? What is the path for that? If one keeps on sitting and contemplating, will his suffering come to an end? No, one has to make an effort for that. One has to practise some rules of self-discipline and that is the fourth noble truth, which says *duḥkha-nirodhagāminī pratipat*. There is a way, there is a path that one has to follow if one wants to get his suffering eliminated for ever. This is known as *aṣṭāṅga-mārga*.

Philosophy of the Buddha is also known as *aṣṭāṅga-mārga*. There is a path which has eight limbs and one has to follow these eight limbs. Then slowly and slowly by practising these eight limbs, one can reach a state which is the state of *nirvāṇa*. What are these eight *aṅgas*? These are: *samyak dr̥ṣṭi*, *samyak saṅkalpa*, etc. everywhere *samyak* is added. *Samyak* is an undeclinable term which we use as an adjective in Sanskrit. *Samyak* means proper, appropriate, upright. The eight limbs are following:

- *Samyak Dr̥ṣṭi*: If we would like to evolve, we have to adopt a vision, a viewpoint which is proper and what is proper? That is all listed in the later literature of Buddhism. We have to look into that. It means that we have an approach which is proper, which is befitting to the path that we want to follow. In other words, *samyak dr̥ṣṭi* is proper vision.
- *Samyak saṅkalpa:* Where is *samyak dr̥ṣṭi* rooted or where does it lead to: *samyak saṅkalpa.* It means that

our thoughts have to be appropriate, if we want to have a proper approach, proper vision, then our thoughts should be accordingly appropriate because approach is based on our thoughts. If we have good and noble thoughts, if our vision is right and appropriate, then what will happen?

- *Samyak Vāk*: We should speak in a proper way so that nobody feels hurt, nobody feels bad because of our terse statements or distasteful words — these should be avoided at all costs.
- *Samyak Karmānta*: This comes after *samyak dṛṣṭi*, *samyak saṅkalpa* and *samyak vāk*. Our actions should be performed in a proper manner. They should be performed according to the rules and they should also be done appropriately.
- *Samyak Ājīva*, our profession should also be proper. If one is following the profession of a hunter, then this will not ordinarily lead to *samyak saṅkalpa*. It is a profession of course, but such professions, such vocations should be avoided and even if they have to be pursued, they should be pursued in a detached manner and not with an idea of hurting someone.
- *Samyak Vyāyāma*: Thus *samyak ājīva* leads to our bodybuilding exercises, they should also be proper and appropriate. If one is building his body, if he wants to raise his stamina to hurt the other person, then it is of no use. So our physical exercises, our health practices should be for the nourishment of our own health, but they should not be for hurting others, so *samyak vyāyāma*.
- *Samyak Smṛti*: Then comes the next one — our memory should also be proper. If one's ideas are not proper, if one's speech is not controlled, if one's profession is not

appropriate or upright, then what will happen? These things will be kept in a sort of fixed deposit which is known as *smṛti*. Obviously one's *smṛti* will also be affected, so for evolving a *samyak smṛti*, one has to adopt the above six proper practices — *samyak dṛṣṭi*, *samyak saṅkalpa*, *samyak vāk*, *samyak karmānta*, *samyak ājīva*, *samyak vyāyāma* and *samyak smṛti*.

- *Samyak Samādhi*: *Samādhi* is the last state when all our mental modes are quietened. This does not happen just by pursuing a few of the physical postures that we are doing today in the name of *yoga*. *Yoga* cannot quieten the mind just by following the *āsana*s although these are helpful in the path of self-control. *Āsana* is only one of the eight parts according to Patañjali's *yoga*.

Interestingly, we have Hindu *yoga*, we have Buddhist *yoga* and we also have Jaina *yoga*, all these schools of thought or all these religious practices, they are meant for the benefit and well-being of humanity. They are all aiming at the same end. Only thing is that their methods are different, their presentation or their viewpoint is different, otherwise they all point out to the way and to the goal. And that goal is common for all. We can see that right from the beginning, from Cārvāka onwards — What is the goal of life for Cārvāka? Enjoyment, which means absence of suffering. Although enjoyment for Cārvāka is limited to the physical enjoyment only. But their idea was also to get rid of suffering while here in Buddhism there is a very balanced, proper code of conduct and if we follow this code of conduct, this *aṣṭāṅga-mārga*, then *duḥkha-nirodha* will follow. If we go into the reverse mode, if we follow the *aṣṭāṅga-mārga*, the elimination of suffering will be possible and elimination of suffering will also destroy the cause of suffering and then whatever was *duḥkha*, that *duḥkha* will be pacified. We shall have no more suffering, this is the promise of the Buddha and his philosophy.

Evidently, there is a fixed route for this in Buddhism and that is known as *triratna* (three gems). After this *aṣṭāṅga-mārga*, we have three more steps to follow and these are *śīla*, *samādhi* and *prajñā*. *Samādhi* has already been covered as the eighth step, but here *samādhi* is coupled with *śīla* and *prajñā*. *Śīla* is conduct or nature as we all know, Here *śīla* means conduct, *samādhi* is a mental state, but if it is coupled with *pañca-śīla*, then it bears fruit of calmness or *nirvāṇa*. *Prajñā* is wisdom, the ultimate level of *prajñā* is known as *prajñā-pāramitā* and in later Buddhism *prajñā-pāramitā* is also given the status of a goddess. Every religion, every philosophy evolves in different modes. So, later on, this *prajñā* became such a coveted deity (Goddess) that it is known as Prajñā-Pāramitā and the Buddhist followers started worshipping Prajñā-Pāramitā. But the idea of the Buddha in his earliest philosophy was very practical; obviously Buddhism is not pessimism as alleged by several scholars. It is a realism of its own kind. It can be understood as empiricism but it is not rational in the sense of rigid rationalism as that of the Cārvāka.

The Buddha's philosophy is very much rational and logical, but it is not just exclusive rationalism because it focuses on *karuṇā* (compassion) as well, so much so that in the later stage of Bauddha philosophy this *karuṇā* also evolves into the state of *mahā-karuṇā*. We have two schools of Buddhism as a religion, these are known as Hīnayāna and Mahāyāna, Hīnayāna is the lesser vehicle, Mahāyāna is the great vehicle. *Yāna* is a vehicle, so Hīnayāna and Mahāyāna are the two schools of Buddhist religion. Hīnayāna is known as a lesser vehicle because according to Hīnayāna, the follower aspires for his own *nirvāṇa* only; he is aiming at his own release or liberation. He does not bother or he does not have the capacity to uplift others but in Mahāyāna, which is associated with the idea of *bodhisattva*, and the *bodhisattva* aims for liberation of all — not only for himself, but for every being of the universe. He says that I do not want to be liberated unless each and every being of the universe is liberated. That is known as Mahāyāna or the ideal of *bodhisattva*. Besides these two traditions known as Hīnayāna and Mahāyāna, these days we also have other branches such as international Buddhism: we have Sri Lankan Buddhism, Burman Buddhism, Korean Buddhism, and Vietnamese Buddhism, Pāli Buddhism and Sanskrit Buddhism. Many countries of Asia are still following Buddhism religiously, we can see that Hīnayāna or Theravāda is popular in Sri Lanka, Mynmar, Thailand and Java.

On the other hand, Mahāyāna is more altruistic and it is very much close to Hinduism. In fact, there is a text titled *Bodhicaryāvatāra* authored by Śānti Deva which is based on Mahāyāna principles. It is very much like the *Bhagavadgītā*, some researches have been done on *bodhisattva*, Mahāyāna and the *Bhagavadgītā*. Most of the ideas of the *Bhagavadgītā* are available in the *Bodhicaryāvatāra*, so it can be said that a stage came when ethical practices or the ultimate aim of Buddhist and Hindu followers appeared to be common. In fact, all of them wanted that more and more human beings should be relieved of suffering.

It is worth mentioning here that there are four *brahmavihāras* according to Mahāyāna. These are mentioned as: *maitrī*, *karuṇā*, *muditā* and *upekṣā:* More importantly it is to be noted that the same terms and the same order of enumeration are also available in Patañjali's *Yogasūtra*:

i. *Maitrī* is friendship, friendship with those who are equal to us. We usually and naturally develop friendship with those with whom we share common ideas, common interests, common hobbies, and *maitrī* develops.

ii. Next is *karuṇā*. *Karuṇā* is the central idea of Mahāyāna Buddhism. We should have compassion for those who are lesser than us in anyway; in finance, in health or in education. If friendship is with those who are equal to us, *karuṇā* or compassion is for those who are lesser than us.

iii. Then comes *muditā*: we should be happy for those who are above us and beyond us, those who have more money, those who have more wisdom, those who have more education, those who have more capacity. We should not feel jealous of them, rather, we should be happy for them, i.e. *muditā*. This is the third *brahmavihāra*.

iv. The fourth is *upekṣā*. There are people with whom one cannot have friendship. There are those for whom one does not feel like having compassion due to certain inexplicable reasons and there are people for whom one cannot even feel happy. There are always such people in every society, such people should only be neglected or ignored. So *upekṣā* is the fourth *brahmavihāra*: *maitrī*, *karuṇā*, *muditā* and *upekṣā*, these four are available in the same nomenclature, same sequence in Patañjali's *Yogasūtra* and in the Bauddha Mahāyāna theory. In Buddhism, they are known as Brahmā-vihāras while Patañjali calls them tools for cleansing *citta*.

Significantly, later on, Buddhist philosophy became very intricate and several doctrines developed, which were classified under four schools of Buddhist philosophy. These four schools are:

i. Mādhyamika, this is also known as Śūnyavāda (nihilism). Notably, this is not absolute nihilism, the term is used here in a technical sense. The Mādhaymika school was propounded by Nāgārjuna. He has written a text known as the *Mādhyamikakārikā*. In Hinduism, we have a text known as the *Māṇḍūkyakārikā*. The *Māṇḍūkyakārikā* and *Mādhyamikakārikā* — if one looks at both the texts together, studies them together, one will feel that both of them have reached at the same point of conclusion. There is so much of reciprocation of ideas. In fact, Śaṅkarācārya was labelled as *pracchanna bauddha*, he was said to be a Buddhist in disguise because the theories of Mādhyamika Buddhism and Advaita Vedānta of Śaṅkara have much in common. Later on, Śāntarakṣita wrote a text called *Tattvasaṁgraha* which also belongs to the Mādhyamika school.[1]

---

[1] For those who want to study more or know more about the Mādhyamika school, there is a secondary source in English written by T.R.V. Murthy titled, Central Philosophy of Buddhism which will be very helpful for them.

ii. Then we have the Yogācāra school,[2] which is also known as Vijñānavāda (subjective idealism). *Vijñāna* here means consciousness because according to Buddhists there is no reality outside, everything is a projection of our own understanding and our own understanding is termed as *vijñāna; vijñāna* is the idea or the consciousness within us. Diṅnāga is the propounder of this school and Dharmakīrti is his follower.

iii. Then we have the third school, which is known as Vaibhāṣika and propounds Kṣaṇabhaṅgavāda (theory of momentariness). The *pratītya-samutpāda* (theory of causation) is based on this idea of momentariness and this is related with the first noble truth *sarvaṁ duḥkham*; *duḥkha* is there as everything in the world is suffering, but everything is momentary as well. So one should not get disheartened over suffering, as this moment of suffering will not stay forever, this will go away very soon. In this way, Kṣaṇikavāda[3] also gives us an idea of hope that whatever we are suffering, will go away.

iv. There is another aspect of this Kṣaṇikavāda (momentariness), represented in the fourth school of Buddhism which is known as Sautrāntika.[4]

Mādhyamika, Yogācāra, Vaibhāṣika and Sautrāntika — these four schools of Buddhism were developed later on and a lot of literature was created pertaining to these four schools, their commentaries and then arguments with other schools of thought

---

[2] Those who want to study more about this school, they should refer to a book by Dharmendranath Shastri titled *A Critique of Indian Realism.*

[3] Those, who want to study more about this school of Buddhism, a book titled Buddhist Theory of Universal Flux by Satkari Mukhopadhyaya will be useful.

[4] For further study in this regard, see Essentials of Sautrāntika Philosophy by Milan Shakya, and The Sautrāntika School of Buddhism by P. Maneewong.

and counter arguments. There is a text of Mīmāṁsā called the *Mānameyodaya* where the definition of all these four Buddhist schools is narrated as follows:

mukyo mādhyamiko vivartamakhilaṁ śūnyañca mene jagad,
yogācāramate tu santi matayastāsāṁ vivarto 'khilah ।
artho 'sti kṣaṇikastvasavanumito buddhyeti sautrāntikaḥ,
pratyakṣaṁ kṣaṇabhaṅguraṁ ca sakalaṁ vaibhāṣiko bhāṣate ॥
— *Mānameyodaya* 31

The Mādhyamika, who comes foremost, considers the entire universe as an illusory transformation of the void; according to the Yogācāra view, cognitions exist and everything is their illusory transformation; the Sautrāntika holds that there are objects which are momentary, and which are inferred from cognitions; and the Vaibhāṣika says that everything is perceptible and momentarily perishable.

It is not possible to discuss all details pertaining to these schools further since we have to discuss Jaina philosophy too, but it may be briefly mentioned that there is a theory of Saṅghātavāda in Bauddha philosophy as nothing is essentially related to other things. In Nyāya — Vaiśeṣika, in Sāṁkhya and in Vedānta — all the six schools of Hinduism, everything is interrelated or intertwined in one way or the other. But Buddha says that nothing is intrinsically related to another. *A* is not related to *B*, *B* is not related to *C* — there is only a continuity and conglomeration called *saṅghāta*. This body is not real, *ātman* is also not real in the sense that Hindu philosophers conceive, it is not eternal; if we feel and think that *ātman* is eternal, we shall always be attached to it. To put an end to this attachment, the Buddha says nothing is interconnected, only plausible connection is the continuity which is based on succession so that every moment leads to the next, but it will never be there for the second one, inherently they cannot be related. In fact, no relation between entities of the world is possible according to Bauddha philosophy. There is Saṅghātavāda, the conglomeration theory of *pañca-skandhas* which signifies that there are only conglomerates of different entities. Path and goal are also not connected, they are one and the same thing. One moment it is path, then next moment comes and it will be new path. The whole is not a new beginning and so there is no relation between parts and the whole also. Therefore, *ātman* cannot be held as eternal. In short, Saṅghātavāda, Santānavāda, Anātmavāda, Śūnyavāda and *nirvāṇa* these are the main concepts of Buddhism. In the words of Nāgārjuna, *nirvāṇa* is:

> *aprahāṇam asamprāptam anucchinam aśāśvatam* ।
> *aniruddham anutpannam etannirvāṇam ucyate* ॥
> — *Mādhyamikakārikā* 25

> *Nirvāṇa* can neither be forsaken nor acquired; it can neither be destroyed nor it is eternal; it is neither restricted nor produced.

It needs a lot of time to explain all these concepts, but to put it in simpler terms, it would be better to refer to Nāgasena in his text *Milindapañha* where he says that *nirvāṇa* is deep like the ocean. It is high like the mountain, sweet like honey, but it cannot be explained. It can only be realized, it can only be experienced. The same thing Śaṅkarācārya says in Advaita philosophy that the ultinate reality cannot be explained, it can only be experienced.

The Buddha's discourses were originally in Pāli language. So a lot of literature in Bauddha philosophy was produced in Pāli. Later on, in Mahāyāna tradition, most of the literature was composed in Sanskrit, so we have Pāli Buddhism and Sanskrit Buddhism. Actually, there is a lot more which needs to be said, but let us now move on to Jainism.

II

Jaina philosophy is also very rich and deep in itself. There is a lot of commonality in Buddhism and Jainism; some people believe that Jainism is only an offshoot of Buddhism and vice versa but it is not so, because as we shall see, there are many theories which have been contributed by Jaina philosophy to the stock of Indian philosophical tradition. The title Jaina is based on the term Jina, just as Bauddha is based on the title Buddha. "Jina" is a person who has controlled himself and his sense organs, who has conquered all the attachments and the Jaina philosophy is so titled as it is propounded by Jina.

Pārśvanātha is known as the propounder of Jaina philosophy, but his historicity is yet to be proved. So Vardhamāna Mahāvīra, the last of the twenty-four prophets of Jaina philosophy is an authentic and historic personality who gave a lot of propagation and popularity to Jaina philosophy. Talking about the literature of Jaina philosophy, we have the *Tattvārthasūtra* of Umāswāti, he is also known as Umā Swāmī. This is the sourcetext of Jaina philosophy and then we have four more ancient texts by Ācārya Kundakunda, which are known as the *Niyamasāra*, *Pañcāstikāyasāra*, *Samayasāra* and *Pravacanasāra*. We have the *Āptamīmāṁsā* of Samantabhadra and the *Pramāṇamīmāṁsā* of Hemacandra. Hemachandra has written extensively. He has authored so many texts that it is impossible to enumerate all the names; there are a lot more scholars in the history of Jaina philosophy but it is more important to focus on two theories which are the most significant contributions of Jaina philosophy.

First, the metaphysical aspect: According to Jaina philosophy, the reality is multifaceted, while for Bauddha philosophy, there is no external reality, which can stay for even two moments. Everything, that is there, exists for one moment. For the Bauddha, the real had only one aspect of momentariness, for Jaina philosophy, it has three aspects, and so three moments are there: *Utpāda*, *Vyaya* and *dhrauvya*. *Utpāda* means that it is produced; then *vyaya* signifies that it gets deteriorated or transformed, but there is some amount of it which is constant and stays as it is. *Utpāda* is production, *vyaya* is decay and *dhrauvya* is stability:

> *utpādavyayadhrauvyayuktaṁ sat* ॥ — *Tattvārthasūtra* 5.30
>
> Reality consists of production, decay and stability.

Sat is reality, a real is that which is born, which is decaying constantly but part of which is also staying for a longer duration.

In other words some aspects of everything are getting destroyed continuously like cells of our own body, we know that cells of our body are changing every moment, but still the name and the form of a person stays constant during his/her lifetime. In fact, there is some aspect of reality which is constant or stable but there are some aspects which are changing and decaying every moment. According to Jaina philosophy, there are three aspects of a real: *utpāda*, *vyaya* and *dhrauvya.*

Incidentally, Hinduism believes in six stages of existence which are mentioned by Yāska in his *Nirukta* as follows: *jāyate*, *asti*, *vardhate*, *vipariṇamate*, *apakṣīyate*, *vinaśyati* –

- *jāyate* (a new thing is born),
- *asti* (it is there now, it is existent),
- *vardhate* (it grows),
- *vipariṇamate* (thereafter it transforms, it changes),
- *apakṣīyate* (then it decays and),
- *vinaśyati* (finally it is destroyed).

These are the six stages of existence according to Hindu philosophy.

For Jainas, there are only three steps: that something is born, some part of it is decaying and some part of the same is stable. So, reality has three aspects but there is another definition of reality which is more important from the metaphysical point of view for Jaina philosophy. That is as follows:

anantadharmātmakaṁ vastu ı — *Ṣaḍdarśana-samuccaya* 57

A real has infinite attributes.

anekāntātmakaṁ vastu ı
— *Syādvāda-mañjarī*,
Quoted in *Sarvadarśanasaṁgraha*, chap. 1

A real is constituted of multiple aspects.

Every real has infinite attributes, every small entity has infinite aspects and no human being, no person of a limited capacity can ever claim that "I have known reality". In fact, reality is endowed with infinite attributes, so it presupposes that nobody can know it completely. This is the most significant assertion of Jainism on their theory of epistemology which is based on the types of real, but can not be defined and described in detail here. There are different views in Jaina philosophy. In this respect some Jaina scholars say there are only two types of reals — *jīva* and *ajīva* (conscious and unconscious) — while for others, there are five reals. These are *jīva, ākāśa, dharma, adharma* and *pudgala. Pudgala* means matter: *pūrayanti galanti ca, pudgala* means anything which occupies space and decays in itself. Matter is that which occupies space but it also gets decayed in course of time. So, broadly there are only two *tattvas* — *jīva* and *ajīva* — but in popular Jaina view there are five types of reals. From another point of view, these are mentioned as seven: *jīva, ajīva, āsrava, bandha, nirjarā, saṁvara* and *mokṣa.*[5]

As far as Jaina epistemology is concerned, it is held that there are two types of knowledge: direct and indirect (*pratyakṣa* and *parokṣa). Pratyakṣa* is also known as *aparokṣa* and anything else than *pratyakṣa* is known as *parokṣa.* Then there are different type of knowledge which have been defined. There is also a type of knowledge through which one can know the ideas available in any other person's mind. From this point of view psychology is also there but more important is the epistemological theory, which is known as Syādvāda or Anekāntavāda. The Jaina definition of reality is already quoted above: *anantadharmātmakaṁ vastu* i.e. reality is multifaceted. Therefore, nobody can understand reality in its entirety. When one says "this is a pen", has he/she known everything about the pen? No. According to Jaina view, one cannot know all the aspects of this pen, which is visible, which can be touched, but there are many latent aspects of this pen because

[5] For details, see *Bhāratīya Darśana*, Baldev Upadhyaya, pp. 111-12.

reality has infinite attributes, this leads us to Syādvāda. *Syād* means "may be". But Syādvāda is not scepticism, it is not agnosticism; it is relativism. This is the relativity theory of knowledge, which is also known as Anekāntavāda. Syādvāda and Anekāntavāda are two sides of the same theory. Anekāntavāda is the metaphysical aspect while Syādvāda is the epistemological aspect of the same. This theory is expressed in seven modes of predication, seven types of statements can be made according to it.

Broadly speaking, there are three viewpoints regarding the nature of reality in Indian philosophy:

- First of all, there are the Naiyāyikas who believe that reality exists: *sat*, it means that reality is present and it stays for a while — so it is *sat*;
- then there are some people like Buddhists who say that there is nothing which stays beyond a moment so this is known as *asat* — therefore, we have *sat* and *asat*.
- Then there is Vedānta which says that empirical reality is neither *sat* nor *asat*, while transcendental reality is inexplicable (*anirvacanīya*).

In this way, these are the three viewpoints which are available in different schools of Indian philosophy. If one takes up any object, for example, this mobile phone. Is it *sat*? Is it real? What do you think? If you say it is real, then what is the definition of real. Real, according to Vedānta philosophy, is that which stays constant in past, present and future. Will this mobile phone stay the same in the past, present and future? Obviously, one does not even know whether next moment it will exist or not. In this sense, it is not *sat*. Therefore, the Buddhist says this is only a conglomeration of different entities. There is some chip, some wire, some plastic case — this is nothing different than these, so it is not real, it is *asat* because it is only a conglomeration of both the aspects: *sat* and *asat*. Advaita Vedānta will say this is not real in the true sense of the term, as the Ultimate Reality is something beyond these visible objects and that reality can never be explained. It is inexplicable (*anirvacanīya*). So we have three broad classes of scholars – some say it is *sat*, then some say it is *asat* and the rest say it is *anirvacanīya*. Taking these three standpoints and mixing and matching them, the Jainas have brought out seven modes of predication, which is known as *sapta-bhaṅgī naya*. It means that any judgement can be put up in seven forms in the same order as follows:

1. *Syādasti.*
2. *Syānnāsti.*
3. *Syādasti ca nāsti ca.*
4. *Syādavaktavyaṁ.*
5. *Syādasti ca avaktavyaṁ ca.*
6. *Syānnāsti ca avaktavyaṁ ca.*
7. *Syādasti ca nāsti ca avaktavyaṁ ca.*

First is *syādasti*. The numerous quarrels and struggles in the world are happening because everybody claims something and insists that only this is true. That is why there is so much of tension and friction. The Jaina philosophy focuses on *ahiṁsā* (non-violence). Just as Buddhist philosophy is focusing on *karuṇā*. Mahāvīra's philosophy is focusing on non-violence. Non-violence, not only at the physical level but also at the mental level. The Jaina philosophy propounds that whenever you have to make any statement, never make a claim, like an imperative that only this is true and everything else is false. To illustrate they cite an example of four blind persons and an elephant. Four persons are visually handicapped and none of them can see the entire elephant. They can only touch one part or the other, somebody who touches the feet of the elephant will describe it in one way, somebody who touches its trunk will say something else and somebody who touches its tail will explain the elephant in some other way. Similarly, because all of us have limited capacity to know the reality in some way or the other, like these four persons, so we cannot see anything in entirety.

Whatever we are saying is from our own positioning, from our own capacity and from our own understanding. Therefore, whatever we say, we should always prefix it with *syād* signifying that (may be from this point of view) it is true or it is relatively true. It can be like this:

- *Syādasti* (maybe it is like this).

  But then we should also say:

- *Syānnāsti*: It is not so from other point of view. From my point of view, it is like this but from your standpoint, it may not be like this.
- *Syādasti ca nāsti ca*: *Syādasti* is based on *sat*, *syānnāsti* is based on *asat* and obviously, the third one is a mixture of these two: *syādasti ca nāsti ca* – maybe, it is like this. Maybe, it is not like this.
- Fourth is *syādavaktavyaṁ;* maybe, we cannot explain it.

  Then another mixture:

- *Syadasti ca avaktavyam ca*: Maybe, this is so, but cannot be explained.
- *Syānnāsti ca avaktavyam ca*: Maybe, it is not so, but this can also not be explained.

  And lastly,

- *Syādasti ca nāsti ca avaktavyam ca.* Maybe, it is like this and not like this, and maybe it can never be explained.

The Jaina philosophy propounds that these seven modes of predication will lead us to a totally non-violent ideology in the arena of philosophy. The Jainas emphasize on this theory since it is so much crucial for their philosophy – in the field of causation, in the field of epistemology, in the field of ethics; everywhere they apply this. In fact, Jaina ethics is so popular and so pervasive because of this theory of non-absolutism or Anekāntavāda. Syādvāda is also known as relative pluralism. Any assertion should not be of unipolar type, it should always be multidimensional because reality is multifaceted by nature.

What is *mokṣa*? According to Jaina viewpoint, *mokṣa* is that stage when all the fruits of our action, *karma-phalas* are totally eliminated — then *mokṣa* occurs. State of *mokṣa* is the state of bliss. How can we reach that? There is a *mokṣa-mārga*; just like *triratna* in Buddhism, we have *triratna* in Jainism:

- *samyak darśana*,
- *samyak jñāna*, and
- *samyak caritra.*

Darśana, our vision or our faith (*śraddhā*),[6] should be proper, our knowledge (*jñāna*) should be proper and our *caritra* (conduct) should also be appropriately matching to our vision and knowledge. There are two schools in Jainism — Śvetāmbara and Digambara and their theories are also different according to their view points. Their code of conduct is also different but for understanding that we have to go to the original sources.

The most important contribution of Jaina view to Indian philosophical tradition is undoubtedly the theory of non-absolutism; much before Einstein propounded the theory of relativity in the arena of science, the Jaina philosophy had given us a theory of relativity in respect of knowledge. It means that human knowledge can never be absolute. It will always be relative. So, this relativity is to be expressed through seven modes that have been enunciated as above.[7]

---

6 *tattvārtha-śradhānaṁ samyagdarśanam* । — *Tattvārthasūtra* 1.2

7 Suggested readings for those who are interested in knowing further are: *Jaina Philosophy of Non-Absolutism* by Satkari Mukhopadhyaya and *Central Philosophy of Jainism* by B.K. Matilal . Besides these, there are many books in Hindi by Sagarmal Jain which are published from Parsvanath Vidyasrama Shodha Sansthan, Varanasi.

Question and Answer Session

SPEAKER: With these words, I stop here. I do not know whether I have been able to explain these two schools adequately for the audience present here, but I have myself benefited a lot because I studied these two schools as *siddhānta* and I am thankful to the VIF and Dr Gupta once again for giving me this opportunity.

MR ANURAG SHARMA: Ma'am *jaise ye* phenomena *hotā hai ki* happiness is followed by suffering and suffering is followed by happiness and this circle is ongoing for the infinite period and it is essential to human existence. In Hinduism, it is believed that it has been created or manifested by the *yoga-māyā*, which is an illusionary power of God. So, can we say that suffering plays an important role to experience happiness and to put efforts for the *ātmabodha* (self-knowledge) that will further goals to the self-enlightenment.

SPEAKER: Thank you Anurag. Actually the Buddha does not talk of happiness in clear terms. He only talks of *duḥkha* and cessation of *duḥkha*, *duḥkha-nirodha*. The clear exposition of *sukha* is not there. That is there in other schools, but in this case because *sukha* can only be experienced when *duḥkha* is not there. Therefore, it is implied but it is not explicitly mentioned or discussed in Buddhism. According to Buddhism, there is a state when every suffering will be over, i.e. *nirvāṇa*, but there is no promise or no statement about the presence of happiness in the state of *nirvāṇa*. So, it is not that elimination of suffering gives rise to happiness, not necessarily. *Duḥkha-nāśa* is not *sukha*. I mean to say *sukha* and *duḥkha* are not related in the Buddhist view. For experiencing *sukha*, there are different discussions in other schools, in Jainism, for example, they have discussed the idea of happiness in detail and the ultimate state of *mokṣa* is narrated as the state of infinite happiness, but in Buddhism, it is more on the causal side of suffering and the preparation and practice for *nirvāṇa*. So you can say there are two ways of explaining things: negative and positive, so they are going *via negativa*. Right? And the idea of self-enlightenment is implied there. *Ātmānaṁ viddhi* is the discourse of the Buddha: "know thyself" that is the idea, but *ātmā* is not of the nature of *sukha* as it is in philosophy of Vedānta where it is held to be *ātmā* as *sat, cit* and *ānanda*. But according to the Buddha, it is only *cit*, not even *sat* in the technical sense of Vedānta, *ānanda* is not mentioned here, only *cit* is focused.

DR PRAVESH KUMAR GUPTA: Thank you, Ma'am for such an enlightening presentation. Though my question is slightly off the topic, on Buddhism as a religion. So I want to know your views on Shamanism and rituals in Buddhism. Please share your views.

SPEAKER: I am sorry that I cannot share my views on the theme of Buddhist religion at the moment because I know very little about Buddhism and that too about philosophy, not about religion. I was focusing on Buddhist philosophy only, so I cannot immediately tell you about rituals in the religion of Buddhism, but might get back to you later after reading and going into the sources.

PROFFESSOR SUJIT DUTTA: I enjoyed your lecture very much. My question is on the philosophical side since we discussed about the six schools of Indian philosophy. Why don't we include or expand those to include Buddhism and Jainism because these are interrelated schools of Indian philosophy from the ancient times. So why we restrict ourselves to six schools and not include Buddhism and Jainism as well and whether Advaita philosophy or later Sikhism would qualify as schools in their own right? So what I mean to say is that can we expand our notion of Indian philosophy? Since we are not looking at the ritual side of it, but in graphical side to include these schools as well.

SPEAKER: Thank you for your very basic and important question. Jaina philosophy and Buddhist philosophy are not excluded; they are very much an integral part of Indian philosophical tradition and they are being taught in all the departments of philosophy, wherever we are teaching Indian philosophy. We are always covering Cārvāka, Jaina and Buddhist philosophy in our fold. It is part of the *Sarvadarśanasaṁgraha*, the seminal text which is a compendium of all the schools of Indian philosophy existing in fourteenth century. It has sixteen schools in it and Jaina and Bauddha are very much there; in fact, Bauddha philosophy is covered in two chapters: the basic ancient Buddhist philosophy and the four later schools of Buddhism because they are so wide and so comprehensive that they cannot be covered in one chapter. Therefore, they are very much a part of Indian philosophy. Not only that, they have enriched Indian philosophy, so much so that Nyāya — Vaiśeṣika, Sāṁkhya and Mīmāṁsā would not have been the same if there was no inclusion of Jaina and Bauddha schools because long debates between all of them have happened. There is a book titled *The Philosophy of Nyāya — Vaiśeṣika and Its Conflict with the Buddhist Dinnaga School* (*A Critique of Indian Realism*), authored by Professor D.N. Shastri. When I started studying for my PhD on Vaiśeṣika, I was not able to understand some portions of the original Vaiśeṣika texts in Sanskrit which were not even translated. At that time, I had to go to this book for clarifying certain textual portions because as I said *pūrva-pakṣa* is intermingled with *siddhānta-pakṣa*. And it is very difficult at places to separate *pūrva-pakṣa* from *siddhānta-pakṣa*. This is again a PhD thesis of a senior scholar whom I knew personally. He went to Russia to study Buddhism from the great Buddhist scholar T. Stcherbatsky, who had written a book called *Buddhist Logic* (two volumes), a pioneering work in the area of Buddhism.

In fact, Buddhism and Jainism are so closely connected with other schools of Indian philosophy that we cannot even think of rejecting or excluding them. I think I have answered one question.

As regards your second query, I already mentioned in the beginning that everybody cannot study everything: *na sarvaḥ sarvaṁ jānāti* and as the Jainas have themselves said that we are all having limited capacity of knowing. So anybody who is specializing in something, for example, I am studying Vaiśeṣika for the past four decades and still I have not been able to cover all the texts of Vaiśeṣika. In fact, it is difficult for an ordinary human being like me to read and know everything but I know the basics of Bauddha, the basics of Jaina as presented in the texts of Vaiśeṣika or Nyāya. However, for this lecture, I went to study some of the original sources of Jaina and Bauddha, that too only one or two sources; mostly through the *Sarvadarśanasaṁgraha* because for a lecture of one hour you cannot have more than what I could explain here. I agreed to this lecture because it is the title of the series in "Indian Philosophy for Beginners"; I am also a beginner in the area of Jaina and Bauddha philosophy.

MR SUKANTA: Has Indian philosophy always associated knowledge of reality with consciousness? Can non-living objects attain knowledge of reality?

SPEAKER: To the best of my knowledge, non-living objects do not have cognition according to Jaina or Buddhist school, the very idea of knowledge or cognition presupposes consciousness. Because, till now, it has not been proven that the non-living objects have knowledge. In Hindu philosophy, knowledge is defined as *satyaṁ jñānam anantam brahma*. Accordingly, knowledge itself is consciousness and *jñāna* is cognition. In fact, cognition and consciousness are so closely related in Indian philosophy that we cannot think of one without the other. And an object, I do not know whether this pen has a knowledge of itself or not. But whatever we are experiencing on the basis of our experience and also on the basis of wisdom transmitted to us by our earlier scholars till now, we only associate living beings or consciousness with cognition or knowledge and not the non-living things. For example, trees are there, trees have some feelings and so they have been enumerated as living beings; this has been clearly stated in some texts of Indian philosophy.

They have been classified in Jaina philosophy also as *trasa* and *sthāvara* or *jaṅgama* and *sthāvara*: two types of *jīvas* are there, but they are *jīvas* (living beings). So knowledge is mostly associated with conscious or living beings to the best of my knowledge. Thank you.

MS AKRITI VINAYAK: What is the definition of the self in Buddhism?

SPEAKER: The definition of self in Buddhism is not given as such, but the concept of each school is different. For example, in Jaina philosophy, it is *caitanyalakṣaṇo jīvaḥ*. *Jīva* is conscious, but in Vedānta it is not only conscious; it is also *sat*, *cit* and *ānanda*. In Bauddha as I mentioned earlier, it is *cit* only, it is in the form of consciousness only; *sat* only in the Nyāya and Vaiśeṣika because in Nyāya and Vaiśeṣika, consciousness is held to be an adventitious attribute of the self. Self is not conscious by nature according to Nyāya and Vaiśeṣika. According to Sāṁkhya, it is of the nature of consciousness. According to Vedānta, it is consciousness, it is also bliss and it is also truth: *satyam jñānam anantam,* three epithets in Vedānta; in others only one, either *sat* or *cit*. So, there are different definitions in different schools. And these definitions depend on the metaphysical ideas that they are going to propound and therefore their epistemology is dependent on the ideas of metaphysics that they have projected. First thing is that each school defines reality in its own way. What is real? Once they have defined a real, then they go back to classify the real into living and non-living or any other mode. Then they will also talk about the nature of self and how the self gets to know objects or the beings or other aspects of the universe.

MS PRERNA GANDHI: What does the Buddhist philosophy enunciate on power and political organization?

SPEAKER: Power and political organization — I do not know much about these aspects in Buddhist philosophy because, as I mentioned earlier, I have not studied Buddhism from that aspect in depth. But this question I will keep in mind and try to explore it later.

DR ARVIND GUPTA: OK. Now there is no other comment, then we can close this session. Thank you Dr ShashiPrabha ji. Thank you so much.

Nyāya and Vaiśeṣika Philosophy

LET us now begin to deliberate upon the six systems of Indian philosophy which are known as *āstika ṣaḍdarśanas* The schools are termed as *āstika*, because all of these six systems believe in the authority of the Veda and testimony of the Vedic word.

Nyāya

First of all, we take up Nyāya philosophy, which is known as logical realism. The school of Nyāya is also known as Indian logic. The propounder of Nyāya system of philosophy is Maharṣi Gautama Akṣapāda. He was a sage-scholar from Mithilā and it is well known that the school of Nyāya flourished in Mithilā for many centuries. The definition of Nyāya given by the commentator of Gautama's *Nyāyasūtra* is as follows:

> *pramāṇairarthaparīkṣaṇaṁ nyāyaḥ* । — *Nyāyabhāṣya* 1.1.1
>
> Nyāya is an investigation into the evidences for knowing an object.

What is Nyāya? Nyāya is the examination of an object or issue with the help of evidences. *Pramāṇa* is the evidence, *artha* is the object or issue and *parīkṣaṇa* is the investigation or examination. So Nyāya is what the judiciary is doing today. Nyāya is known as jurisprudence today and jurisprudence depends on investigation of the evidences; this is the precise definition provided by Vātsyāyana, the commentator of *Nyāyasūtras* propounded by Maharṣi Gautama.

There are several other terms also which have been used to denote the Nyāya school of logic. One of these is *ānvīkṣikī*. *Ānvīkṣikī* is derived from the word *anvīkṣā*. *Anu* means afterwards and *īkṣā* means examination or investigation. So after the realm of perception is over, then the scope of reasoning or argumentation begins and that is known as *anvīkṣā*. In the science and the intellectual tradition too, the process which begins after perception is known as *ānvīkṣikī*. The same is also termed as *hetu-vidyā* because the whole discussion revolves around the *hetu*, the reason; Vādaśāstra is another name for Nyāya because ancient Indian rules of dialectics have been propounded in this stream of Indian logic.

What is the goal of Nyāya? Each system of Indian philosophy begins its discourse by setting up a goal because no human endeavour is usually started without anticipating the goal. The goal of Nyāya according to the *sūtrakāra* is *apavarga*. *Apavarga* is the concept which is also known as *niḥśreyasa, kaivalya* or *nirvāṇa* in other schools. In Nyāya, this is explained as *apavarga*. *Apavarga* signifies a state when the whole chain of suffering has been stopped and this chain, according to Nyāya, is like this: *duḥkha* (suffering), *janma* (birth), *pravṛtti* (activity), *doṣa* (fault) and *mithyā-jñāna* (erroneous cognition). When all of these stop working one by one, then *apavarga* is possible. How is *apavarga* to be attained? How can we reach this state of *apavarga*? Each school of Indian philosophy presupposes a goal and also envisages a way or a path to reach that goal. According to Nyāya, there are sixteen objects that have been enumerated and it is proclaimed that by knowing these sixteen objects or categories, one can reach the ultimate goal of *apavarga*.

What are the sixteen objects (*ṣoḍaśa padārthas*). These sixteen entities are very important; although they are mentioned as sixteen in number, yet the whole focus is on the first one and that is *pramāṇa* (means of knowing). Accordingly, the first object is *pramāṇa*; then *prameya* (object of knowing) is the second and *saṁśaya* is the third, which is very significant, because just as we start to know something, a doubt arises. If there is no doubt, then there is no quest for knowing. We would never start our effort for knowing if there is no doubt. So doubt is the starting point of investigation according to Nyāya. Then comes *prayojana*, even if there is doubt but one does not have any goal or aim of discussion, there is no use in wasting time and effort. Hence there should be some *prayojana* (purpose). And how shall one know what is correct and what is not? What is valid? What is invalid? This is to be understood through *dṛṣṭānta* (an example or illustration). To re-iterate these five — *pramāṇa*, *prameya*, *saṁśaya*, *prayojana* and *dṛṣṭānta* — are the background of Nyāya. In other words, these five *padārtha*s prepare the initial stage of Nyāya and then comes *siddhānta*. *Siddhānta* is the theorization or accepted conclusion, what one may also call hypothesis or presupposition: this is what is to be proved. So *siddhānta* is the accepted conclusion and then comes *avayava*. *Avayava*s are the five members or the premises of syllogism: *nyāya-vākya*. Just as in Western logic we have a three-tier syllogism, in Hindu Nyāya we have five members or five steps. These are known as *avayava*s or the *pañcāvayava vākya* (five-membered syllogism):

- *pratijñā* (exposition),
- *hetu* (reason),
- *udāharaṇa* (illustration),
- *upanaya* (application), and
- *nigamana* (conclusion).

In fact, this is the hallmark of Indian logic. Next comes *tarka* (hypothesis), just as a *siddhānta* is set and a *vākya* or *pañcāvayava vākya* is framed, similarly *tarka* is to be provided first and then a *nirṇaya* is to be presented; *nirṇaya* is the ascertainment or verification of what was put as hypothesis. *Vāda* is debate or continuation of argument, this is also very important; then comes *jalpa*. When one starts debating or arguing, then many false arguments also emerge which are known as *kutarka*s in Sanskrit. *Kutarka* is again of many types and one of these is *jalpa*. *Jalpa* means disputation or ranting. After *jalpa* comes *vitaṇḍā*, *vitaṇḍā* is destructive criticism. There are two sides — one is for the motion and other is against the motion, *vāda* (dialogue or debate) can take place only when the ongoing debate has a *vādī*, he who has put up his *siddhānta* and the *prativādī* who is opposing the *siddhānta*. One of them uses *vitaṇḍā* (destructive criticism) as he wants to derail the discussion; this term *vitaṇḍā* is for false arguments or destructive criticism. Next comes *hetvābhāsa* (fallacies of arguments, fallacies of reasoning). These fallacies are studied in Western logic also. But in Indian logic and especially in Nyāya school of Indian philosophy, these *hetvābhāsas* have occupied the central place because success of the debate depends on avoiding all types of fallacies (*hetvābhāsas*). After the fallacies, comes *chala*. *Chala* is quibble. Next is *jāti*, *jāti* is futile refutation. And lastly *nigraha-sthāna* is the point of defeat when one of the discussants is defeated and the other is declared as winner. To re-capitulate, these sixteen *padārthas* are: *pramāṇa*, *prameya*, *saṁśaya*, *prayojana*, *dr̥ṣṭānta*, *siddhānta*, *avayava*, *tarka*, *nirṇaya*, *vāda*, *jalpa*, *vitaṇḍā*, *hetvābhāsa*, *chala*, *jāti* and *nigraha-sthāna*.

Once a student of Nyāya masters all the above sixteen *padārthas*, then only he can expect to achieve liberation or *apavarga* — this is the promise of Maharṣi Gautama. Obviously this does not seem quite into the fitness of things because these sixteen *padārthas* — they are not directly related to the goal of *apavarga* (liberation). As mentioned earlier, they are enumerated as sixteen, but the whole focus is on the first one, i.e. *pramāṇa*. All the other *padarthas*, except the second one *prameya*, will be discussed later. All other fifteen *padārthas* of Nyāya are related to the domain of logic or to the process of knowing, i.e. *pramāṇa*. Therefore, Nyāya is also known as *pramāṇaśāstra*. It is dealing with the epistemological issues to the extent of fifteen *padārthas* and *prameya* is the only one which deals with metaphysics. In other words, *prameyas* are the objects to be known, which are not the main theme of Nyāya.

Let us briefly discuss the literature or the sources of Nyāya. What are the sources of Nyāya school? First of all, Gautama's *Nyāyasūtras* are the most original and most ancient texts of Nyāya; then the *Nyāyabhāṣya*, commentary of the *Nyāyasūtra* is written by Vātsyāyana. As stated already, almost all the schools of Indian philosaphy, be it *āstika* or *nāstika*, follow a pattern or a format of literature. They begin with the *sūtras* (small precise statements) pronounced by the propounder. Then the commentators explain these *sūtras* and thus the earliest exposition after the *sūtras* is known as *bhāṣya*. *Sūtra*, *bhāṣya* and then come other types of commentaries called *ṭīkās*. Actually, in Indian intellectual tradition, three *bhāṣyas* are very significant. These are known as authentic commentaries: one of them is the *Nyāyabhāṣya* of Vātsyāyana (this Vātsyāyana is different from the one who authored the *Kāmaśūtra*); this is the logician Vātsyāyana who extolled the study of Nyāya. He has expounded the methodology of Nyāya. He has also explained that the Nyāya school envisages four aspects. First of all, it is to enunciate the utility or the significance of Nyāya. Why should one study Nyāya? What is the purpose? Vātsyāyana says:

> *pradīpaḥ sarvavidyanamupāyaḥ sarvakarmaṇām* ।
> *āśrayaḥ sarvadharmāṇaṁ vidyoddeśe prakīrtita* ॥
> — *Nyāyabhāṣya* 1.1.1

> Nyāya or *ānvīkṣikī* is like a lamp (*pradīpa*); it is a light for all other branches (*sarvavidyānām*). It is the means for accomplishment of all activities. It is the supports for all duties; it has been elucidated (by Kauṭilya) under the section of *vidyās* (domains of knowledge).

If one has to master any of the domains of knowledge in Indian tradition, he/she needs to study logic or Nyāya first, because this is like a lamp. If one wants to see objects put in a room, first he/she has to have some light in that room. Hence, Nyāya is like a *pradīpa* for all the *vidyās*; *upāyaḥ sarvakarmaṇām* — all human endeavours need a foundation of logic, they anticipate or presuppose the study of logic because if one does not know logic, then he might undertake any action, he might perform many deeds, but they will not be fruitful since they are not done in a proper logical manner.

All our duties or obligations are prescribed in the Dharmaśāstras and they are in turn based or rooted in Nyāya. This science of logic, this school of study is very significant. It sharpens one's intellect through arguing and questioning; in Indian tradition questioning has been an important mode of imparting knowledge. Education system was mainly in the mode of a dialogue between the teacher and the taught, and it was basically the student who raised questions, he came well prepared and he raised searching questions to which the preceptor would provide answers. It is not like today that the teacher or the preceptor comes prepared and he starts delivering a lecture. It was the other way round. Therefore, if one is well equipped in the science of logic, then he will have many more sharp questions. If one masters this science — this domain of knowledge — it will definitely sharpen his intellect. Hence, logic is very important for any branch of learning. This is what Vātsyāyana has said. Then the question arises, who should study Nyāya and when should one begin with the study of Nyāya? As mentioned earlier, it is when there is a doubt. If there is no doubt, then no use of studying Nyāya. The scope of Nyāya begins only when there is a doubt. Even in modern judicial system, the argument starts when there is a doubt, if the doubt is already dispelled, then there is no utility of argument. So Vātsyāyana says:

> *nanupalabdhe 'rthe nyāyaḥ pravartate na nirṇīte 'rthe* ׀ *kiṁ tarhi? saṁśayite 'rthe* ׀ — *Nyāyabhāṣya* 1.1.1
>
> Nyāya does not deal with the objects which are not available, it does not also dwell upon those issues which have already been settled because the decision has already been taken, no use of arguing. Where should Nyāya apply to: where there is *saṁśaya* — when there is a dilemma or when there is doubt — whether this is right or this is not right.

The Nyāya should be applied in case of doubt and that should also be applied in a very proper or appropriate method. What is the method? That method is Nyāya or *pañcāvayava vākya* (five-membered syllogism).

Vātsyāyana further mentions that there are four aspects of *nyāyaśāstra*, which are as follow:

- First one is the agent (*kartā*); there has to be a conscious agent who has some doubt, he is also known as ***pramātā***. A person who wants to know the valid means of knowing, he is known as *pramātā* (agent) — from this point of view *pramātā* is a technical term.
- Next is ***pramāṇa*** - when a desire to know arises in *pramātā*, what should he do? He should proceed further — whither? He should first master the *pramāṇas*. *Pramātā* is the knower or the agent. *Pramāṇas* are the means or methods of knowing like *pratyakṣa*, *anumāna*, *upamāna* and *śabda*.
- Obviously the question arises here: but what should he know? Shall he start with knowing all the objects of the world? Can he do that? No, he should start in a very proper and logical manner to know the valid objects which are known as ***prameya***s (objects) and which have been enumerated by Maharṣi Gautama in his *Nyāyasūtra*. Only those objects should be discussed which are known as *prameyas* in Nyāya. Those objects should be known and those should be mastered.
- So, when these three *pramātā*, *pramāṇa* and *prameya* are in place, then the result will be valid knowledge and that result is known as ***pramiti* or *pramā*** (valid knowledge or correct knowledge). If one wants to achieve correct knowledge, then he has to begin with *pramātā*, a person who is well prepared to master that science. That is what is done today in the aptitude test. If someone wants to go for management training, he has to qualify the MAT or CAT; common aptitude tests like CAT or MAT exams are held to ascertain the eligibility of the *pramātā*.

In short, *Pramātā* is the *adhikārī*, the eligible person (*pātra*). *Pramāṇa* is the method or the means of knowing. *Prameya* is the object of knowing and *pramiti* or *pramā* is the result of knowing. So, this is the methodology of knowing, this is known as *pramāṇaśāstra* (epistemology). Nyāya epistemology incorporates above four aspects within its fold.

Now, what are the *prameyas*. We have already enunciated sixteen *padārthas*. But what are the *prameyas*, the second *padārtha*. *Prameyas* are twelve and these are the objects of knowledge. What are these objects which one should try to know? These are twelve as enumerated by Maharṣi Gautama. To elaborate them as under:

1. *Ātman*, the first object worthy of knowing is *ātman* because unless we know ourselves, unless we know the self or the soul who is the *pramātā*, no cognitive activity will begin. *Ātman* is the first *prameya*.

2. *Śarīra* (body) is next. If *ātman* is disembodied, then there is no way to know it. *Ātman* can be known only when it is embodied. Therefore, body is held to be very significant in Indian philosophy, not in the sense that we understand it today — as an object of enjoyment, as an object of decoration, as an object of sensuous gratification. No, *ātman* is the knower and *śarīra* is the abode of that knower where *ātman* is situated. So *śarīra* is very important.

3. *Indiriyas* (sense organs) are the instruments of experiencing various objects.

4. *Arthas* are the objects (*viṣayas*), viz. *rūpa, rasa, gandha, sparśa* and *śabda*. These five are the *viṣayas* of five sense organs (*indiriyas*).

5. *Buddhi* (intellect)

6. *Manas* (mind)

7. *Pravṛtti* (activity)

8. *Doṣa* (fault)

9. *Pretyabhāva* or *punarjanma* (rebirth)

10. *Phala* (result of our action)

11. *Duḥkha* (suffering)

12. *Apavarga* (release)

These are the twelve objects of knowing which have been termed as *dvādaśa prameyas* in Nyāyaśāstra. In essence, the above four aspects, explained earlier, are: *pramātā*, *pramāṇa*, *prameya*, and *pramā* or *pramiti*.

What about God? He has not been listed in the twelve *prameyas*. So a question may arise whether the system of Nyāya accepts God or not. God is included under the first object *ātman*. *Ātman* is stated to be of two types: *jīvātmā* and *paramātmā*. In fact, theism of Nyāya is also a very important topic which has been well explained by a traditional Nyāya scholar Udayanācārya.

This brings us back to the sources or literature of Nyāya. As already mentioned, the *Nyāyasūtra* by Gautama and the *Nyāyabhāṣya* by Vātsyāyana are the two original sources. Then, we come to the *Nyāyavārttika*. In Indian philosophical tradition, when *bhāṣya* or the primary commentary on *sūtras* was also found as inadequate, then the later scholars needed some more clarity about theories of Nyāya. Therefore, in around sixth century, a scholar named Udyotakarācārya wrote the *Nyāyavārttika*, a compendium of Nyāya which is very technical and very rich in its content. So the *Nyāyasūtra*, *Nyāyabhāṣya* and *Nyāyavārttika* came into existence. And when even *vārttika* was not sufficient to completely explain the theories of Nyāya, then after a period of hundred (or more) years, another scholar emerged who was known as Vācaspati Miśra, he wrote a commentary on the *vārttika*. The original *sūtras* were propounded by Gautama. Vātsyāyana wrote a commentary on *sūtras* known as *bhāṣya*. Udyotakarācārya wrote a treatise called the *Nyāyavārttika*. Notably these are all technical terms of Indian philosophy.[1] The scholars of those times were so highly endowed that they found even the *vārttika* of Nyāya was not sufficient

1 Each school of Indian philosophy does have a bhāṣya, each school does have a vārttika. Accordingly, the Nyāyavārttika in Nyāya, Ślokavārttika in Mīmāṁsā, Pramāṇavārttika in Buddhism. Vārttika is a type of text and bhāṣya is also a type of text. For details, see the Epiloge in this book. pp.

to explain certain abstruse concepts. So Vācaspati Miśra wrote another commentary on the *vārttika* which explains the intent of Udyotakarācārya in detail. This is known as the *Nyāyavārttika-Tātparya-Ṭīkā*. It explains the *tātparya* of *Nyāyavārttika*; this is a *ṭīkā*. *Ṭīkā* is another mode or another form of writing an exegetical text in Indian philosophical tradition. These are the types of texts: just like these days we have paperback edition, hardbound edition, online editions, etc. similarly, in ancient times in Indian philosophical tradition, these types of texts were prescribed and the scholars would start writing a type of book in any school of philosophy they were trained in. In this series, after these four seminal texts, the fifth significant text of original Nyāya is authored by Udayanācārya which is named as *Nyāyavārttika-Tātparya-Ṭīkā-'Pariśuddhiḥ'*.

In fact, these five texts are known as *pañca-granthikā* of Nyāya. If one wants to master the Prācīna Nyāya or the ancient Nyāya, one has to go through these five seminal texts. When Udayanācārya found that there are some complexities in the *Nyāyavārttika-Tātparya-Tīkā* (of Vācaspati Miśra) due to new development of thought, then he wrote the *Nyāyavārttika-Tātparya-Ṭīkā-Pariśuddhiḥ*, a correct interpretation of the *Nyāyavārttika-Tātparya-Ṭīkā*. We must mark the growth of our tradition. It is alleged that Indian tradition has been very rigid and dogmatic, but it needs to be appreciated how the later scholars not only added to the earlier stock of knowledge, but they also revised the knowledge which goes on developing as times keep on changing. So, according to the contemporarity of the problems and fresh challenges, the scholars wrote new texts, but they did not write as individual philosophers as happened in the West. In the West, we have philosophers like Nietzsche. Whatever Nietzsche writes is not necessarily related to Plato or Aristotle. He is writing as an individual. But in Indian philosophy, if one is writing a Sanskrit text of scholastic type, a treatise of the Indian philosophical tradition, then he will try to ascribe himself to a sage or belong to a clan of thought, a *sampradāya*, a school of thought — either one should be belonging to the school of Nyāya or to the school of Mīmāṁsā, or to the school of Sāṁkhya. But one would always belong to a particulare school, This was a tradition, continuity of tradition.

These five texts that have been mentioned above, cover a period of almost 1,000 years, or a little more than that. In a period of 1,200 — 1,400 years, these five texts were composed. After that, there are many more of texts which are available in the tradition of Nyāya but there came a deviation. Why this deviation came? Because in between this duraction the conflict with Buddhist scholars started. The Nyāya is devided as Hindu Nyāya and Bauddha Nyāya. Scholars started confronting each other regarding their thoughts and theories - *siddhāntas*, and their views were disputed. The Bauddhas started refuting the Nyāya theory and Nyāya scholars produced counter arguments to respond to their criticism and that way in the 1,000 years of Middle Ages when this conflict was at its climax, then the development of Indian philosophy is a feat to observe and study. Growth and development of Indian philosophy in those times of intellectual conflicts went through the modes of *vāda-prativāda*, *pūrva-pakṣa-siddhānta-pakṣa*, *praśna* and *uttara*, and *khaṇḍana* and *maṇḍana.* This way, theories were being improved, the styles were being changed. And the change of style occurred to such an extent that a new school of Navya-Nyāya emerged. Nyāya is chronologically understood in two types — Prācīna Nyāya and Navya-Nyāya. The five texts mentioned above are known as the sources of Prācīna Nyāya.

Around thirteenth century, a great scholar Gaṅgeśa Upādhyāya, (emerged in Bengal) propounded Navya-Nyāya which flourished in Mithilā and Bengal.[2] Vasudeva Sārvabhauma was the first scholar of Navya-Nyāya in Bengal. He had several students and all of them carried forward the legacy one by one. Just like the five ancient texts we have the Navya-Nyāya series of *granthas*. Gaṅgeśa Upādhyāya

---

2 For further details, see "A Historical Survey of Indian Logic", M.R. Bodas in his Introduction to *Tarka-Saṁgraha* of Annamhaṭṭa, pp. ix-lii, Bhandankar Oriental Research Institute, Poona, 1974.

wrote a book known as the *Tattva-Cintāmaṇi*. It was a trend-setting work in the field of Navya-Nyāya. Anybody who has not mastered the *Tattva-Cintāmaṇi* or the style of *Tattva-Cintāmaṇi*, which is known as Navya-Nyāya, he will not be an expert Naiyāyika. One will be surprised to know that this style of Navya-Nyāya is being studied in many of the Western universities even now. Western scholars like Stephen Phillips, Jonardon Ganeri and many others are working in this area currently. Earlier H.H. Ingalls from America wrote a book titled *Materials for the Study of Navya Nyāya Logic*. All these Westerners started studying it and worked very hard to master the method and the style of Navya-Nyāya, which is very technical and mathematical. Why this style was adopted? It was to respond to the Buddhist arguments and to put their own arguments in such an abstruse style that nobody can find a fault with their theories. So the school of Nyāya has grown into two streams — Prācīna Nyāya and Navya Nyāya. Navya-Nyāya begins with the *Tattva-Cintāmaṇi*. The *Tattva-Cintāmaṇi* was commented upon by a great scholar Raghunātha Śiromaṇi from West Bengal. He wrote a commentary on the *Tattva-Cintāmaṇi*, which was known as the *Dīdhiti*. Then came Jagadīśa Bhaṭṭācārya who wrote *Jāgadīśī* on it. After that came Gadādhara Bhaṭṭa who wrote another commentary, the *Gādādharī*. These texts are not being popularly taught or studied by many scholars and students in many Indian universities these days because they are highly technical and very tough. But imagine the calibre and the capacity of these scholars who were totally immersed in the study and growth of Indian philosophy, especially Indian logic.

What did Gaṅgeśa do? The Nyāyaśāstra propounded sixteen categories and *vāda* is one of them. *Vāda* is a theory or an argument. Gaṅgeśa started theorization of the concepts. Prācīna Nyāya conceptualized the idea and Navya-Nyāya put the concepts into the form of theories like Maṅgalavāda. Even today we start our programme or our study with an invocation as per our tradition.

All the Sanskrit writers whether they are writing poetry (*kāvya*) or they are writing *śāstra* — they begin with an invocation which is known as *maṅgalācaraṇa*. Gaṅgeśa wrote a chapter in his *Tattva-Cintāmaṇi* which is known as Maṅgalavāda (theory of *maṅgala*). It discusses as to why we should perform invocation? What is the result of invocation; if we do not perform an invocation, what will happen? Will the text or the work be complete or not? Thus, he propounded a theory called Maṅgalavāda. Many options were given like: why *maṅgala* is the goal or if there is an other goal, then why not *maṅgala*, if one does not do *maṅgala* then what will happen? Like Maṅgalavāda, he put several other theories like Īśvaravāda, Vidhivāda, Apūrvavāda and Adṛṣṭavāda. These theories were developed by later scholars in very abstruse and abstract manner, and they are being explained by scholars till date, very highly gifted scholars. Ironically, on the one hand, the style was raised to such a high intellectual podium, but on the other hand, the original and innovative conceptualizing started declining. Indian philosophy reached its pinnacle in the form of Navya-Nyāya and after seventeenth or eighteenth century the original thought process which was taking place till now with the commentaries and sub-commentaries came to a certain halt.

In short, this is the story of Indian logic. It was just an outline because now we have to discuss the other school also which is known as Vaiśeṣika and this has been my own area of specialization. But before that, we should also remember that there are many more *prakaraṇa granthas* (handbooks) in Nyāya tradition. These are very useful texts because they are small treatises which can be read by beginners. For example, the *Tarkasaṁgraha* or *Tarkabhāṣā*. For Nyāya, there is the *Tarkabhāṣā* of Keśava Miśra, a very popular text, small one which covers all the theories of Nyāya in a nutshell; we can say these are ready reckoners or the primers of Nyāya philosophy like the *Tarkabhāṣā*. Interestingly, the *Tarkabhāṣā* was written by Buddhist scholars also. We have Bauddha *Tarkabhāṣā* by Mokṣakara Gupta and we have Jaina *Tarkabhāṣā* by Yaśovijaya

Gaṇi. Significantly, there was first a Hindu *Tarkabhāṣā*, by Keśava Miśra, which is, of course, based on Hindu Nyāya, but as stated earlier, like Hindu Nyāya, Bauddha Nyāya and Jaina Nyāya were also very popular. In this way we have many *prakaraṇa granthas*. The *Tarkabhāṣā*[3] is one of them which is very elementary, very precise and very useful for entering the domain of Nyāya school of philosophy.

Nyāya school of philosophy is known as logical realism, because it propounds that the objects we want to know, they exist in the external world. The basic question of knowledge is whether objects are different than the knower. We have already discussed that in the Nyāya philosophy *pramātā* is different, *pramāṇa* is different and *prameya* is different; they all exist independently, they all are interconnected and interdependent, but they exist of their own. So this is called logical realism because it deals with the problem of logic, with the problem of knowing, the process of knowing, the result of knowing, the fallacies that may come in between the process of knowing and the format of knowing. The last one is *pañcāvayava vākya*. What is the form of syllogism? The form of syllogism is known as *pañcāvayava*, this is again very technical and very methodical. The first statement is *pratijñā*. *Pratijñā* is the enumeration of what we want to prove and the usual example of *pratijñā* that is given in Nyāya is:

1. *Pratijñā*

sādhyanirdeśaḥ pratijñā ।	*parvato vahnimān* ।
Pratijñā is the statement of what we want to prove.	The hilltop contains fire.

Suppose two-three persons were going for a morning walk, they were walking and they saw that on the top of the hill there is *dhūma* (smoke), but they did not see fire. They could

---

3 Recently a small treatise titled *Mīmāṁsātarkabhāṣā* of Kashinath Nyaupane has been published from Jayatu Sanskritam, Kathmandu Nepal, VS 2056 (2000 CE).

see smoke and they wanted to prove something. What did they want to prove?

parvato vahnimān ।

That there must be fire on the hilltop.

This is *pratijñā* as this is to be proved. How do we prove it?

For that, we give a reason: How can you say that there is fire? Other one will ask and the first one will answer as follows:

2. *Hetu*

sādhyasādhanaṁ hetuḥ ।	*dhūmavattvāt* ।
Hetu is the reason for proving the *proban*.	because there is smoke

First one is *pratijñā*, second one is *hetu*. There is fire on the hilltop. Because there is *dhūma* (smoke) that we can see. We are not seeing fire. So from seen to the unseen, we are progressing one by one because everything cannot be seen, there are some objects we can see and from those seen objects, we assume or presume that there is something else, but there should be a connection between the two like *dhūma* and *agni*. Are they related and the person will say yes, they are related. How? That willl be illustrated by an example.

3. Next is *dṛṣṭānta* (or example). (*Pratijñā* is the first *vākya*, *hetu* is the second *vākya*) and *udāharaṇa* or *dṛṣṭānta* is the third *vākya* which will be like:

yatra yatra dhūmastatra tatra vahniḥ yathā mahānase ।

Wherever there is smoke, there is fire, just as in the kitchen.

As we all know the old-time kitchens had both — smoke and fire. Although modern kitchen does not have smoke, it does have fire but smoke is not there. So the connection between smoke and fire cannot be proved in our modern kitchen, but the examples given in these classical texts are correct as they were written long back.

4. Fourth is *upanaya* or application, which signifies the application of relation between smoke and fire; we have observed it many times in the kitchen, but we should also apply it to the hilltop. How shall we do that? The proponent would say:

   tathā cāyam ।

   The smoke on the hilltop is likewise related to the fire.

   How can you say that? Because I have observed it everyday in the kitchen. I observe that if there is smoke, there is fire, so smoke cannot exist without fire. If there is smoke, there has to be fire.

5. Last one is *nigamana* or conclusion:

   tasmāt parvato vahnimān ।

   Therefore, the hilltop has fire.

   To recapitulate, the first was *parvato vahnimān* and the last is *tasmāt parvato vahnimān.* In the first, we are putting it as a hypothesis; in the last we are giving a conclusion because we have observed the invariable relation (*vyāpti*) between smoke and fire. We have illustrated it with the example of our kitchen and we have applied it to this specific smoke on the hilltop. Why hilltop? because it is not possible for everyone to go and climb the hilltop and see fire for oneself. If one could go and watch that there is fire, then it will not be a case of inference. It will be a case of perception. Whatever one can experience directly with the sense organs, that is the domain of perception (*pratyakṣa*).

   The question is: does our knowledge stop beyond *pratyakṣa;* or do we know many more things which are not to be known by sense organs? This is the basic question. We know many more things which are not directly perceived by us. *Anumāna* is there, but even the scope of *anumāna* is limited, so when *anumāna* also fails to work, then we go to the third means of knowing and that is termed as *upamāna. Upamāna* is based on analogy or similarity. Sometimes, we try to know an unknown object through similarity (*upamāna*) with a known object.

Last comes *śabda-pramāṇa* (verbal testimony), which is the most important and which is the hallmark of these six systems of Indian philosophy due to which they are known as *āstika darśanas*. Everything else falls if Vedas says so or if the teacher says so or if a trustworthy person says so — we will believe his word because he is reliable; this is known as *śabda-pramāṇa*. The realism of Nyāya is specially evident in the fact that Nyāya not only believes in the authority of the Vedic word, it also believes in the authority of common persons if they are trustworthy. Bhāṣyakāra Vātsyāyana has clearly stated:

> *ṛṣyāryamlecchānāṁ samānaṁ lakṣaṇam* । — *Nyāyabhāṣya* 1.1.7
>
> The reliability of a sage, a noble person and even an uneducated person is equal as far as their statement is trustworthy.

In short, what is *śabda*? The answer of Nyāya is:

> *āptopadeśaḥ śabdaḥ* । — *Nyāyasūtra* 1.1.7
>
> The statement of a reliable person is known as *śabda-pramāṇa*.

Who is that reliable person? Anybody can be a reliable person, be it a *ṛṣi* or an *ārya* or even an uneducated person (*mleccha*). He is to be held reliable if he knows the object with which he is dealing. So *śabda-pramāṇa* is the supreme *pramāṇa* for Nyāya school and there is a lot of debate regarding *śabda-pramāṇa*, its mode and its validity. Some of the schools accept it in some other ways; like Mīmāṁsā and Nyāya have long debates regarding *śabda-pramāṇa* because Mīmāṁsā deals with Vedic word only, while Nyāya deals with the word of a reliable person — it may be Vedic or it may be non-Vedic. It may be spoken by anybody in the world but if he is a reliable person, then we have to take his word as testimony.

Vaiśeṣika

The next school of Indian philosophy is Vaiśeṣika, which is known a sister school (*samānatantara*) of Nyāya. In these six *āstika* schools we have three pairs like Nyāya and Vaiśeṣika are known as *samāna tantra* because both of them agree upon many theories. Similarly, Sāṁkhya and Yoga is a *yugala sampradāya* — both of these are also sister schools, and then Mīmāṁsā and Vedānta — there are some similarities and some common presuppositions to which both of them agree. As we have already seen, Nyāya is a theory of knowledge, it mainly deals with *pramāṇas*; it is known as *pramāṇaśāstra*. But it has not dealt with *prameyas* in as much detail as was expected. Vaiśeṣika fills in this lacuna. Vaiśeṣika deals basically with the *padārthas* (objects) of knowledge and it is known as *padārthaśāstra* or *prameyaśāstra*. Therefore, Nyāya and Vaiśeṣika became complementary to each other. Although from their beginning up to the tenth century, for 1,000 years or 1,500 years, both the schools developed independently. They originated separately and they grew independently, but in around tenth century, when the struggle with the Buddhists became intense, then Nyāya and Vaiśeṣika joined hands to fill in the deficiencies of their sister school and become stronger together. Nyāya provided the logical platform and Vaiśeṣika provided the metaphysical explanation, and both of them came to the same level. However, in this amalgamation process the loss was of Vaiśeṣika and not that of Nyāya. Because Nyāya overshadowed Vaiśeṣika; consequently, not many people know much about Vaiśeṣika or its significance. Vaiśeṣika is a very important school for a study of the six systems of Indian philosophy as has been stated in the following popular statement:

> *kāṇādaṁ pāṇinīyaṁ ca sarvaśāstropakārakam* ।
>
> If one wants to master all the Śāstras, one must study at least two Śāstras if not all: which are: Kāṇāda, the school propounded by Kaṇāda, that is Vaiśeṣika and the school propounded by Pāṇini, that is Vyākaraṇa.

Evidently, Pāṇini's grammar talks of *padas*, it is *padaśāstra*. And Vaiśeṣika of Kaṇāda is known as *padārthaśāstra*. *Pada* is the name or the word, and *padārtha* is the meaning of that word: *padasya arthaḥ padārthaḥ*.

If somebody says "this is a pen", then the Pāṇinian school will deal with the term pen, how is it constituted and how is it derived. What is its morphological structure? But the system of Kaṇāda will deal with the essence of this pen as an object; this is made of plastic, plastic comes from which element and what are its properties? Will it be extinct after being broken? Or will something remain of it? These are the issues that Kaṇāda discusses about the *padārthas*. We see that there are hundreds and thousands of objects in the world. Is there anybody who can claim that he has seen and known all the objects or can know all of the objects? No human being has the capacity nor can anyone claim that he or she has known everything. Then how should we know all these objects? To this, the Vaiśeṣika would say that we should classify things into groups that are possible. In science also the some process is followed and this is done in our practical life as well. We divide and classify objects, so that protecting and managing them is easy and convenient. Accordingly, what did Kaṇāda do? He divided the whole of this world into six *padārthas* and the later Vaiśeṣika scholars claim that everything can be covered well under these six elements; nothing remains out of the domain of these six *padārthas*, if one knows these six, then he knows everything. What is the goal of knowing in Vaiśeṣika? Just as it is held to be *apavarga* in Nyāya, similarly in Vaiśeṣika, the ultimate goal is termed as *niḥśreyasa*. But the Vaiśeṣika definition of this goal is even broader. In the first statement of the *Vaiśeṣikasūtra*, Kaṇāda says:

athāto dharmaṁ vyākhyāsyamaḥ । — 1.1.1

Now, therefore we shall begin with explaining the nature of *dharma*.

What exactly is *dharma*? These days, lots of discussions are going on the nature of *dharma*. And what is this *dharma* that we shall be discussing under Vaiśeṣika? Kaṇāda say *dharma* is the basic *dharma* of the universe and that *dharma* is very broad.

Accordingly the next *sūtra* defines *dharma*, where Kaṇāda says:

yato 'bhyudayaniḥśr̥eyasasiddhiḥ sa dharmaḥ ।

— *Vaiśeṣikasūtra* 1.1.2

Dharma is that means by knowing which both *abhyudaya* and *niḥśreyasa* are accomplished.

Abhyudaya is material progress and *niḥśreyasa* is spiritual fulfilment. In fact, no amount of material possessions can give one the sense of fulfilment. Therefore, *abhyudaya* is important but *abhyudaya* is not all, it needs to be followed by *niḥśreyasa*. *Abhyudaya* is the worldly progress and *niḥśreyasa* is the spiritual perfection. *Dharma* incorporates both of these. What can be a more secular and comprehensive definition of *dharma* than this? This definition is quoted by one and all without knowing that this is provided by Kaṇāda in his *Vaiśeṣikasūtra*. When a disciple of Kaṇāda asks him: how can we know that *dharma*. How can we master that? Kaṇāda says if you know the six *padārtha*s enunciated by me, then you will reach *niḥśreyasa*, the ultimate goal. The knowledge of six *padārtha*s will provide you *abhyudaya* and will also lead you to *niḥśreyasa*.

What are the six *padārthas*? *Dravya* (substance), *guṇa* (attribute), *karma* (activity), *sāmānya* (generality or the generic attribute), *viśeṣa* (ultimate particularity) and *samavāya* (inherence). These are the six categories clearly mentioned by Kaṇāda. But, later on, a seventh category *abhāva* was also added to the list. Subsequently, Vaiśeṣika theory came to be known as Saptapadārthavāda: *dravya*, *guṇa*, *karma*, *sāmānya*, *viśeṣa*, *samavāya* and *abhāva* are the seven *padārtha*s, and the previous Vaiśeṣika claim is revised that nothing remains out of these seven *padārtha*s. Everything that is here in the world can be covered under these seven; everything in the world can be put under one or the other *padārtha*. From this point of view, this classification, this categorization done by Kaṇāda has been so comprehensive, historically it has been so significant that till today it cannot be superseded; you accept it or not, you agree with it or you disagree with it, but the historical significance of this classification is very well established. And this is primarily the theory of matter — just like Nyāya is a theory of knowledge; although the Vaiśeṣikas bring in *ātmā* and *paramātmā* also into this discussion. But basically this is the theory of matter and mind motion, of course, is there in the form of *karma*.

Significantly, the Vaiśeṣikas provide some basic insights into the scientific investigation of the ancient Hindus when we go into details of these theories. The theory of atoms, for example, Kaṇāda was the first to give us a theory of atomic creation. The creation or production of any object begins with the minutest atoms. Atoms are the ultimate constituents of matter. Four types of atoms are there in the universe according to Vaiśeṣika: *pṛthivī*, *jala*, *teja* and *vāyu*. They are of four types pertaining to these four *dravyas* (substances). When two atoms of a particular substance combine, a *dvyaṇuka* (dyad) is produced. When three dyads combine, a *tryaṇuka* (triad) is produced and when four *tryaṇukas* combine a *caturaṇuka* is produced and so on and so forth, all the objects of the world are created like this from their respective atoms. On the one hand, we have the system of Vedānta in Hindu philosophy, which says that each entity of the universe is permeated by the single reality-consciousness, and on the other hand, Vaiśeṣika propounds that each entity of the universe, even each atom of the universe is discrete, is an independent entity. Each atom is different from the other. Although they are held to be of four types: earthly atoms, airy atoms, watery atoms and fiery atoms; yet even among earthly atoms, earthly atom *A* is said to be different from earthly atom *B*. So there are two strings of the same thread only, one side of the string is Vaiśeṣika and the other side of the string is Vedānta. According to Vaiśeṣikas, each of us has a different *ātman*, *ātmans* are innumerable, with innumerable bodies, innumerable minds and innumerable atoms. So Jīvabahutvavāda is the theory of Vaiśeṣikas, same is stated by Sāṁkhya also. Sāṁkhya accepts Puruṣabahutvavāda, so plurality of selves is accepted there as well.

The nomenclature of Vaiśeṣika is in fact derived from the term *viśeṣa*. *Viśeṣa* is a category according to Vaiśeṣikas. The name of the system comes from this category *viśeṣa*. This category is also an innovative concept of the Vaiśeṣika which is available only in the eternal substances. Accordingly, substances or *dravyas* are of two types: *anitya dravyas* and *nitya dravyas*. There are nine *dravyas*. First four *dravyas*: *pr̥thvī*, *jala*, *teja* and *vāyu* are held to be *anitya* in the form of products but their atoms are *nitya*. The last five — *ākāśa*, *kāla*, *dik*, *ātman* and *manas* — are *nitya dravyas* only and these do not have any atoms or parts of them. *Viśeṣas* inhere in the *nitya dravyas* only and not in *anitya dravyas*. In other words the products like this book — this is *anitya*, this does not have the *viśeṣa* because it will perish. Whatever is produced will perish, *anitya*. This is a production, this is an effect: so this does not have a *viśeṣa*, but when we go on breaking or destroying the book, it will not be totally extinct. What will be left? According to Vedānta, only pure consciousness will be left, according to Vaiśeṣika minutest material in the form of atoms will be left. Those atoms are eternal and each atom will have its own *viśeṣa*. Just after *pralaya*, when all the bodies will be destroyed because they are produced, but all the *ātmans* will be there as they are *nitya*. All the *manas*-s will be there because *manas* is also said to be *nitya*, *manas* is *aṇu* and atoms are *paramāṇus*, the minutest while *ātman* is *vibhu* (ubiquitous). So all the *manas*-s will have their own *viśeṣas*. All the *ātmans* will have their own *viśeṣas* and all the atoms will have their own *viśeṣas*. This is the theory of *viśeṣa* and the name Vaiśeṣika to the system of Kaṇāda is given by the category of *viśeṣa*. It is also known as Kāṇāda system, Kāṇāda Darśana or Vaiśeṣika Darśana, besides being known as Pailuka Darśana because *pīlu* is another name of atom.

One more notable aspect of atomic theory is there: when these earthly atoms are put into heat, there occurs a change in their properties. Pīlupāka and Piṭharapāka are the two theories based on the chemical changes in attributes of earthly atoms due to the application of heat. This is pure chemistry. We put some elements into heat, first in normal temperature, and then increase the level of heat; the properties of the earthly substance start changing. Vaiśeṣikas have explained it like this — that when we apply heat to the earthly atoms, then some of the properties of that earthly object change. For example, in summer season, we observe the fruit of mango. Why did we innovate refrigeration, to avoid the direct and excessive contact with heat so that we can use the mango or the tomato for many more days, if there was no refrigeration, if this mango was put into constant heat it would get softer in touch and its taste will also change. It will be soft to such an extent that we will not be able to eat it. So, chemical action or *pāka* changes its properties. What is *pāka*. *Pāka* is the application of heat. Which properties of earthly objects change? Only four — *rūpa*, *rasa*, *gandha* and *sparśa* — these four properties of an earthly object change due to the application of heat. It does not happen in case of water or air, we can see ourselves — if we heat water even in summer, if we apply heat it will get hot but if we leave it to itself it will again cool down. If we fill a bucket of hot water and leave it till evening, water will get cool on its own. Because coolness is the property of water while earth has this unique capacity to change its properties due to application of heat (*pāka*). In other words *pāka* is possible only in the case of earthly objects.

How does *karma* (motion) take place? According to Vaiśeṣikas, *karma* (motion) can be of five types: *utkṣepaṇa* (throwing upward), *apakṣepaṇa* (throwing downward), *ākuñcana* (contraction), *prasāraṇa* (expansion) and — *gamana* (going). All other types of motion come under the last one *gamana*. These five are the forms of *karma* (motion) or activity which occurs in physical objects. Vaiśeṣika has tried to describe and explain the visible and physical material world. Maybe, that is the reason why this school was neglected in traditional circles of Indian philosophy. To substantiate one could see that Vācaspati Miśra ignored this school to an extent that he wrote a commentary on Nyāya; not only Nyāya, he wrote commentaries on all the other five *āstika* schools also; he is known as *sarvatantra–svatantra* but he ignored the school of Vaiśeṣika. He wrote a commentary on the Sāṁkhya, another on Nyāya and also on Mīmāṁsā, Vedānta and Yoga, but he did not write any commentary on Vaiśeṣika because he did not find it worthwhile. Why? Probably because it deals with the visible and material world; it does not talk much of the spiritual side. To put it more precisely, this system was not very well received earlier by our traditional scholars, but now-a-days due to its rational outlook, its secular approach and the scientific insights that it provides, this system has become very popular. I have been working on the philosophy of Vaiśeṣika for the past five decades, I can quote names of some twenty or twenty-five scholars from outside India who are currently working on Vaiśeṣika: from Japan, from Russia, from Germany and from America.[4] Evidently, this is a very significant system but it has not been studied much in its original texts. There are many commentaries and texts of Vaiśeṣika which are still lying unexplored. One of the texts of Vaiśeṣika which is again a ready reckoner or a primer and which is very popular, is the *Tarkasaṁgraha*; just like the *Tarkabhāṣā* for Nyāya. The *Tarkasaṁgraha* of Nyāya–Vaiśeṣika is very popular *prakaraṇā-grantha*. As many as thirty or forty commentaries have been written on the *Tarkasaṁgraha*, a small text; the author Annambhaṭṭa himself has written a commentary on *Tarkasaṁgraha*. He wrote the *Tarkasaṁgraha*, a treatise, then himself wrote a commentary on his own work known as the *Tarkadīpikā*.

Recently, there was a proposal to prepare a critical edition of the *Padārtha-Dharma-Saṁgraha* on the *sūtras* of Kaṇāda, also known

[4] For details, see ShashiPrabha Kumar, 2019 "Vaiśeṣika Studies Across the World" in *Categories, Creation and Cognition in Vaiśeṣika Philosophy*, pp. 171-86.

as the *Praśastapādabhāṣya* on *Vaiśeṣikasūtra*. Significantly, till date, no critical edition has been made available of this text. When we started looking for its manuscripts, we came to know about a scholar from Japan, his name is Norihiko Tanaka. He has collected some thirty-five or thirty-seven manuscripts of the *Padārtha-Dharma-Saṁgraha* of Praśastapāda. When we asked him as to when will you bring out the critical edition? He responded that he is still busy in collecting and in digitizing all these manuscripts. So thirty-seven manuscripts of the text out of which many are not easily available, although he collected all the manuscripts from India only. Ironically, many of us, Indian scholars, do not know about so many manuscripts of this particular text. Likewise, many more texts of Vaiśeṣika will be lying in the manuscript libraries, which are awaiting to be explored.

Question and Answer Session

SPEAKER: While teaching at Jawaharlal Nehru University, I used to ask my research students to work upon manuscripts and they brought some new commentaries. Some three or four of my students have worked on the manuscripts of Vaiśeṣika texts.

I think that is all I can say about Vaiśeṣika in such a short time. More than 2,000 years of history in case of Nyāya and Vaiśeṣika cannot be covered in such a short duration, so I have just given you a sketch of what is possible. Those of you who want to delve deeper, please do so; if I can be of any help. I will be available always. Thank you so much.

DR ARVIND GUPTA: Thank you Dr ShashiPrabha ji. I think this was really very interesting what you just mentioned about long history of these philosophies, more than 2,000 years and it is a sad commentary that you do not have digitization of all the manuscripts available. No interest, only some people like you are working on this branch of Indian philosophy, but broadly, people know absolutely nothing about it, but listening to you, we saw that these Indian thinkers of the yore, they came very close to the modern scientific method of inquiry, and whether it was metaphysics or the methodologies. Scholars like Kaṇāda also came up about atoms (*paramāṇus*) and categories (*padārthas*), the issues or the objects that need to be studied and the method of studying. This tradition seems to have continued up to seventeenth-eighteenth century and, yet, how is it that India missed the modern discoveries, you see if you look at the Western philosophical thought — they had like Aristotelean properties and categorization, etc. that it had started. Ptolemy had some model of the universe and even on Indian side we had mathematicians and good astronomers. We had people who were observing the body, alchemy or Āyurveda, etc. No doubt, there was this emphasis on the technical side of it and there was this highly evolved philosophical discourse. If they had been combined, then perhaps the revolution in science and technology would have come to India much earlier than it came to Europe, which was really in the fifteenth century. When Galileo, Newton, Kepler and other people applied their focus on a lot of observations or empirical knowledge and then, of course, theorizing it and categorizing it and understanding the basics and giving the theories of how the various elements of the universe are working. Of course, the nature is explained by these fundamental forces and that method is continued. We can have many explanations. Probably today these methods are still relevant. But I do not see any application of these or even knowledge of this in the modern teaching of science in our schools or universities. This is really a very sad story and probably it is continuing even today. So anyway, let me put my short question: what is the importance of observation? Because, you observe through the empirical method and build theories around it through experimentation. All this seems to be highly evolved and as you mentioned that Vācaspati Miśra did not write a commentary on Vaiśeṣika which is materialistic. So people who are interested only in spiritual aspects, probably the *apratyakṣa* ones, whether there was focus on empirical observation in these philosophies or any other philosophy that may have led to the modern scientific method which finally took off. This is my first question and the other is that the Arabs who translated a lot of Indian knowledge texts and then they took it to the West in Europe. And that became the basis of the modern scientific method in Europe. And the knowledge that they translated was about astronomy or trigonometry or mathematical knowledge, but I am not very aware whether they also translated this Nyāya and Vaiśeṣika or any of these philosophical texts. And whether these are being taught in the Western universities. Of course, you mentioned about some Western scholars, but they may be only isolated. If it is not a case for studying in a comparative manner, the Western philosophy and the Indian philosophy, Buddhist and Jaina systems included, so that a complimentary philosophy emerges and that addresses many of the problems which were not addressed in one system or the other. So that is my question and then there are a couple of questions on the chat box. I will come to that in a moment. You might like to answer this.

SPEAKER: Sir, I answer your second question first. As regards the question about observation, I think the Vaiśeṣika was, of course, focusing on this method because Kaṇāda typically uses the word while describing two types of objects — *dṛṣṭa* (observed) and *adṛṣṭa* (not observed) —, and he was candid enough to admit that he had not been able to explain so many things or processes which he mentions as *adṛṣṭa*. Under *adṛṣṭa*, he mentions a lot of physical phenomena like why the needle goes towards the magnet (*cumbaka*)? Why does the earthquake occur? Why does the air move in curvilinear motion? Why does the fire go upwards? Like these, many other physical activities, he says they are all *adṛṣṭa* (unseen). He means to say that I have been able to explain only the *dṛṣṭa* ones. You have rightly mentioned that the tradition of Indian philosophers or Indian scholars had been more towards introspection or inner experience. That is why this system, the school of Kaṇāda did not receive the type of attention that it deserved. There are three types of methods that we employ: observation is one of them, introspection is the first and experimentation is the third, which leads to scientific innovations. And I am sure by studying these theories of Vaiśeṣika that some sort of experiments might have also been conducted. Maybe one or two, that too, not at the scale of modern scientific experiments, but Kaṇāda must have made some experiments. Only then, he would have been able to propound the *pāka* (chemical) theory, i.e. how a pot is baked into the hot fire. Also regarding metals, like gold and silver, he holds that, metals are not earthly objects. They are fiery objects: *suvarṇādayo dhātavaḥ taijasāḥ*, because if you put the metals into fire, they will change their form from solid to the liquid, they will transform a little but the nature, the colour, etc. will not change and they will not be extinct while the earthly objects will change their form and their properties totally if they are put into fire. But as you rightly said that Āyurveda has employed the theories of Vaiśeṣika in its discipline. In fact, the whole of Āyurveda is based on *dravya-guṇa-vijñāna* of Vaiśeṣika. There are three types of *doṣas* – *pitta*, *kapha* and *vāta;* the prescription or the treatment is based on *dravya-guṇa-vijñāna* and that *dravya-guṇa-vijñāna* is totally founded on the theories of Vaiśeṣika and research has also been done on Vaiśeṣika influence on Āyurveda. Similarly, Vaiśeṣika with regard to mathematical notions, because they have a very peculiar theory of numbers. How the number two arises and how it gives rise to the further numericals? *Dvitvotpatti-prakriyā* is very typical of Vaiśeṣika, I think their scientific insights were based on observation, but they did not get due recognition and support. If they would have got the desired support, then maybe, we would have done some progress in the field of scientific spectrum, but now many scientists are focusing on these and especially this theory of *padārtha*s, the categorization and they are working in the area of artificial intelligence as well.

Now I come to the next question you mentioned about the Western and Indian philosophy. Some studies have been made and one of the European scholars whose book was published in 1918, probably the earliest book on Vaiśeṣika, was a Dutch scholar – B. Faddegon. He wrote *The Vaisesika System* (1918). Unfortunately, the book by Faddegon was not available in India when I started working on Vaiśeṣika but now it is available online and it is being republished also. I must say that 1980 onwards, or even before that, some German scholars have worked on Vaiśeṣika theories. Comparative philosophy is also emerging, epistemology of Vaiśeṣika and the Western philosophy — a work has been done. Especially one of the German scholars who had settled in America — Wilhelm Halbfass. He wrote a book on Vaiśeṣika titled as *On Being and What There Is*? This shows that the Western philosophy also discusses the concept of being and Kaṇāda deals with this concept very technically. He talks of being and becoming, *astitva*, *tattva* and *bhāva*. What is common among the six *padārthas*. There are three things *astitva*, *abhidheyatva* and *jñeyatva* — all the six categories that he has mentioned, they all are existent, they have being; the ones that can change they are the *bhāvas*; *bhāva* is the transformation or becoming. They are all communicable through language (*abhidheyatva*) and these six are also the objects of our knowing (*jñeyatva*).

In fact, the above-mentioned book by Halbfass proved to be a pioneering one for the study of Vaiśeṣika and the Western world rose towards it.[5] Now this is being studied in comparison with the scientific theories — they are studying Vaiśeṣika system and taking some inputs from here. There are works going on this theory of molecular medicine. Now-a-days we have this discipline of molecular medicine, which is also applied in the treatment of cancer — that is based on the Vaiśeṣika theory of *pāka*; if you apply heat to a few atoms their properties change, so this cheemotherapy is also based on the theory that the cells which have been damaged, they should be exposed to extreme heat, to burn those diseased cells. This theory of *pāka* is being employed in the medical treatment too. The scientists in such departments must include and examine traditional Indian ideas in their research. Likewise, this method

---

[5] In between Faddegon and Halbfass, the works of another European scholar Erich Fravwallner needs to be noted, particularly his book *History of Indian philosophy*, Vol. II (*On Nature Philosophical Schools*).

of experimentation, I am not sure how they will use it but many scholars are using Vaiśeṣika theories. As far as the scientists and the mathematicians are concerned, the name of Professor Subhash Kak is worth mentioning and many more scientists are studying Vaiśeṣika from this perspective. Sanskritists like me can only provide original and ancient inputs in Vaiśeṣika. We do not have the background of scientific experiments or theories but this is the need of the hour and many students are doing their research in these areas.

MR SUKANT: Actually my question got answered. My question was that it seems that Nyāya was more concerned with mind and less with matter, and then you of course explained that how Vaiśeṣika was concerned more with matter because logical realism, you know, when it is applied to the study of matter, it is the science. So in Nyāya the logical realism is being applied more to the mind rather than to the matter.

SPEAKER: You are right because the Naiyāyikas were dealing only with the *pramāṇas*, so they were applying it to the mind while Vaiśeṣika applied it to the material aspect or the visible aspect of the world.

DR ARVIND GUPTA: You see it is also important, if you have to do observations in an experimental set-up, you also need instruments. Galileo used telescope to look and that changed science completely. I do not know whether in Indian science and philosophy there was a stress on the measurements.

SPEAKER: Not on exact and specific measurements because as you said they did not have advanced instruments. In fact, they were the sages (*ṛṣis*) living and working in the field of nature, but they have clearly talked of measurement, the basic nature of measurement as an attribute. There are measurements of four types, known as *aṇu*, *mahat*, *hṛsva* and *dīrgha* both length and breadth have been discussed but they are not going to the exact measurements. Similarly, regarding this *gurutva* (gravitation) — *gurutva* is one of the twenty-four *guṇas* and Kaṇāda has mentioned that anything which falls from above, when it is thrown from above, it falls down because there is *gurutva* in *pṛthivī*. So, he has clearly mentioned about the gravitational pull of the earth and one of the contemporary scholars has worked on this theory of gravitation; he has tried to show that Newton's Laws of Gravitation are definitely suggested in the *Vaiśeṣikasūtra*. But it is only the basic classification of measurement — like *aṇu* (minute), *mahat* (gross), *hṛsva* and *dīrgha* (long and short) — these four types of measurements are described but they did not go into the exact measuring because they did not have any instrumental support and that was not their area also. I would say that rather than *upakaraṇa* (instruments), they were depending more on their *antaḥkaraṇa* (internal instrument or mind).

MS ANUSKHA: Though my question is not topical, I still use my limited knowledge and analysis to just ask the question. Since you mentioned that the Nyāya philosophy is about logic and fallacies, and that it is about logical realism, so you know that today's world is a world of unlimited information — we consume so many articles, texts and books on a daily basis, but that has also given rise to fake news, disinformation and propaganda, and why people fall prey to these kind of things is that because maybe they do not have the intellectual capabilities to distinguish between a trap and the reality. So in that way, I wanted to know, that how the methodologies that have been talked about in the Nyāya philosophy can be used to address this issue of the current information age, which is fake news.

SPEAKER: Very good question. And you are right that this notion of fallacies is very tricky; if this concept of logic is taught to students at a younger age, I think this will help because if they are not taught logic, they are more prone to believe whatever is made available to them. Isn't it? Our teacher who taught us logic in the class twelfth, he used to say that throughout our life we do not speak a single sentence which is logically correct. So logic is quite significant and if logic or philosophy is taught (because logic is a part of philosophy), it should be taught at least at the secondary level, if not at the elementary or middle level; it should be made a part of the curricula. Now with the New Education Policy, we have understood the importance of philosophy. Philosophy is a foundational subject and this should be taught to young minds so that they are trained in discrimination of whatever knowledge is received by them. That is why the validity of knowledge is also a very important question in Indian intellectual tradition — Jñāna-prāmāṇyavāda. It is not that whatever we see with our eyes is correct, even *pratyakṣa* can be *ābhāsa* (illusion) and the theory of *hetvābhāsa* occupies the central stage in Nyāya. So this theory of fallacies, in the West that is very limited, if you see the extent of *hetvābhāsa*s that are discussed in Nyāya, I think that should be made available; at least the basic structure of argumentation or whatever is written or spoken is not reliable, while only the reliable word is to be trusted. This basic premise has to be imprinted on young minds. They should not trust anything which comes to them as valid. First the validity of it needs to be tested. There are means of testing which have been given, how to test the validity of a statement, how to test the validity of a thing which is visually perceived — we have to check and then we should trust it. I think that is a very relevant question, especially with regard to social media and fake news these days.

DR ARVIND GUPTA: You mentioned that New Education Policy will regard philosophy as a foundational subject. What does it mean? Will they teach it in schools?

SPEAKER: Yes, actually it is being taught in some of the schools, but people discourage students from studying philosophy. Now they are putting philosophy on centre stage already and also other branches of it like logic, ethics, aesthetics and metaphysics — all these are parts of philosophy. All these aspects of study are very important for the young minds. At least at the 10th or 12th levels; philosophy is already there but it is not available in many schools. It should be made more widely available now. It should be offered in more and more schools. For example, I studied logic and psychology in class 11th and 12th. So just like mathematics, if you study mathematics your brain becomes logically oriented, similarly if you study logic you will not trust anybody or anything. You will always have a check on whatever is being offered to you.

ANURAG SHARMA: Ma'am my question is: जो महाभारत में संजय उवाच और भगवानुवाच है उसमें शब्द ही हैं मतलब कोई लिखित स्क्रिप्ट हमारे पास नहीं थी और बाद में वेद व्यास एंव भगवान् गणेश के द्वारा महाभारत लिखा गया। तो क्या शब्द-प्रमाण हम कहते हैं वो इस कॉन्टेक्स्ट में सही बैठता है जो संजय उवाच और भगवानुवाच हुआ और अगर ये सही बैठता है तो क्या शब्द-प्रमाण को हम क्रेडिबल इन्फॉर्मेशन मान सकते हैं इसी टेक्स्ट में क्योंकि एक वर्बल ट्रान्सफॉर्मेशन होता किसी कम्युनिकेशन का तो प्रोबेबिलिटी ज्यादा होती ताकि उसमें इन्टरप्रिटेशन आ जाए। तो क्या फिलॉसॉफी का कॉन्टेक्स्ट हम लेकर चलें तो भगवानुवाच और संजय उवाच को हम सही मानते हैं एज़ ए क्रेडिबल इन्फॉर्मेशन?

SPEAKER: This a very good question Anurag. केवल जो कोई कुछ बोलता है और तुम सुनते हो वह वास्तव में शब्द-प्रमाण नहीं है। वह तो श्रावण प्रत्यक्ष (auditory perception) है। इसके लिए तो न्याय-भाष्य जरूर पढ़ना चाहिए। जो कुछ कोई बोल रहा है और हम सुन रहे हैं वह केवल महाभारत ही नहीं हैं वह तो हमारी सारी श्रुति-परम्परा है। वेद से लेकर उपनिषद् तक और महाभारत में भी आपने बता दिया और पुराण में भी — इन सब में बोलकर ही बताया गया है। यह शब्द-प्रमाण नहीं है यह तो शब्द का प्रत्यक्ष, श्रावण प्रत्यक्ष है, ये ऑडियो परसेप्शन है, उन्होंने मुँह से बोला और हमने कान से सुना। यह शब्द प्रमाण नहीं है, शब्द-प्रमाण की परिभाषा न्याय दर्शन में दी गई है –

> *āptopdaeśaḥ śabdaḥ* । — *Nyāyasūtra* 1.1.7
> The statement given by a reliable person is *śabda-pramāṇa.*

Now the question is who is an *āpta*? तो उसका भी स्पष्टीकरण दिया है कि जिसका कोई भी स्वार्थ नहीं है, जो जैसी वस्तु है, वैसी ही बताता है। आप्त व्यक्ति अपने छात्रों को बताना चाहता है कि पीछे से, यानि अपने गुरुओं से यह सुना है और यह आपके लिए मैं दे रहा हूँ। तो जो सबसे बड़ा टेस्ट है "आप्तता" या रिलाएबिलिटी का, वह है यथार्थ-वक्ता का। ही हू स्पीक्स इट एज़ इट इज़ (जैसा है वैसा बोलने वाला)। और यह बात हमें पहले चैक करनी पड़ेगी। जब आप यूनिवर्सिटी की क्लास में जाते हैं, जो आज आप मेरा लेक्चर सुन रहे हैं। यह आप VIF के पोर्टल पर सुन रहे हैं। तो आपको लगता है जो कोई यहाँ पर बोल रहा है वह ठीक बोलेगा, रिलाएबल बोलेगा। लेकिन कहीं भी किसी मंच से कोई कुछ बोलता है उसको सुन तो रहे हैं आप कान से। लेकिन वह सब शब्द-प्रमाण नहीं हैं। जब कोई बात आप्त पुरुष कहता है वही शब्द-प्रमाण होता है। आप्तता की परीक्षा बहुत महत्त्वपूर्ण है जैन दर्शन में तो पूरा ग्रन्थ लिखा गया इस प्रमाण पर — *आप्तमीमांसा*। तो आप्त की परीक्षा, रिलाएबिलिटी का जो टेस्ट है, वो हमारे यहाँ वही है जो न्याय दर्शन में बताया गया है –

ṛṣyāryamlecchānāṁ samanaṁ lakṣaṇam ।
— *Nyāyabhāṣya* 1.1.7

वात्स्यायन कह रहे हैं कि सब लोग आप्त हो सकते हैं ऋषि भी, आर्य भी और म्लेच्छ भी। शर्त क्या है कि वे जो कुछ जानते हैं वैसा ही बताएं और उनका कोई स्वार्थ ना हो वे दूसरों के हित की चिन्ता से ही बता रहे हैं। जब कोई स्वार्थवश कुछ बोल रहा है वह शब्द-प्रमाण नहीं है। सबसे पहले आप उनकी यह परीक्षा करें। जैसे स्टुडेण्ट की परीक्षा होती है वैसे वक्ता की परीक्षा होती थी आप्तता की — स्टुडेण्ट की पात्रता की परीक्षा और वक्ता की आप्तता की परीक्षा।

MS KAJRI KAMAL: Please illustrate six *padārtha*s or the scheme of categorization with an example of each — especially the category of universal, particular and inherence.

SPEAKER: There are six *padārtha*s as already mentioned: *dravya*s are nine — *pṛthivī*, *jala*, *vāyu*, *teja*, etc. so all the variety of the world that you see, you touch, you hear and taste the objects — all these are *dravyas*. All the objects you smell, that is *pṛthivī*, then the water you drink or air you breathe, it is a *dravya*. Agni, Sūrya they are all there. *Ākāśa* is a *dravya* due to which we are able to listen to the words being spoken. *Kāla* and *diśā* are *dravyas*. *Ātmā* — it is a *dravya* because I am speaking and you are listening. What is *ātmā* according to Vaiśeṣika?

jñānādhikaraṇam ātmā । — *Tarkasaṁgraha* 17

Ātman is the abode of consciousness and cognition.

We are able to know and we are able to communicate because we are embodied *ātman*s and are endowed with a *manas* (mind) each. You see there are the external objects, sense organs and in between the sense organs and the *ātman*, there is *manas*. *Manas* is the mediator. It is the mediator between the external world and the internal realm. I cannot take this pen straight to the *ātman*, but the image of the pen will be conveyed to my *ātman* or my consciousness with the help of my mind. In other words, mind is the instrument (*antaḥkaraṇa*). When we internalize the external world, then we need a mediator who can work within the external as well as internal realms and mind has that capacity. It can go to the external world and it can reach to the internal world without any effort. That is why it is always running from outside to inside and from inside to outside. So *manas* is the *antaḥkaraṇa*. These are the nine *dravyas*.

Then we come to *guṇas* (properties) of *dravyas*, there are twenty-four *guṇas* according to Vaiśeṣika and each of the *dravyas* has some particular *guṇas*. Some have fifteen *guṇas*, some have fourteen, some five. *Rūpa, rasa, gandha, sparśa, saṅkhyā, parimāṇa, pr̥thaktva* (separateness), *saṁyoga-vibhāga* (disjunction and conjunction). *Paratva-aparatva*, and *buddhi, sukha, duḥkha, icchā, dveṣa, dharma, adharma, prayatna* and *saṁskāra* — these are twenty-four *guṇas*. The last nine *guṇas* of this list are pertaining to the *ātman* while the first fifteen *guṇas* pertain to the physical world. So, there are lots of classifications and many types of narratives in the texts of Vaiśeṣika — for that you have to go to the original sources.

Karma is the third category as already mentioned — there are five types of *karma* — motion or activity:

> *utkṣepaṇamapakṣepaṇamākuñcanaprasaraṇagamanānī pañca karmāṇī* ।   — *Vaiśeṣikasūtra* 1.1.7
>
> Throwing upward, dropping downward, contraction, expansion and going in general — are five kinds of motion.

This is a proven fact that physical activity can be possible in five directions. Even our mind keeps on moving. It is constantly in motion. *Ātman* cannot move because *ātman* is of the unlimited magnitude. It is *vibhu* or of *parama mahat parimāṇa*, anything which moves needs a limited magnitude — this pen can move because it is limited to only this much of height and this much of space. But if the room is full with bricks and pens to such an extent that there is no vacant space at all, then there cannot be any movement. Then its motion is not possible as it requires some space and the object which has to move should be of a limited magnitude, then only motion is possible. *Dravya, guṇa* and *karma* are easy to explain, easy to understand.

Now we come to the fourth category *sāmānya*. *Sāmānya* is not ordinary commonality. This pen *A* and this pen *B* are common. But this is not *sāmānya*, visible commonality is not *sāmānya*. This is similarity (*sādṛśya*). This is not *sāmānya* as *sāmānya* is eternal. It is not created. It is always there. For example, all of us are Bhāratīya and all of us are *manuṣya* — what will be *sāmānya*? — *manuṣyatva* or *bhāratīyatva*? *manuṣyatva* will be *sāmānya* according to Vaiśeṣika, but *bhāratīyatva* is not *sāmānya* because it can change — if one goes to USA and accepts the citizenship of America, then he/she will not be a Bhāratīya in the technical sense of the term. Hence *bhāratīyatva* is an *upādhi*. *Manuṣyatva* is a *jāti*. One becomes American or German or Swedish — one can even change his/her gender, one can change his/her name, one can change his/her religion; but despite all the changes, still he/she will be a *manuṣya*. So *manuṣyatva* is a *jāti* and not these imposed commonalities. Neither visible commonality nor imposed commonalities are *sāmānya* but natural commonality, eternal commonality is *sāmānya* according to Vaiśeṣika.

Then comes *viśeṣa*. It is particularity but not ordinary visible particularity. I am different from you. But this is not the particularity (*viśeṣa*) that the Vaiśeṣika is talking about. Vaiśeṣika is talking about the *viśeṣa*, which is available in the ultimate eternal substances. What are the eternal substances? These are five — *ākāśa*, *kāla*, *dik*, *ātman* and *manas*. So *viśeṣa* is the particularity which is available in these five substances and eternal atoms of the first four substances — *pṛthivī*, *jala*, *teja* and *vāyu*. This *viśeṣa* is a technical term of Vaiśeṣika.

Then comes *samavāya*. *Samavāya* is a relation, an inherent relation. See there are two types of relations accepted in Vaiśeṣika: *saṁyoga* and *samavāya*. *Saṁyoga* is conjunction which can be made available and which can be disjoined any time. I hold a pen in my hand. It is *saṁyoga*, but I leave the pen, no change in the pen and no change in the hand. But the relation between wood and the table is different; if I want to separate wood from the table, I have to break the table. Similarly, this body and its parts have an inherent relation, if I want to remove or separate one part from the whole, then I have to cut the part; the whole will also get deformed and part will also be changed. So this is *samavāya*. *Samavāya* relation is an internal relation and this relation changes the nature of its relata. While *saṁyoga* pertains to two objects, which do not change even after they are disjoined. So *saṁyoga* and *samavāya* are different.

The last and seventh *padārtha* in the list of Vaiśeṣika is *abhāva* — as we already know *abhāva* is different and is dependent on *bhāva* — anything which existed earlier, but it does not exist now. There was a refrigerator in this corner yesterday. Today we can see there is no refrigerator; earlier *ācāryas*, sages and scholars of ancient India, would say: *ghaṭa āsīt*, there was a pot, now there is no pot. Nowadays, we do not use *ghaṭa* so we can say here was a refrigerator, now it is not. So, there is an *abhāva* of *ghaṭa* or refrigerator — that which would have been here, but it is not. *Abhāva* is again of four types, *prāgabhāva*, *pradhvaṁsābhāva*, *anyonyābhāva* and *atyantābhāva* — anything which is not yet produced, its *prāgabhāva* is there. Till such time, that the effect is not produced, its *prāgabhāva* exists. *Prāk* means before and *abhāva* means absence. Second is *pradhvaṁsābhāva*. Whatever is produced, will definitely perish — absence after its destruction is called *pradhvaṁsābhāva*. *Anyonyābhāva* is mutual negation — *A* is not *B* and B is not *A*. This is mutual negation, *anyonyābhāva*. *Atyantābhāva* is universal absence or universal negation: e.g. absence of colour in air (*vāyu*). I do not know what today's science says. But Kaṇāda has said that *vāyu* does not have any colour. Air cannot be visually perceived. Can it be? No. So *abhāva* is of four types. There is no time to explain all the details of these theories. I think that I could at least make these seven *padārthas*[6] understandable.

DR ARVIND GUPTA: So another question I had was about the *Tarkabhāṣā* as you mentioned by Keśava Miśra. Are English translations available?

SPEAKER: Yes, both Hindi/English translations of the *Tarkabhāṣā* and *Tarkasaṁgraha* are available online also.

---

[6] For details, see (i) *Vaiśeṣika Darśana mein Padārtha-Nirūpaṇa*, Delhi, D.K. Printworld, 2013 and, (ii) *Classical Vaisesika in Indian Philosophy*, Routledge, UK, 2019;

MS SOMYA AVASTHI: मैम मेरे दो सवाल थे एक तो ये जो बताया कि NEP के संदर्भ में जो लॉजिक पढ़ाया जाएगा क्योंकि मैने भी ग्रेजुएशन में लॉजिक पढ़ा है लेकिन उनका जो तरीका पढ़ाने का है वो बहुत मैथेमेटिकल है तो मेरा पूछना था कि हमारी इण्डियन फिलॉसॉफी का जो लॉजिक है उसका मैथोडोलॉजी क्या है। और दूसरा सवाल था कि हम बोलते हैं "प्रत्यक्षं किं प्रमाणं" लेकिन जो अप्रत्यक्ष है उसके लिए क्या प्रमाण है। हमें कैसे पता चलेगा कि जो अप्रत्यक्ष है, उसका क्या प्रमाण है?

SPEAKER: पहले तो जो आपका सवाल है कि इण्डियन लॉजिक की मैथोडोलॉजी क्या है। मैंने जो पञ्चावयव-वाक्य बताया, वो है इण्डियन लॉजिक का मैथड/प्रतिज्ञा, हेतु, उदाहरण, उपनय और निगमन। वही हमारा फॉर्मेट है, वही इण्डियन लॉजिक का मैथड है और और दूसरा सवाल है "प्रत्यक्षं किं प्रमाणं", उसका मतलब है प्रत्यक्ष को किसी प्रमाण की क्या आवश्यकता है। वह सबसे बड़ा प्रमाण है उसमें गलती की कोई सम्भावना नहीं है जैसे कि कहावत है- "हाथ कंगन को आरसी क्या"। क्योंकि जो चीज सामने है तो उसके लिए प्रमाण की क्या जरूरत है। लेकिन जहाँ तक प्रत्यक्ष की पहुँच है उससे परे हमने जाना है तो अनुमान की जरूरत है। सारा जो न्यायशास्त्र, और सारी जो लॉजिक है और सारा जो तर्क है वह तो अनुमान का ही क्षेत्र है। प्रत्यक्ष में कोई बहस नहीं है। बहस अनुमान में होती है। तो उसकी आपूर्ति के लिए हमारे पास चैक्स एण्ड बैलेंस है जो हमने डिस्क्स किए हैं कि इसमें कोई फैलेसीज़ तो नहीं है, उसमें यह दोष तो नहीं है, वह हेत्वाभास तो नहीं है। जब सारी परीक्षा हो जाती है उसके बाद अगर हमने अनुमान किया है तब वह प्रमाण बनता है वही प्रमाण है — मीन्स ऑफ़ वैलिड नॉविंग। यदि गलत नॉलेज़ पर हम पहुँच रहे हैं तो वह प्रमाण नहीं है। प्रमाण के साथ-साथ चार तरह की अप्रमा भी मानी हैं; erroneous cognition. So theory of error is as important in Indian logic as theory of knowledge. Theory of error propounds five types.[7] न्याय कुछ कहता है।, सांख्य कुछ कहता है; सो एरर-थ्योरी भी सबकी अलग-अलग है। तो उन सबकी परीक्षा करके तब हम किसी निर्णय पर पहुँचते हैं।

7 इसे "ख्यातिपञ्चक" कहते हैं। विस्तृत विवरण हेतु देखें इसी ग्रन्थ के अध्याय 10, के मीमांसा दर्शन भाग में पृ० 249-50.

Sāṁkhya and Yoga Philosophy

We shall now discuss some basic tenets of Sāṁkhya and Yoga philosophy. In the *ṣaḍ-darśanas*, just like Nyāya and Vaiśeṣika are sister schools, similarly, Sāṁkhya and Yoga are complementary schools.

Sāṁkhya

The term *sāṁkhya* is derived from *saṁ* + *khyā*. Sāṁkhya also signifies *saṁkhyā* or a number because Sāṁkhya enumerates twenty-five entities in all; moreover, the dictionary meaning of the term *saṁkhyā* is "discussion or consideration", i.e. *Saṁkhyā, carcā, vicāraṇā*

These three meanings of this term are given in *Amarakośa.*[1] So, this term signifies *saṁkhyā* (number), *carcā* (discussion) and *vicāraṇā* (thinking or consideration). The *Mahābhārata* says:

> *sāṁkhyāṁ prakurvate caiva prakṛtiṁ ca pracakṣate* ।
> *tattvāni ca caturviṁśat parisaṅkhyāya tattvataḥ* ॥
> — 12.306.42-43

> In Sāmkhya, number (of entities) are enumerated, first *Prakṛti* is propounded and then-twenty four entities are explained in detail.

The word *sāṁkhya* is derived from *saṅkhyā* because it accepts two basic entities and twenty-five entities in all. It is a dualist system, it accepts *puruṣa* and *prakṛti*, *puruṣa* is the self or the consciousness and *prakṛti* is the matter. Everything in this material world is derived or evolved from *prakṛti*. So the whole world and its variety that

1 *Amarakoṣaḥ (Nāmaliṅgānuśāsanam)* of Amarasiṁha, I.5.3, Chowkhamba Surabharti Prakashan, Varanasi, 1992 (IVth edn).

we see — is all the play of *prakṛti*. Sāṁkhya theory of creation is known as theory of evolution; not creation but evolution. Why so? and what is the difference — that we will discuss later. Right now, this much is enough about the nomenclature of the term *sāṁkhya*.

The propounder of this system of Sāṁkhya is said to be Maharṣi Kapila. He is very well known and his name appears in the *Mahābhārata* also. We have *Sāṁkhyasūtras* which were propounded by Sage Kapila. Although the sanctity or authority of the available *Sāṁkhyasūtras* is doubtful. Scholars feel that the *Sāṁkhyasūtras* which that are available today are not the original *Sāṁkhyasūtras*. The original ones have been lost and the ones that we have today were compiled at a very later stage but there is no doubt about the fact that they are propounded by Kapila. We also have a commentary on the *Sāṁkhyasūtras*, the *Sāṁkhyapravacanabhāṣya* by Vijñānabhikṣu who was a sixteenth-century scholar and his work is held in high easteem in the Sāṁkhya tradition. There are some other well-known scholars who are believed to be the disciples of Kapila like Āsuri, Pañcaśikha, Vindhyavāsa and Vārṣagaṇya. But, unfortunately, all the texts authored by these scholars have been lost. Much of the ancient Sāṁkhya literature is not available today.

The current theories of Sāṁkhya are found in the *Sāṁkhyakārikā*, a small treatise, authored by Īśvarakṛṣṇa; that is a very popular and authentic source of Sāṁkhya being studied today. The *Sāṁkhyakārikā*, as its name indicates, is composed in verses, the technical verses — theories of Sāṁkhya have been put into *kārikā*s, the *kārikā* is a technical name given to the verses employed in *śāstra* and the verses that we find in *kāvya* like the *Rāmāyaṇa* and *Mahābhārata*, they are known as *śloka*. So there is a difference between these two types of verses. Just the very term *kārikā* denotes that this is a *śāstra* while *śloka* means that this is a *kāvya*. The *Sāṁkhyakārikā* has been very popular, so many commentaries have been written on it; the most important one being Vācaspati Miśra's *Tattvakaumudī*.

As mentioned above, Sāṁkhya is a dualist and a realist school. It is assumed to be an orthodox school because it accepts the sanctity of Vedas; the Vedic authority is acceptable to Sāṁkhya. As regards the two basic elements accepted in Sāṁkhya, these are *puruṣa* and *prakṛti*.

Puruṣa is the conscious principle, just conscious and a mere witness. It is like a *sākṣī*, it is just there; it doesn't do anything; it is not a doer, not an enjoyer, not an experiencer. It is not affected by the three *guṇa*s that belong to *prakṛti*.

Prakṛti is constituted of three *guṇas*. The term *guṇa* lexically means secondary, because *prakṛti* itself is primary. The other name for *prakṛti* is *pradhāna*. As compared to *prakṛti* or *pradhāna*, these three *guṇas* are secondary because they are the constituents of *prakṛti*. *Prakṛti* is the matter or the material principle, the original primal cause of the world. *Prakṛti* is unconscious and it is an object. The most important theory that Sāṁkhya provides is the theory of three attributes or three *guṇas*: *sattva*, *rajas* and *tamas*, these three are the constituents of *prakṛti*. Any object of the world, maybe a pen, water, bottle, human body, anything for that matter, is composed of *prakṛti* and therefore it has triple attributes: *sattva*, *rajas* and *tamas*. The same object can be having predominance of *sattva*, *rajas* and *tamas* at different moments. The same object can be felt as *sāttvika*, *rājasa* and *tāmasa* by any one of us. For example, someone is listening to music, the same song can be very pleasing to him/her now, but at some other moment, when one is not inclined to listening music, the same song will irritate him/her and there are times whether music is playing or not, that does not matter to him/her. Therefore, pleasure, pain and neutrality (*prīti*, *aprīti* and *upekṣā*), these three are our reactions to various objects. We react in three ways because everything that we experience is constituted of these three *guṇas*. But before discussing these *guṇas*, it is noteworthy to mention that Sāṁkhya begins with the promise of eradication of three types of suffering. Just as the Buddha says *sarvaṁ duḥkham*, Sāṁkhya begins with an enumeration of *trividha duḥkha* and promises freedom from them. According to Sāṁkhya, the ultimate goal of life is getting rid of three kinds of suffering, forever and for sure. Sāṁkhya has used two terms: *ekāntika duḥkha-nivṛtti* and *ātyantika duḥkha-nivṛtti*:

> *atha trividhaduḥkhātyantanivṛttiratyantapuruṣārthaḥ* ।
>
> — *Sāṁkhyasūtra* 1.1

> Now, therefore, the ultimate aim of life is to get rid of three types of suffering for ever and for sure.

This is the first *Sāṁkhyasūtra*. According to it, suffering is of three types:

- *ādhyātmika*, i.e. the suffering experienced within one's body is *ādhyātmika* suffering.
- *Ādhibhautika*, the physical suffering that we feel outside the body is physical; there is excess of rain, excess of heat, these are the *ādhibhautika duḥkha*s.
- and the third one is *ādhidaivika* which is invisible and over which we have no control.

While going through these three types of sufferings, one is not sure as to where should we classify this corona virus currently troubling the whole world. There is an adjective used here — invisible, since this corona virus is invisible to us, ordinary people, it should be classified under *ādhidaivika* but since it is a part of matter and it is physical, it can also be classified in *ādhibhautika*. As we all know that corona is the most dreaded disease for humanity and it can be covered under all the three types of *duḥkha*s it is a matter of common experience that when corona enters somebody's body, then it becomes *ādhyātmika* because one has to undergo inner pain and suffering. Unfortunately, there is the psychophysical aspect of it as well. So everybody wants to get rid of this suffering. But what happens when we have a disease, we go to the doctor, we take a medicine and the pain subsides. Is it *duḥkha-nivṛtti*? Yes, but it is temporary *duḥkha-nivṛtti*, which is not forever. No doctor can ever claim that this pill will cure a disease forever. Nobody can guarantee that. Maybe the same disease develops again after some period. Therefore, the *duḥkha*, the suffering keeps on recurring. There is no way that we can get rid of suffering forever. Second, there is no way of ensuring that suffering is removed for sure, the same medicine is taken by hundreds of people. Problem of somebody is cured, but there are many others whose pain persists; despite taking a pill for every three hours, or four hours, their fever does not get cured. So *duḥkha-nivṛtti* is neither sure (*ekantika*) nor forever (*ātyantika*). But Sāṁkhya claims that all these three kinds of sufferings can be removed — that too forever and for sure. This is the promise of Sāṁkhya and this is the goal of every human being. Therefore, Sāṁkhya is a very popular system, mainly because of this claim that if you want to get rid of *trividha duḥkha*, then you must follow what Sāṁkhya describes and prescribes.

How do we get rid of this *trividha duḥkha*? Sāṁkhya gives us the clue; there is a technical term for this techique, this is termed as *vyakta-avyakta-jña-vijñāna*. It means that this is a *vijñāna*, a *viśiṣṭa jñāna*. This is a specific knowledge which propounds that there are three types of entities; basically, there are only two (*puruṣa* and *prakṛti*), but since *prakṛti* can again be classified into two types, therefore, they become three types:

(i) *vyakta* (manifested visible world) *prakṛti*,

(ii) *avyakta* (unmanifested *prakṛti*), and

(iii) *jña* (conscious *puruṣa*).

No epithet. No adjectives. *Jña* means just knowledge or *jñāna* (consciousness). The one who knows, who just knows, who is conscious, but who does not act, who does not feel, who does not enjoy, who does not suffer, it is just there. In this way, *puruṣa* (conscious principle) in Sāṁkhya has no role to play except that it is there. And because it is there, activity in *prakṛti* starts. Matter cannot get activated if there is no consciousness. So just the proximity of the conscious principle, activates matter in such a way that the equilibrium of *prakṛti* is disturbed and the dance among these three *guṇas* — *sattva*, *rajas* and *tamas* — starts; consequently the evolution takes place. Therefore if we want to get rid of suffering, we should have *vyakta-avyakta-jña-vijñāna*; i.e. we should know that these three are different types of entities. What happens when we confuse these three to be identical? When the *jña* (conscious principle), the *puruṣa* or the self thinks that whatever is happening is happening to me; if there is suffering, I am suffering; if there is pain, I am the sufferer, if there is happiness or pleasure, I am the enjoyer. This false notion, this is the crux or the real cause of bondage and if is broken, then there will be freedom. Freedom from suffering will start the moment we realize that this body is not me. This suffering does not belong to me, I am away from all this — this is the wisdom of Sāṁkhya: *vyakta-avyakta-jña-vijñāna*.

Here a question arises as to what is *vyakta* and what is *avyakta*. *Prakṛti* as mentioned earlier is known as *pradhāna*; *prakṛti* is also *avyakta*, invisible in its real nature. In its original form, matter is unmanifest; in its primordial nature, *prakṛti* is not manifested. *Prakṛti* is *triguṇātmikā*. All the three *guṇas* — *sattva*, *rajas* and *tamas* — they are there in it, but they are in a stage of equilibrium. They are in their own basic nature. None is disturbing the other, and none is propelling the other. So, when this equilibrium is broken or disturbed, only then evolution starts. How does this equilibrium break? It breaks just when there is the vicinity or the proximity of *puruṣa* (conscious principle). Although the conscious principle is devoid of these three *guṇas*, it is not affected by *sattva*, *rajas* and *tamas* in reality and in essence, but it thinks erroneously or it imposes on itself that I am being affected by *sattva*, *rajas* and *tamas*. This false notion is the root cause of its bondage.

In this way *avyakta prakṛti* becomes *vyakta*; it becomes manifest and manifestation is the beginning of evolution. How does it evolve? Significantly we do not use the word "create" in Sāṁkhya because according to it no creation is real, it is just the difference between manifestation and unmanifestation. The theory of causation that

Sāṁkhya propounds is known as Satkāryavāda. Accordingly, when *avyakta*, the original cause or the primordial cause starts manifesting, then evolution begins; the first *vyakta* evolute of *avyakta prakṛti* is *mahat. Mahat* is the intellect (*buddhi*) and there is predominance of *sattva* in this state. Three *guṇas* — *sattva, rajas* and *tamas* — they have different properties. *Sattva* is transparent, *sattva* is calm, it is quiet, the symbolic colour of *sattva* is said to be as white: *sattvaṁ laghu prakāśakam*; it is very light in weight and it is *prakāśakam* — it illuminates everything. Here Sāṁkhya gives the example of a mirror which is very clean; a clean mirror presents clean images.

Mahat is the first evolute of *prakṛti.* This is said to be *buddhi* because it is predominant in *sattva*, it is transparent. It is clean as a mirror and the reflection of *puruṣa* in this clean mirror appears; when we watch a mirror, we see our image in it. How do I realize that this is me. I see the mirror and think that this reflection in the mirror is me. But is it real? Is the image real? No, nobody can ensure that the image is real. Everybody sees his or her own image in the mirror and he or she thinks that this is me; same happens in the Sāṁkhya scheme of the world with the spirit, the self or the *puruṣa.* Significantly, *puruṣa* here is gender neutral. It is not masculine *puruṣa, puruṣa* means *puri śete saḥ* — *puruṣaḥ*. Who is a *puruṣa*? *Puruṣa* is the principle of consciousness, that which is staying or resting in this body, in this city or abode which is known as body. *Puruṣa*, the term also appears in Puruṣa Sūkta of the *Ṛgveda* (10.90). *Puruṣa* means the embodied self and when it sees its image in *mahat* or *buddhi* (an evolute of *prakṛti*), the bondage starts; the bondage has two senses here — bonding or a relation starts between *prakṛti* and *puruṣa,* and the bondage in the sense of *bandhana* begins. The very root cause of *bandhana* is mixing up of the two different entities. That is why there must be *vyakta-avyakta-jña-vijñāna* or discriminating knowledge among *vyakta-avyakta* and *jña* — this discriminating knowledge is also known as *viveka. Viveka* means discriminating power; when *puruṣa* loses its *viveka* and imposes the image of *mahat* on oneself, then the bondage starts and once the bondage starts, the entanglement gets more and more dense and *puruṣa* or the self gets tied into all these chains of suffering.

Mahat gives rise to *ahaṁkāra*; *ahaṁkāra* is the second evolute of *prakṛti*. *Mahat* is *vyakta* while *prakṛti* is *avyakta*. *Prakṛti*, *pradhāna* and *avyakta*, these three are parallel terms; *mahat* is the first evolute of *avyakta*, it is *vyakta*. *Mahat* onwards, *vyakta* (manifest world) is evolving. *Mahat* is also known as intellect or *buddhi*. *Ahaṁkāra* is egoism. Just when I see an image in the mirror and I think this is me (*aham*) — then *ahaṁkāra* (egoism) arises and the manifestation of ego begins. In other words *mahat* is pure *sattva*. *Ahaṁkāra* is *rajas* mixed with *sattva*. *Rajas* has a tendency that it is active and restless. It moves everything that is around it. It is the *rajas*, which helps in different types of motion. If I am moving my hand, it is because of *rajas*, if I am speaking or understanding, what is being said, that is because of *sattva*. If somebody is feeling sleepy or sluggish, that is due to *tamas*. So *sattva* is light and transparent; *rajas* is restless and moving; red colour is the symbol of *rajas* while *tamas* is heavy and it is the enveloping principle which engulfs everything in darkness and, therefore, it is heavy. Black colour signifies *tamas*. These three *guṇas* are determining the nature of every object that we experience in this world. From *mahat* we move on to *ahaṁkāra*. From *ahaṁkāra* evolve the *pañca-tanmātras*. In the term *tanmātra*, *tan* means that, and *mātra* means only; so there is only an essence, the subtlest essence of material objects, subtle form of matter is known as *tanmātra*.

From *mahat*, evolves *ahaṁkāra*. *Ahaṁkāra* gives rise to five *tanmātras*. *Tanmātras* are minute forms of matter like atoms of Nyāya and Vaiśeṣika. Although Sāṁkhya does not use the word atoms but actually these *tanmātras* are equivalent to the subtlest forms of matter. These are five, viz. *rūpa*, *rasa*, *gandha*, *sparśa* and *śabda tanṁātras*. These are caused by *tamas* or *tamoguṇa*. Next come *pañca-mahābhūtas*. *Tanmātra* is the subtle form of matter and *mahābhūta* is the gross form of matter; from the subtle form of matter are manifested the gross *pañca-mahābhūtas*: *pṛthivī*, *jala*, *teja*, *vāyu* and *ākāśa*, these are also discussed in Nyāya and Vaiśeṣika. Earth, water, air, fire and sky, these are the five gross forms of matter and from these gross forms of matter (*mahābhūtas*) the eleven organs are manifested.

What are the eleven organs? Five motor organs (*kārmendriyas*), five sense organs (*jñānendriyas*) and one mind (*manas*). In the beginning there are two basic entities: *puruṣa* and *prakr̥ti*. First one is *puruṣa*, second is *prakr̥ti*. From *prakr̥ti*, *mahat* is manifested. *Mahat* gives rise to *ahaṁkāra*; so *triguṇātmikā prakr̥ti* or *avyakta* is manifested into two entities now: *mahat* and *ahaṁkāra*. From *ahaṁkāra* to *pañca-tanmātras*, they are seven; from *pañca-tanmātras* to *pañca-mahābhūtas* they become twelve and eleven *indiriyas* are added to them; so twenty-three — if we add one *prakr̥ti* and one *puruṣa* to these, then they are twenty-five in total. So this is the Sāṁkhya enumeration of twenty-five entities. Therefore, the nomenclature Sāṁkhya is justified because it counts and enumerates twenty-five entities. Out of these twenty-five two are eternal: *puruṣa* and *prakr̥ti*. They are the basic entities which remain even after dissolution. But the remaining twenty-three are manifested, they evolve out of *prakr̥ti* and they dissolve into *prakr̥ti* too. They are not created, they are not destroyed, they are evolved and they just dissolve. That is the term that Sāṁkhya uses: *vyakta* and *avyakta*.

Now, if we examine these twenty-five entities minutely, they are again divided into the following four categories in Sāṁkhya:

i. *Prakr̥ti*, the category that is only the cause of something, *kāraṇa* or *prakr̥ti*. *Prakr̥ti* also means the cause. *Prakr̥ti* is the original cause. So there is a type of entity in Sāṁkhya, which is just the cause, it is never caused, but it causes many more and that entity is *prakr̥ti*, *pradhāna* or *avyakta*. It is *anādi*, it is *nitya*, but it is the cause of everything that is manifested. In other words, *prakr̥ti* is *avikr̥ti*, *prakr̥ti* is the cause of everything but not caused by anything. So: *mūla prakr̥tiravikr̥ti*. It is not a *vikṛti* of anything. *Vikṛti* is the effect and *prakṛti* is the cause. It is not the effect of anything. It is the cause of everything.

ii. *Prakṛti-vikṛti*: Next is *prakṛti-vikṛti. prakṛti* means a cause and *vikṛti* means an effect. So there are some entities, which are the causes of something, and which are also the effects of something. Seven entities are in this category; which ones? These are: *mahat*, the first evolute of *prakṛti*, *mahat* is *prakṛti* as well as *vikṛti*. It is *prakṛti* to *ahaṁkāra* and it is *vikṛti* of *prakṛti*. So it is *prakṛti* as well as *vikṛti* — *prakṛti* of *ahaṁkāra* and *vikṛti* of *prakṛti*. Similarly *ahaṁkāra*, *ahaṁkāra* is the *vikṛti* of *mahat* and it is the *prakṛti* of *pañca-tanmātras* — so the seven evolutes of *prakṛti* are: *prakṛti* as well as *vikṛti*. *Mūla prakṛti* is only *prakṛti* and not *vikṛti*. But there are some entities which are *prakṛti* as well as *vikṛti* — *mahat*, *ahaṁkāra* and *pañca-tanmātras* are placed in this second category.

iii. *Vikṛti*: the third type of entities is *vikṛti* only; it means that they are just the effects and not the cause of anything. What are these? These are sixteen: five *mahābhūtas* and the eleven sense organs — these sixteen are caused from *pañca-tanmātras*, but they are not the cause of anything — therefore they are termed as only *vikṛti*.

iv. *Na prakṛti na vikṛti*: This is the fourth and last category which signifies *puruṣa* — the whole game is played by *prakṛti*; *puruṣa* is there but it is not *prakṛti*, it is not *vikṛti*; it is just a witness. It is just a spectator. It is observing the game but not part of the game. So *mūla prakṛti*, i.e. *avikṛti*, *prakṛti-vikṛti*, *vikṛti* and *na prakṛti na vikṛti* — all the twenty-five entities[2] can be classified in these four causal categories.

Now we come to the theory of causation. But before that, let us understand that in its liberated form, *puruṣa* might be one principle, one entity; but at the practical or empirical level *puruṣas* are

---

2 *Mūlaprakṛtiravikṛtirmahadādyāḥ prakṛtivikṛtayah sapta Śoḍaśakastu vikāro na prakṛtirna vikṛtirna puruṣaḥ.* — *Sāṁkhyakārikā* 3

accepted to be innumerable. *Puruṣa-bahutva* (plurality of *puruṣas*) is the accepted principle in Sāṁkhya. Just as Nyāya and Vaiśeṣika accept plurality of souls, similarly Sāṁkhya accepts plurality of *puruṣas*. *Prakṛti* is one but *puruṣas* are innumerable. Why so? They have given reasons for everything they have propounded. Why should we accept *puruṣas* as innumerable? The *Sāṁkhyakārikā* has given three arguments to support of this theory:

1. We all see for ourselves that the birth, death and sense organs are different for each person in the world; its not that everyone is born, dead or disabled simultaneously.[3] So it is evident that there are innumerable number of selves (*puruṣas*).

2. It is also a matter of common experience that each individual engages in activity separate; it is not that when A is active, then B is also active. Therefore plurality of selves (*puruṣas*) is a logical postulate.[4]

3. Moreover, the diversity among human beings due to three *guṇas* namely *sattva, rajas* and *tamas* is also quite visible. Some persons are endowed with predominantly *sāttvika* attributes while others are mainly *rājasika* in nature and the remaining are primarily *tāmasika*. This diversity also proves that the selves (*puruṣas*) are innumerable.[5]

The theory of causation propounded by Sāṁkhya has three names — Satkāryavāda is the most popular name. This is also known as Pariṇāmavāda and its third appellation is Vikāravāda. Satkāryavāda, Pariṇāmavāda and Vikāravāda, these are the three names given to the Sāṁkhya theory of causation. But before explaining the technical terms, let us just take an example. We see that curd is prepared out of milk. We just add some small portion of

---

[3] *Jananamaraṇakaraṇānāṁ pratiniyamāt.* — *Sāṁkhyakārikā* 18

[4] *Ayugapat pravṛtteśca.* — *Sāṁkhyakārikā* 18

[5] *Puruṣabahutvaṁ siddhaṁ traiguṇyaviparyayāccaiva.*
— *Sāṁkhyakārikā* 18

curd to milk and milk solidifies into curd. Now the question arises: Is the curd a new product, or is it just the transformation of milk? That is the basic question. According to Nyāya and Vaiśeṣika, curd is a new product; it is a different entity than milk. Of course, it is coming out of milk, but it is not milk. It is a new beginning, so milk and curd, *kāraṇa* and *kārya* are different. Curd was not there when milk was there; this view is known as Asatkāryavāda, the Nyāya-Vaiśeṣika theory of causation; Satkāryavāda is the Sāṁkhya theory. According to Nyāya, curd or the effect was not there before it was produced anew. Here the Nyāya objection is that if it was already there, then what is the logic in its production? To this, Sāṁkhya says that it was already there; curd was already there in the milk. The only difference is that it was unmanifested when milk was there. But now it is manifested when it is appearing as curd. The essence is the same, the attributes are also the same, only the name and form have changed. So this is known as *pariṇāma*. *Pariṇāma* means transformation, milk has transformed into curd. It is not a new beginning, it is not a new product, it is just a transformation. *Vikāra* also means the same, *vikāra* means the change; milk has changed into curd. Cause has changed into effect, but both are one and the same according to Sāṁkhya. According to Nyāya–Vaiśeṣika they are two different entities, the product or the effect is a new beginning, their qualities are different, their purpose is different. Also in Āyurveda, the attributes of curd are held to be different than milk, those who cannot consume milk or who are allergic to milk, they can digest curd easily. In this case, Nyāya–Vaiśeṣika seems to be more realistic than Sāṁkhya. Although Sāṁkhya is also known as a realistic school but Sāṁkhya is leaning towards Vedānta, it is in the middle way. Nyāya–Vaiśeṣikas are at the beginning level, the most commonsensical level. Vedānta is at the highest pedestal of the idealistic philosophy, in between is Sāṁkhya. In fact, Sāṁkhya is preparing the ground for Vedānta.

Vedānta also accepts Sāṁkhya theory of Pariṇāmavāda at the empirical level. But at the transcendental level, they differ,

Sāṁkhya accepts Pariṇāmavāda while Vedānta propounds Vivartavāda. According to Vedānta, neither milk nor curd is real. They are only an imposition of one thing on the other. This is just an illusion. So, there is something in real while something else is manifesting itself in various forms. As a result, Vedānta has a different theory called Vivartavāda, but it is based on the Sāṁkhya theory of Satkāryavāda. There are four positions propounded in Indian philosophy regarding the theory of causation. Vācaspati Miśra has quoted them all in his commentary *Tattvakaumudī* on the *Sāṁkhyakārikā*. Let us briefly understand these four positions, because these are the basic principles of Indian philosophical thought regarding the theory of causation:

I. *Asataḥ sat jayate*: *Sat* (existent) is produced out of *asat* (non-existent). There was nothing earlier. But now something is produced. This is the Buddhist theory of *asataḥ sat jayate*; *sat* is produced out of *asat*. There was nothing because the earlier moment had vanished, there is no cause and effect in real. It is only a theory of dependent origination. The first moment has vanished and it has given rise to the second moment, so there was something which is not there, *asat* now. Just after that, *sat* has been born; *sat* has been produced, *asataḥ sat jayate*. We have two things: one is the cause and the other is the effect. According to Buddhism, by the time the effect is born, the cause has already vanished, it is destroyed. It has already been extinct. No two moments can coexist. So cause and effect cannot coexist. By the time, the effect has been produced, the cause has already become extinct. It has become *asat*, so from *asat*, *sat* is born. By the time one is talking of *sat*, it has also become *asat*. The theory is known as Pratītyasamutpādavāda (theory of dependent origination) — this is the Buddhist view.

II. *Sataḥ asat jayate*: Next view is of Nyāya–Vaiśeṣika. According to them The effect was non-existent earlier and it is born out of the existent cause. The cause was existent, but the effect was non-existent (*asat*) earlier. Now, that the effect is produced, it has become *sat*, so *sataḥ asat jayate*. Therefore, it is known as Asatkāryavāda. When milk was there, milk was *sat* but curd was not there — so curd was *asat*, *sataḥ asat jayate*, so — the effect was *asat* (non-existent). Now it has become existent (*sat*) from being non-existent (*asat*) in the form of cause; cause was existent, but effect was not there. Hence *sataḥ asat jayate*. This is the second viewpoint of Nyāya–Vaiśeṣika.

III. *Ekasya sataḥ vivartaṁ kāryajātam*: This is Vedānta view. Vedānta says *ekasya sataḥ*: there is only one *sat*, the reality is only one, all that we say as *kārya* (effect) is just an imposition or illusion. I say, this is a table, this is a mobile phone, this is a pen, this is a book — but all these are impositions because reality is only one. These impositions are known as *vivarta*.

All the effects of the world are just an illusion or an imposition on one single reality that is *Brahman*. No effect is true, nothing is a true production, only one reality is there and it is being manifested in different forms. The Vedāntins give an example, famous example of rope and snake: there is darkness in the night and there is something hanging on the window, constantly moving due to the wind. It is a rope, but throughout the dark night the whole family is scared of the moving object, the inhabitants of the house are sitting, standing or crying outside because they think it is a snake. When sunlight comes, they all see that there is a rope and there was never a snake. This was just a rope and it was moving due to the movement of the wind. So, the snake was imposed on the rope due to darkness. Similarly, due to our own ignorance, we impose everything on reality and then we suffer, when this imposition and that covering is removed, the covering of our ignorance, then the light and the knowledge both emanate. This is based on the Vedānta view which is known as Vivartavāda.

IV. *Sataḥ sat jayate*: Sāṁkhya propounds *sataḥ sat jayate*, which means that all these causes are real and effects are also real. The cause was existent, it is existent and the effect is also existent. None of them is unreal. So Sāṁkhya says, we are the greatest realists because according to us cause is *sat* and effect is also *sat*. Therefore, Satkāryavāda (theory of causation) is the most logical theory in which both the cause and the effect, the *kāraṇa* and the *kārya* are *sat*. Milk was *sat*, curd is *sat*. As far as the relationship between the cause and the effect is concerned, according to Nyāya–Vaiśeṣika, there is an intrinsic relation, which we have already discussed as *samavāya*. But according to Sāṁkhya (also Vedānta), the relationship between the cause and the effect is *tādātmya* (identity). Both the cause and the effect share an identity, which is the same. They do not have a different identity. Essence is same, only the name and form have transformed. In short, there is a transformation, which is real while according to Vedānta that transformation is also unreal, but according to Sāṁkhya it is real, this much is the difference between Sāṁkhya and Vedānta. Vedānta says:

> *vyavahārabhūmau pariṇāmavādaḥ* ।
> *paramārthabhūmau vivartavādaḥ* ॥
>
> At the empirical level we accept Pariṇāmavāda, but at the transcendental level even Pariṇāmavāda is not real, it is Vivartavāda.

In fact, this theory of causation and different conceptions of it are very crucial to discriminate and understand the standpoint of various schools of philosophy. Above interpretation of these four viewpoints in brief has been given by Vācaspati Miśra.

According to the Sāṁkhya theory of causation, Satkāryavāda, the process of evolution starts from *Prakṛti* which is the original cause. *Prakṛti* is *sat* and every evolute, that is being manifested, is also *sat*, nothing is *asat*. Here one is reminded of the popular verse of *Gītā*

nāsato vidyate bhāvo nābhāvo vidyate sataḥ । — II.16

The above view is representative of the Sāṁkhya theory and it means that which was there can never perish and that which has perished means it was never there. So, anything that is real, it will never perish and what is real? Only *ātman* is real, if body is perishing, that means it is not real. This is the teaching of the *Gītā* as well.

This theory of Satkāryavāda is in brief a theory of transformation, theory of change because it is the backbone of metaphysics for Sāṁkhya.

Let us now discuss the epistemology of Sāṁkhya. It accepts three *pramāṇas*: *pratyakṣa*, *anumāna* and *āpta vacana* or *śabda-pramāṇa*. According to Sāṁkhya, there are three means of valid cognition: first is perception, which was also accepted by Nyāya. *Anumāna* (inference) and the verbal testimony are also accepted. Although there are differences in these conceptions, but in principle, they accept three *pramāṇas*.

Sāṁkhya ethics can be discussed under Yoga because Yoga is essentially not different from Sāṁkhya. Yoga is just the practical aspect of Sāṁkhya. The theoretical aspect of Sāṁkhya is accepted by Yoga in totality. There is no change except one addition, i.e. God in its scheme. It needs to be noted here that conjunction of *prakṛti* and *puruṣa*, is not an ordinary conjunction. According to Sāṅkhya, it is the *saṁyoga* between *prakṛti* and *puruṣa*, this *saṁyoga* is of a different kind, this is known as *sannidhi*; *sannidhi* means just being close or in proximity. The proximity of conscious principle *puruṣa* activates the material principle *prakṛti*. All the evolution, all the play, all the suffering, all the enjoyment, all the variety in the universe is a play of *prakṛti*. *Prakṛti* is the dancer, she is dancing. *Puruṣa* is there, totally awake, totally distinct. But due to ignorance when it feels involved in the activities of *prakṛti*, when it thinks that I am enjoying, I am suffering; then this evolution starts. The covering of ignorance engulfs *puruṣa* just as a black cloth is put on the light, the light is engulfed in darkness. Similarly, the covering of ignorance that engulfs the conscious principle and although it is not the agent, not the doer or the experiencer, it starts thinking that I am the doer, I am the experiencer and the bondage starts, the suffering starts. In essence, if we have to get rid of suffering, what should we do? We should start and try to acquire the discriminating power — *viveka-jñāna*, so that we know that *prakṛti* is different and *puruṣa* is different; all that is being played, it belongs to *prakṛti*, it pertains to *prakṛti*, and not to us. That is all that the *Gītā* teaches in the last chapter; in chapter 18, the *Gītā* explains *kartṛtva-abhimāna* and *kartṛtva-visarjana. Puruṣa* imposes the egoism (*ahaṁ*) on itself; although *ahaṁkāra* is an evolute of *prakṛti,* but *puruṣa* imposes it on oneself and gets into the trap of *prakṛti. Prakṛti*, when it starts activity, then the evolution begins and *mahat* evolves from *prakṛti. Ahaṁkāra* from *mahat*, *pañca-tanmātra*s from *ahaṁkāra*, *pañca-mahābhūtas* from *pañca-tanmātras* and the eleven organs — five sense organs, five motor organs and one *manas* — from *pañca-mahābūtas.* These are the twenty-five entities, enumerated and explained in Sāṁkhya.

Now, before we come to Yoga, we must acknowledge that this is a very important system, not metaphysically, but ethically. Yoga is also known as the *seśvara* Sāṁkhya. As we have seen in the Sāṁkhya philosophy, it does not talk of God. Sāṁkhya is an atheistic system because there is no need for God in its world view. Two elements are there, two entities are there, they join, they come into combination and evolution starts. When they disjoin, when *puruṣa* realizes its own true nature, then *prakṛti* starts dissolving; just like evolution, dissolution starts. The *manas* and the sense organs dissolve into the *pañca-mahābhūtas*. *Pañca-mahābhūtas* dissolve into *pañca-tanmātras*, *pañca-tanmātras* dissolve into *ahaṁkāra, ahaṁkāra* dissolves into *mahat* and *mahat* dissolves into *prakṛti* or *pradhāna* — then remain *puruṣa* and *prakṛti* — both of them stay independently.

Both of them are eternal. Both of them are omnipresent, but the combination *saṁyoga* is not there because now *prakṛti* is in the state of equilibrium. That equilibrium has to be maintained:

> *sattva-rajas-tamasāṁ sāmyavasthā prakṛtiḥ* ।
> — *Tattvakaumudī* on *Sāṁkhyakārikā* 3

This is the definition of *prakṛti*, when it is *sāmyāvasthā* (equilibrium), then it is *prakṛti*, *pradhāna* or *avyakta*. When the *sāmya* is disturbed, then *vaiṣamya* (disequilibrium) starts. Sometimes *rajas* is predominant and the person gets very restless, very aggressive. And sometimes the same person is very calm, very happy and very cool — that time it is *sattva*'s predominance; sometimes the same fellow is in a mood that Arjuna felt, it is known as *viṣāda-yoga*, *tamoguṇa* has engulfed the *citta* of Arjuna and he does not know what to do. Although he knows everything, he was even taught everything, all the planning was done in consultation with him and now he says, I do not know what to do. Because *tamas* has engulfed his mind. This happens with each one of us. We experience *sattva*, *rajas* and *tamas*, the interplay of these three at different stages of our lives, because we are under bondage of *prakṛti*. So, if we want freedom from this bondage, then we have to attain this distinction between consciousness and matter. *Puruṣa* (consciousness) is not *prakṛti* (matter) — they are two different entities and they are not to be imposed upon each other. This is the crux of knowledge that Sāṁkhya propounds: *sattvapuruṣānyatākhyāti* (distinct knowledge of *prakṛti* and *puruṣa*).

Yoga

Now, we shall briefly discuss the school of Yoga philosophy. The term *yoga*, as we all know, is derived from two Sanskrit roots:

- *yujir yoge*: to combine or to unite is *yoga*; and
- *yuj samādhau*: the term *yoga* is also used in the sense of *samādhi*.

Samādhi is the consideration or rather the ultimate level of consideration, profound concentration or trance, one might say.

Samādhi is translated in various ways. In simple terms, *samādhi* is *yoga*, at the higher level, but the basic meaning of root *yuj* is to combine or to unite; when two things combine, it becomes *yoga*. If we add prefix *sam* before it, it becomes *saṁyoga*, we add prefix *vi* before it, it becomes *viyoga*. So, *yoga* is the union of two entities. What are the two entities? Yoga adds the principle of God to the twenty-five entities enumerated by Sāṁkhya and accepts twenty-six entities. It is also known as *seśvara* Sāṁkhya. Sāṁkhya is *nirīśvara* Sāṁkhya and Yoga is *seśvara* Sāṁkhya. When the individual self is in communion with the divine or the higher self, then it is Yoga. Even in *samādhi*, the individual self is in communion with the divine self, that is known as *samādhi*.

Patañjali is the propagator of Yoga; he is not the propounder like Kapila is the propounder of Sāṁkhya, Gautama is the propounder of Nyāya and Kaṇāda is the propounder of Vaiśeṣika. Patañjali is not the first propounder of Yoga because Yoga is a very ancient tradition. Right from the *Ṛgveda* and coming through several seers, Yoga was instructed from one to another generation. Patañjali has only systematized it. And he has proclaimed it his first statement:

> *atha yogānuśāsanam* । — *Yogasūtra* 1.1
>
> Now the system of Yoga will be presented.

He does not say that I will explain *yoga* just as Kaṇāda says:

> *athāto dharmaṁ vyākhyāsyāmaḥ* । — *Vaiśeṣikasūtra* 1.1.1

The first *sūtra* of the *Yogasūtras* simply states that now, the system of Yoga is being discussed; the system which has been handed over to us from generation to generation. It is said that Hiraṇyagrabha or Prajāpati Himself was the original teacher of Yoga, thus it was of divine origin. As we shall see later, *Īśvara* is held to be the *ādi-guru* according to Yoga. So Yoga is held to be of divine origin. Yoga is so popular and so pervasive in Indian tradition that be it Jainism or Buddhism, they all have the idea of Yoga in their philosophy. They may differ in their theorization, in metaphysical orientation, but Yoga is accepted by all of them. Actually the principles of Yoga are found in all the schools of Indian philosophy because these are principles of universal ethics. They are acceptable to Buddhism and Jainism also. The scholars of these traditions have also written texts on Yoga. The Jainācārya Hemacandra has written the *Yogaśāstra* and the Jain scholar Umāswāmī has discussed the principles of Yoga in his *Tattvārthasūtra*. It is noteworthy here that Buddhists have talked of *catvāri āryasatyāni* and the concept of *triratnas* which pertain to their idea of Yoga only.

The literature of Yoga is also very wide. To begin with, the *Yogasūtra* is divided into four sections:

1. Samādhipāda begins with the idea of *samādhi*,
2. Sādhanapāda explains as to what are the means or *sādhanas* for *samādhi*,
3. Vibhūtipāda elucidates what are the accomplishments when Yoga is mastered, and
4. Kaivalyapāda discusses what is the ultimate goal of Sāṁkhya–Yoga.

Vyāsabhāṣya is the commentary on the *Yogasūtra*. Vācaspati Miśra has written the *Tattvavaiśāradī* on the *Vyāsabhāṣya*. He is the one who has written commentaries almost on all the schools of Indian philosophy. So we have the *Vyāsabhāṣya* by Vyāsa, *Tattvavaiśāradī-Ṭīkā* by Vācaspati Miśra and then *Yogavārttika* by Vijñānabhikṣu. We have many more texts, but this is only one about the basic sources of Yoga. Besides, there are many types of Yoga principles in Indian tradition. The Yoga of Patañjali is known as *rāja-yoga* or *kriyā-yoga*. Why *rāja-yoga*? Because, this describes and signifies the kingly nature of Yoga. The princely nature of Yoga signifies that it can go through all the levels of the mind just as a king can go to any part of his palace. Just like a *rājā*, a *yogī* can enter any place, any plane of his consciousness, any level of his mind. He can enter and he can do different types of activities. Therefore, it is *kriyā-yoga*. Pātañjala-Yoga, *rāja-yoga* and *kriyā-yoga* are one and the same. This is actually the philosophical tradition of Yoga. But we also have *mantra-yoga, laya-yoga, japa-yoga, haṭha-yoga*, etc.

Only the less learned persons think that Sāṁkhya is different and Yoga is different. Actually, they are not different because Yoga does not talk of metaphysics in detail, it just accepts the twenty-five principles and adds one more — God, so they become twenty- six. In the *Gītā* we have a verse, it says:

> *sāṁkhyayogau pṛthagbālāḥ pravadanti na paṇḍitāḥ* ।
> *ekamapyāsthitaḥ samyagubhayorvindate phalam* ॥ — V.4

> Those who are learned, they know that Sāṁkhya and Yoga are not different; he who has mastered one out of these two, he achieves the fruit or the result of both the Sāṁkhya and Yoga.

What is the definition of Yoga? The second *sūtra* after *atha yogānuśāsanam* answers the question as to what is Yoga? Patañjali says:

> *yogaścittavṛttinirodhaḥ* । — *Yogasūtra* 1.2

> Yoga is defined as *nirodha* (cessation), control or restraint of the activities of mind.

When one is able to control the activities of own mind, then he/ she has accomplished Yoga. Yoga is the science of controlling one's mind. Once mind is controlled, everything else can be controlled

> *mana eva manuṣyāṇāṁ kāraṇaṁ bandhamokṣayoḥ* ।
> — *Amṛtabindopaniṣad* 6.34

> Mind is actually the cause of bondage and mind is the cause of release.

In fact, controlling one's mind is the most difficult task and this is what Yoga teaches. Actually, Yoga is pure psychology, Yoga is ethics; in its practical aspect, it is ethics. In its theoretical aspect, it is psychology and it is so fascinating that one can go deeper into one's own mental potencies, one can master one's mental activities and not only one can master, one can witness like a person who stays aloof from his own mind. Mind is working and one can witness how his mind is working — just like an object, one can become a subject. We are the self, the subject, and mind is only an object or an instrument. We always identify with, rather we are controlled by, our mind. Yoga teaches us how to control our mind and become the masters of our mind. Rather than becoming masters of our own mind, we try to master everything around us. Yoga teaches us the technique of happiness and the technique of getting rid of three types of suffering.

Let us discuss the nature of *citta* in *yoga*. What is *citta*? As we have just discussed, *mahat* is the first evolute of *prakṛti* (matter), it is material in nature, *mahat* is known as intellect (*buddhi*) in Sāṁkhya; but in Yoga, *mahat* is *citta*. The term used for *mahat* in Yoga is *citta* because it is transparent; it is the manifestation of *sattva guṇa* and the predominance of *sattva* makes it totally transparent. So, the one whose *citta* is transparent and clean, he is nearing the process of Yoga, he is nearing the process of restraining his mind. But those of us whose minds are enveloped with different types of *kleśa*s are suffering the pangs of bondage. We shall see that Yoga enumerates several types of *kleśa*s, several *citta-vṛtti*s and several *citta-bhūmi*s.

As already mentioned, Yoga is the restraint of mental activity. How many types of *citta-vṛtti*? First of all, they are classified into two: *kliṣṭa* and *akliṣṭa*, *kliṣṭa* is painful and *akliṣṭa* is not painful. When Yoga is accomplished, the activities do not remain painful, but till such time the activities of our mind are painful to ourselves. What are these activities, *vṛitti*s or *citta-vṛtti*s; they are stated to be five:

1. *pramāṇa* (real cognition),
2. *viparyaya* (perverse cognition),
3. *vikalpa* (verbal cognition),
4. *smṛti* (memory), and
5. *nidrā* (sleep).

These are the five *citta-vṛttis: pramāṇa, viparyaya, vikalpa, smṛti* and *nidrā. Nidrā* itself is a *citta-vṛtti*. We do not have control over our *nidrā*. Sometimes we do not get sleep. We take pills to sleep and sometimes we are feeling too sleepy. We do not have control but the *yogīs* have a complete control over their *nidrā*. For some persons, five minutes of sleep can feel refreshing. Army people are trained like that, within five minutes they can fall asleep and get rejuvenated while we, ordinary people do not have control over our *nidrā*, we do not have control over our *smṛti* also. We forget everything that needs to be remembered and we remember everything that needs to be forgotten. So these are *kliṣṭa vṛttis* for us ordinary persons. As already mentioned, there are two types of *vṛttis*: *kliṣṭa* and *akliṣṭa* (painful and not painful). For the *yogī*, they are not painful because he has control over them. For us, they are painful because we are controlled by them.

Again, there are five types of *kleśas* (afflictions). We already discussed three types of *duḥkha* in Sāṁkhya. But in Yoga five types of *kleśas* are enumerated:

> *avidyā, asmitā, rāga, dveṣa and abhiniveśa.*

While *avidyā* (nescience) is that which should be known correctly, we know the objects via incorrect ways. And we think that whatever I know that is correct, but actually that is *avidyā. Asmitā* is egoism. *Rāga* is attachment, *dveṣa* is aversion and *abhiniveśa* is clinging to life. Nobody wants to die. Everybody is clinging to life, that is *abhiniveśa*. So five types of *kleśas* and five types of *citta-vṛttis* have been enunciated.

Then come five levels of *citta* or *citta-bhūmis*. What are these five? They are:

> *kṣipta, vikṣipta, mūḍha, ekāgra and niruddha.*

Kṣipta is restlessness of a wavering mind, this is because there is the predominance of *rajas*. You might have seen people who are always restless, if they get to do something, they will just feel bored and then jump to another. They have a very restless and wavering mind which does not let them stay at rest. Second is *mūḍha*, torpid or forgetful because there is the predominance of *tamas*. *Vikṣipta* is distracted or oscillating mind. Those who have such a mind are not steady-minded because their mind is always oscillating: I should do this, or I should do that. This is because their mind is under predominance of *rajas*. So *rajas* and *tamas* — when they play games, the mind becomes *kṣipta*, *mūḍha* and *vikṣipta*. These three levels are not useful for Yoga. Anybody who has these three types of mind, will be finding it difficult to start the practice of Yoga. But there are remaining two types of *citta*, which are very conducive to Yoga. One is *ekāgra* (concentrated or single-pointed); there are people who are very focused and concentrated. Because their mind is endowed with the predominance of *sattva*. And then there are those whose mind is *niruddha* (controlled) — they have controlled their mind. These last two types of *citta* are really conducive to Yoga.

What are the means for attaining this clarity, this transparency of *citta* (mind)? Four things have been mentioned in Yoga philosophy, these four are the means for *citta-prasāda* (transparency of mind), which is available in *ekāgra* and *niruddha citta-bhūmis*. How can one achieve that? Four attributes have been enumerated in this regard:

maitrī, *karuṇā*, *muditā* and *upekṣā*.

Maitrī is friendship with those who are enjoying the pleasures. *Karuṇā* is compassion towards those who are suffering. One should be compassionate to those who are aggrieved. *Muditā* is joy towards the virtuous, actually the natural human reaction to the virtuous is mostly seen in the form of jealousy, but the Yogic way of reacting to the virtuous is joy (*muditā*). And *upekṣā* is being neutral to those who are vicious. So being joyful towards the virtuous, being neutral towards the vicious, being compassionate towards those who are suffering and being friendly with those who are enjoying — these are the four ways enunciated in Patañjali's *Yogasūtra*, these are the means for *citta-prasāda. Prasāda* is transparency or the clarity of mind. If we want that our mind should be clear of the afflictions, we should practise these four attributes: *maitrī, karuṇā, muditā* and *upekṣā*. They are collectively called *brahmavihāra* in Mahāyāna Buddhism. Interestingly, the same terms, the same explanations are there, but they are available in the Bauddha tradition also. As stated above, Yoga is a very pervasive tradition. It is available in Jainism and Buddhism as well, besides Hinduism.

Now we come to the *aṣṭāṅga-yoga*. Most of us might be knowing of these eight limbs of Yoga. Although these days we practise just the *āsanas*. *Āsana* is only the third limb of Yoga. There are eight limbs:

> *yama, niyana, āsana, prāṇāyāna, pratyāhāra, dhāraṇā, dhyāna* and *samāedhi.*

first is *yama* (control) and five *yamas* are there. These are five types of restraints, for controlling or restraining one's mind as Yoga is all about that: *yogaścittavṛttinirodhaḥ.* How to control one's mind? By practising these five types of *yamas* or abstentions:

> *ahiṁsā, satya, asteya, brahmacarya* and *aparigraha.*

These five *yamas* are in fact universal principles for controlling one's mind. They belong to the whole humanity. Patañjali says that these are *sārvabhauma mahāvaratas*, i.e. they are universal abstentions — for Hindus, for Jainas, for Buddhists and for Christians, for Americans and for Indians. These can be practised by all human beings across the world.

Next is *niyama*, five ethical principles or observances:

> *śauca* (physical hygeine and mental purity), *santoṣa* (contentment), *tapa* (practising of penance), *svādhyāya* (study) and *īśvara-praṇidhāna* (meditating upon the divine).

These are the five *niyamas*. But these days, unfortunately, anybody who teaches Yoga or who practises Yoga, who pursues Yoga, does not talk of *yamas* and *niyamas*, even if he or she talks about these, nobody practises these. But traditionally for mastering Yoga, for accomplishing control over one's minds, one has to practise these *yamas* and *niyamas* first; then comes *āsana* (bodily posture); postures will not be steady if one is not practising *yamas* and *niyamas*. Currently, only physical *āsanas* are understood as Yoga or may be even *prāṇāyāma*, the fourth limb of Yoga.

Prāṇāyāma is controlling one's breath, exhaling and inhaling: then comes *pratyāhāra* (controlling the sense organs), then *dhāraṇā* (steadying our *citta*, focusing our *citta*); next is *dhyāna* (focusing our attention or meditation) and lastly *samādhi* (concentration). *Samādhi* is the last, the eighth, this is the climax of concentration in the course of spiritual discipline. This is termed as *samādhi*. Out of these eight limbs of Yoga, the first five are known as extrinsic (*bahiraṅga*), the last three are known as intrinsic (*antaraṅga*). If one practises these five, then his/her sense organs can be controlled, his/her mind can be controlled. All the five types of afflictions are gone and one can become happy as aspired:

> *yogaścittavṛttinirodhaḥ* । — *Yogasūtra* 1.2
>
> Yoga is the controlling of our mental activity.

How can one do that? Patañjali says:

> *abhyāsavairāgyābhyāṁ tannirodhaḥ* । — *Yogasūtra* 1.12
>
> There are two ways: one is *abhyāsa* (practice) and the second is *vairāgya* (detachment).

Practising meditation and practising detachment from sensual objects. These are the two ways of attaining Yoga. Besides, there is one more aspect, which is very important

> *īśvarapraṇidhānādvā* (even by surrender to God).

If one can neither practise *abhyāsa* nor *vairāgya* to the level one is required to, then one can take another path. What is that? That is profound meditation and total surrender towards God:

īśvarapraṇidhānādvā. That can also help in controlling one's mind. In fact, this is the most important contribution of Yoga that it has included God in the theory of Sāṁkhya. The definition of God is given here as follows:

> *kleśakarmavipākāśayairaparāmṛṣṭaḥ puruṣaviśeṣa īśvaraḥ* ।
>
> — *Yogasūtra* 1.24

> God is a special *puruṣa* who is not afflicted by the *kleśas* or even by the fruits of actions.

Īśvara is also a *puruṣa* in the philosophy of yoga, because it is conscious, but it is *puruṣa-viśeṣa* as it is not affected by the five types of *kleśas* (afflictions). It is not affected by the results of actions like ordinary people. It is, therefore, held as God. He is the earliest among teachers.

> *pūrveṣāmapi guruḥ kālenānavacchedāt* । — *Yogasūtra* 2.26

> He is the teacher of our ancestors too, since he is not affected by time.

It means that I have learned this from my teacher, my teacher learned it from his teacher. We may go on and on, but who is the first and foremost teacher or preceptor? That is *Īśvara*. So, *Īśvara* is the base, the substratum of *samādhi*, *Īśvara* is the earliest teacher. And how can we attain the grace of *Īśvara*, the divine?

> *tasya vācakaḥ praṇavaḥ* । — *Yogasūtra* 1.27

> *Praṇava* is His name.

If you want to remember God, or if you want to concentrate on the divine principle, then you should recite *praṇava*, *praṇava* is also known as *oṁkāra*.

Praṇava is the nomenclature of *Īśvara*. It is the name of the divine, the one-syllable word *oṁ* is connotative of the divine or *Īśvara*.

I would like to conclude with this *śloka* which says:

ayameva paramo dharmaḥ yadyogenātmadarśanam ।

— *Yājñavalkyasmṛti* 1.8

The ultimate duty of human beings is to see oneself through Yoga.

What is the highest *dharma* (obligation). The answer is as given above. This is the highest *dharma*: *yadyogenātmadarśanam* that one should realize oneself. *Ātma-darśana* is the highest goal in all the philosophical discourses. But how do we do that? *Yogena*, with the assistance of Yoga? We can see ourselves through Yoga, the path of perfection, which we have to pursue slowly and slowly with patience, while focusing or meditating upon *Īśvara*, the divine along with physical and mental restraints and observances.

Question and Answer Session

DR ARVIND GUPTA: Compliments.

Lt GEN. SAWHNEY: Compliments.

PROFESSOR GOEL: Compliments.

Mr SUKANT SARAN: Can I ask a question? My question is regarding the Sāṁkhya philosophy, which says *prakṛti* and *puruṣa* are both real and they exist independently; but from modern scientific view, as well as from our common experience, how can we observe matter without self? So, if we cannot observe matter without self, then this independence needs a little more specification. I would like you to comment on this.

ANURAG SHARMA: My question is that in Bishnoi culture we consider Viṣṇu as the ultimate *puruṣa*. In Śaiva culture, Śiva is considered ultimate *puruṣa* and *ādi-yogī*. So, is there any role of *yogī* and *yoginī* which represent the feminine and masculine energy defined in our Vedic culture with reference to *prakṛti* and *puruṣa*. And how does the Sāṁkhya philosophy define *yogī*? Is there any reference available? Thank you ma'am.

SPEAKER: Thanks for the comments, compliments and questions. In fact, this is my first lecture on Yoga. I have taught the *Sāṁkhyakārikā* but had never taught Yoga during these five decades of my career, I never got an opportunity to teach Yoga; unless you teach, you do not get clarity and confidence. So, for this lecture today, I prepared a lot and I read several books on Yoga.[6] I must admit that while preparing for this lecture, I have learnt a lot and I will feel satisfied if you liked whatever I have presented. I also realized that Yoga is much deeper than is being popularized and publicized these days. It is more on the psychological side than on the physical side. And this is what has been expressed by a few of discussants as well. I agree with you. There was a question regarding the independence of *prakr̥ti* and *puruṣa*. In Sāṁkhya, both of these principles are said to be independent. But they are complementary and an example is given pertaining to a lame and a blind person. A lame person cannot walk, but he can see while a blind person can walk, but he cannot see. So, just a combination of a lame person and a blind person makes the walk possible; the lame person is taken over his shoulder by the blind. The lame person can guide the path and the blind person can walk. Similar is the cooperation, coordination and complementarity between *prakr̥ti* and *puruṣa*. That is what makes two independent persons or two independent entities work and coexist; until and unless their cooperation is continuing, the world is continuing. But the moment they realize their independence, through discrimination, that moment itself the process of dissolution starts. Hence this is a beautiful narrative that Sāṁkhya has woven. Although there are some philosophical problems in this theory too. One problem, which I have always faced while studying and teching Sāṁkhya and which has been raised by the opponents of Sāṁkhya is basically the Nyāya–Vaiśeṣika, of whom I have been a student. The

[6] If someone is interested, there is a book by Chatterjee and Dutta — we all know this is for the beginners, and then we have the Sāṁkhyakārikā and Sāṁkhya-Tattvakaumudī-Ṭīkā with English translation. The original text is, of course, the Yogasūtra of Patañjali, a very good interpretation on this is available by Bengali Baba. And last, but not the least, there is I.C. Sharma's *Ethical Philosophies of India*.

Nyāya–Vaiśeṣika has raised an objection against Sāṁkhya theory of *prakr̥ti* and *puruṣa,* and the objection is that the conscious principle *puruṣa,* is inactive and the unconscious principle, *prakr̥ti,* is active. So how can this be explained? Usually, we see that the consciousness and agency — these two are co-extensive, but in Sāṁkhya's case agency is ascribed to *prakr̥ti,* which is unconscious and consciousness is assigned to *puruṣa* who is totally inactive. This poses a problem and the second question which also bothered the Sāṁkhya and which was raised by several other opponents is that while *prakr̥ti* and *puruṣa* are said to be independent, then how can they come together for start of evolution process? Both of them are co-eternal, both of them are coexisting, always in proximity. So what is it that initiates activity and disturbs the equilibrium? For Sāṁkhya, there is no clear cut answer possible. Yoga has tried to give that answer through the inclusion of God. According to Yoga, it is God who is controlling the world. And depending upon the *karma*s of *jīvas*, *Īśvara* begins that coordination and breaks that equilibrium and the evolution takes place.

Mr Ajay Goel has suggested some books on Yoga which are written in a popular style. I think that will be a good reading for the audience here. One question by Anurag Sharma was about *yogī* and *yoginī.* This is again a very valid question. The immediate definition of *yogī* can be as one who has controlled all his idea of sovereignty. Looking into the sources, there are many more definitions. The following definition is worth quoting in this connection:

> *dr̥ṣṭiḥ sthirā yasya vinaiva dr̥śyāt*
> *vāyuḥ sthiro yasya vina prayatnāt* ।
> *cittaṁ sthiraṁ yasya vinavalambāt*
> *sa eva yogi sa guruḥ sa sevyaḥ* ॥
> — *Amanaskayogaḥ* 1.14

Whose sight is fixed without visible object, whose vital air is constant without an effort, and whose mind is controlled without a point he is verily a true *yogī*, a true teacher and worthy of being served.

A lot of research has also been done on *yoginī* tradition. But this is not in the Pātañjala-Yoga tradition. It is a later addition and contribution of scholars from various sects.

Yoga is also an evolving science and till today many new interpretations and new explanations of Yoga are going on. But what I could realize from whatever the discussions and deliberations were made here is that we should reach out to the sources. We must read one or two of the original sources of Yoga which are very simple to understand and once we read and understand the basics of the *Yogasūtra*, then it will be easier for us to begin any practice or any pursuance of Yoga philosophy. Because unless we go to the original source, many deviations are possible as we do not know about the authenticity of practices being taught.

Each school of Indian philosophy accepts *śabda-pramāṇa* and *śabda-pramāṇa* is known as *āpta-vacana*. *Āpta* is one who is reliable. So reliability in this age of social media, is a very important point. For testing reliability of our knowledge tradition, we should go back to the original sources. I would recommend that one should definitely read the *Yogasūtras* which are only 195 in number, Sanskrit of these *sūtras* is so simple and the explanations are so numerous that we can easily understand them. I am glad that with this assignment of delivering a lecture on the Sāṁkhya–Yoga, I have re-read and tried to understand *Yogasutras* in a deeper manner. Now, the last lecture I have to do is Mīmāṁsā and Vedānta and that is a very wide tradition in itself.

VIF LECTURE X

Mīmāṁsā and Vedānta Philosophy

Mīmāṁsā

In Indian philosophical tradition, just like Nyāya and Vaiśeṣika, Sāṁkhya and Yoga are held to be sister schools, similarly, Mīmāṁsā and Vedānta are intrinsically connected to each other although they might apparently seem poles apart in their approach to reality. Mīmāṁsā is known as Pūrva-Mīmāṁsā, while Vedānta is known as Uttara-Mīmāṁsā. Mīmāṁsā deals with the Brāhmaṇa texts of Vedic literature; to be more precise, Mīmāṁsā is based on the Brāhmaṇa texts while Vedānta is based on Upaniṣads; Vedānta is *jñāna-kāṇḍa* and Mīmāṁsā is *karma-kāṇḍa*. In other words, we can say that Mīmāṁsā is ritualistic and Vedānta is spiritualistic. But they are two aspects of the same thread that connects all the schools of Hindu philosophy. The term *mīmāṁsā* itself means investigation, enquiry or deliberation. Enquiry or investigation into the Vedic statements and these statements are primarily injunctive statements that Mīmāṁsā investigates and deliberates upon. The root verb of the word *mīmāṁsā* is *mān: māner jijñāsāyām.* Mīmāṁsā begins with the following *sūtra*:

> *athāto dharmajijñāsā* । — *Mīmāṁsāsūtra* 1.1.1
>
> Now therefore arises the quest for *dharma.*

The Vaiśeṣika also begins with a premise to explain *dharma*:

> *athāto dharmaṁ vyākhyāsyāmaḥ* । — *Vaiśeṣikasūtra* 1.1.1
>
> Now, therefore, we shall explain the nature of *dharma.*

It means that we shall begin with the explanation or interpretation of *dharma.*

Obviously, Mīmāṁsā does not begin with the explanation. It begins with *jijñāsā* (a quest or desire to know). Now we have to know what is *dharma*. More significantly, the nature of *dharma* in Vaiśeṣika as well as in Mīmāṁsā is different. Vaiśeṣika defines *dharma* as:

> *yato 'bhyudayaniḥśreyasasiddhiḥ sa dharmaḥ* । — 1.1.2
>
> *Dharma* is that which leads us to material progress as well as spiritual fulfilment.

But here in Mīmāṁsā, *dharma* is defined as follows:

> *codanālakṣaṇo 'rtho dharmaḥ* । — *Mīmāṁsāsūtra* 1.1.2
>
> *Dharma* is injunctive in nature.

The Vedic statements are injunctive; that injunction, that action to which Vedas enjoin, that itself is *dharma*. So, *dharma* for Mīmāṁsā is ritualistic, *dharma* signifies action and this action does not mean ordinary action but the Vedic rites prescribed in the Brāhmaṇa texts. It is very unfortunate to note that the research work on Mīmāṁsā philosophy has been less as compared to Vedānta. Vedānta has been very popular, but not Mīmāṁsā, even though Mīmāṁsā is very rich in its content and in its thought as we shall see. To quote Professor I.C. Sharma:

> Strangely enough in spite of the comparative disregard of research scholars towards Mīmāṁsā, the practical life of Hindu Society, its religious practices and its jurisprudence have all along followed the injunctions of this system. Mīmāṁsā has propounded and explained those basic principles of life which have been followed and are being followed by millions upon millions of Indians. — 1991: 215

Therefore, the central theme of Mīmāṁsā is the adaptation of *dharma* (duty) as enjoined in Vedas. This is the *dharma* for Mīmāṁsā and it signifies strict adherence to the performance of rituals as enunciated in the Brāhmaṇa texts. Mīmāṁsā is also related to jurisprudence. Even today in the Indian courts, Mīmāṁsā rules of injunctive statements and interpretation are being followed.[1] These rules are propounded in the Dharmaśāstra tradition of India, and that is why they are applicable in the jurisprudence and its legal implications are being adopted.

Coming to the literature of Mīmāṁsā, it is very vast and rich like in other schools of Indian philosophy. The propounder of this school is Maharṣi Jaimini who is said to exist as early as 300 or 400 BCE and his text *Mīmāṁsāsūtras* is very vast; unlike the *Yogasūtra* which is very small and crisp in content. The *Mīmāṁsāsūtra* is divided into sixteen chapters and there are total 2,644 *sūtras* across these chapters. Out of these, the first twelve chapters are known as *dvādaśalakṣaṇī* and the last four chapters are known as *saṁkarṣaṇa-kāṇḍa*. If we go to the commentators on Mīmāṁsā sūtras of Jaimini, Śabara Swāmī is the first well-known commentator who wrote the *Śābara-Bhāṣya* on the *Mīmāṁsāsūtras*. As already mentioned, there are three famous *bhāṣyas* in Indian tradition, which are very important. One of them is the *Nyāyabhāṣya* of Vātsyāyana, the other one is the *Mahābhāṣya* of Patañjali on Pāṇini's grammar and the third one is the *Śābara-Bhāṣya* on the *Mīmāṁsāsūtras* of Jaimini.

After Śabara Swāmī, we have two other great scholars in Mīmāṁsā tradition: Kumārila Bhaṭṭa and Prabhākara Miśra. Actually, there is a popular legend which says that Kumārila was the teacher and Prabhākara was his student or a disciple, but he was so bright that he never subscribed to the views of Kumārila. He always questioned whatever Kumārila had to say and Kumārila never felt offended. This demonstrates that there was so much of liberalism in Indian tradition, that the disciple could freely question the statement of his own teacher. Prabhākara always used to question and Kumārila happily welcomed his questions. And, finally, one day Kumārila said, I am defeated; you are my *guru*, I am your *śiṣya*. Therefore, in the tradition of Mīmāṁsā, the views of Prabhākara

---

[1] For details, see Markandeya Katju, (Retd. Justice), 2013, *The Mīmāṁsā Principles of Interpertation*, Allahabad: Modern Law Publication.

are known as *gurumata*, although he is the *śiṣya* of Kumārila Bhaṭṭa. In other words Kumārila's views are known as Bhāṭṭamata and Prabhākara's views are known as Prābhākaramata. So, these two different streams of Mīmāṁsā are based on the same *sūtras*, on the same *bhāṣya*, but their interpretations are quite different. Kumārila wrote three great texts: first is the *Ślokavārttika*, which is in verse form. And this is based on the first chapter, first section of the *Mīmāṁsāsūtras*. His next work is the *Tantravārttika* which is in prose form. And this is the interpretation from the second section of the first chapter up to third chapter of the *Mīmāṁsāsūtras*. The later nine chapters are interpreted in the *Ṭupṭīkā*. Prabhākara wrote two commentaries, the *Bṛhatī*[2] and the *Laghvī*, these two commentaries are also on the *Śābara-Bhāṣya*. Both these streams had the single sourcetext but they have different commentators, followers and students.Thereafter we have an enormous literature in Mīmāṁsā. It will be surprising to know that in all the six schools of the orthodox Hindu philosophy and the three heterodox schools, except Cārvāka which has almost no literature left, all the other schools have such a long list of textbooks that it is difficult even to list them, what to talk of reading them and understanding them all!

Thus, with this brief introduction to the Mīmāṁsā literature, let us now move on to the *pramāṇa* theory of Mīmāṁsā. Coming to its epistemology, we can say that Mīmāṁsā is also like other schools of Hindu philosophy, it begins with propounding the means of knowledge, the *pramāṇas*. As already mentioned, in Nyāya, there are four aspects: *pramāṇa*, *prameya*, *pramātā* and *pramā* or *pramiti*. *Pramāṇa* is the means of knowledge, *prameyas* are the objects of knowledge, *pramātā* is the subject or the knower and *pramā* is the result of knowledge. Nyāya accepts four *pramāṇas* but Bhāṭṭa Mīmāṁsā accepts six *pramāṇas* and out of these six *pramāṇas*, we have already covered *pratyakṣa*, *anumāna*, *śabda* and *upamāna*. Although the nature of these four *pramāṇas* in Mīmāṁsā and Nyāya is a little different, but we will not go into the details of these four.

---

[2] *Bṛhati of Prabhākara Miśra*, Madras: University of Madras, 1934.

The two new *pramāṇas* that Mīmāṁsā has propounded, are *arthāpatti*, i.e. presumption or implication, and *anupalabdhi* or non-apprehension because the main task for Mīmāṁsā is explaining the Veda. Therefore, everything they are discussing is concerned with the interpretation of Vedic statements; they had to devise some new means of knowledge — *arthāpatti* is very important from this point of view. *Arthāpatti* is required to reconcile the visible inconsistency in two issues. The Mimāṁsakas cite a very popular example: suppose there is a fellow named Devadutta. He does not eat during daytime but he is getting fat day by day. Now-a-days medical science would examine and diagnose it from a different perspective, but the Mīmāṁsakas or the earlier philosophers, they could only reason out or could deliberate upon why Devadutta is getting fat, while he is not eating during daytime: *pīno devadutto divā na bhuṅkte.*

Now there is an apparent inconsistency. How come? Because Devadutta is getting fat while he is not eating during daytime. Everybody is observing him, whether he eats or not during day time; they all know that he is not eating, then how come he is getting fat? Now these two inconsistent facts are to be reconciled with an implication, or with a presumption that he might be eating at night. When everybody else is asleep, then he might be eating.

Mīmāṁsā terms this as *arthāpatti* and argues that this means of knowledge has to be employed for resolving the apparent inconsistencies in the injunctive statements of the Veda. It has been dealt with detail in Mīmāṁsā texts and there are various types of *arthāpatti* like *dṛṣṭārthāpatti* which is visually apprehended. Then, there is *śrutārthāpatti* which is heard and then there are different subtypes of *dṛṣṭa* and *śruta* types as well.

Next *pramāṇa* is *anupalabdhi* or non-apprehension. In Nyāya philosophy, *abhāva* is accepted as a *padārtha.* According to them, *abhāva* or non-existence is visually perceptible. But according to Mīmāṁsā (i.e. Bhāṭṭa Mīmāṁsā), *abhāva* cannot be visually perceived, there has to be a different type of means for its cognition and that is held to be *anupalabdhi*; if there was a pot in this room, it would have been visible. Now that it is not visible, it means that it is not there. So *anupalabdhi* is a separate means of knowing (*pramāṇa*). These are the six *pramāṇas* accepted by Bhāṭṭa Mīmāṁsakas. Prabhākara does not accept *anupalabdhi* as an independent *pramāṇa*; only the above five *pramāṇas* are acceptable to him and his followers.

Beside the above, the theory called *prāmāṇya,* is also very significant in Mīmāṁsā and it needs to be understood. *Prāmāṇya* means validity. Is our knowledge self-valid? Or do we have to corroborate the validity of our knowledge later on? Suppose one sees that there is water on the road. It is a very sunny day and the road is cemented. Someone is driving and feeling thirsty. He looks at the road ahead and see that there is a lot of water. This is visual perception, but is it valid? Is the water actually there? Or is it not, how to prove the validity? For the Nyāya scholar, the validity will be proved when he goes there, and tries to drink some water and the water can quench his thirst, only then its validity will be proved. For Nyāya, validity of knowledge is not intrinsic to knowledge, it is extrinsic, it has to be proved by separate ways, separate means. But for Mīmāṁsā, because it is not dealing with the ordinary cognition, it is dealing with the Vedic content and so cannot have any iota of doubt regarding the import of Vedic statements. Therefore, for the Mīmāṁsakas, knowledge is intrinsically valid. It is *svataḥ-pramāṇa*. For Nyāya, it is *parataḥ-pramāṇa*. In other words, the *prāmāṇya* or validity of knowledge is a debatable point between Nyāya and Mīmāṁsā. Mīmāṁsā is very insistent on this *svataḥ-prāmāṇya* or self-validity of knowledge. Since we cannot go into the details of these debates, hence only an outline is given here for basic introduction.

Related with this validity of knowledge is another important theory of Indian philosophical thought, which is known as the theory of error. Cognition can be erroneous or it can be correct, it can be valid or invalid. So how do we explain an invalid or erroneous cognition? Regarding this erroneous cognition, there are five different views in Indian philosophy. We are not going to delve deep into these five types too but we must know that, they are known as *khyāti-pañcaka.*[3] Out of these, two view points acceptable to Bhāṭṭa and Prābhākara Mīmāṁsā are quite significant. According to Bhāṭṭa Mīmāṁsā, when we apprehend that there is water while in reality there is no water, actually there is mirage of sand seen in the sun. How to explain this? There are two objects — water and sand which are both visible in the sunlight. Obviously these two are mixed up. One would finally come to know that there is no water, there is sand which is shining due to the sunlight or solar light.

This view is known as *anyathā khyāti.* To understand this issue, according to Prabhākara, no cognition can be erroneous. There are only two objects. There is water, and there is sand, both of them are correct but due to our own mental jumbling (*vivekāgraha*) they have got mixed up. Hence, Prabhākara's theory is known as *akhyāti*, it means that no cognition is erroneous. Kumārila's theory is known as *anyathā-khyāti* or *viparīta-khyāti* which means that there is sand, which is cognized otherwise, i.e. as water. I am cognizing it as water due to certain factors like the sunshine. If the sunshine is not there, I will not see water there, then I can see that there is a road and sand is dispersed on it. So *anyathā-khyāti* or *akhyāti*, these are the two theories of both the Mīmāṁsā schools respectively regarding the erroneous cognition. There are three more theories in this regard which are acceptable to Nyāya and other schools of Indian philosophy, namely *ātmakhyāti, asatkhyāti and anirvacanīya khyāti.*

Coming to the metaphysics of Mīmāṁsā, this much can be said that the metaphysics of Bhāṭṭa Mīmāṁsā is not much different from what the Nyāya–Vaiśeṣikas have accepted. Kumārila mostly accepts what the Nyāya–Vaiśeṣikas have to say, the only difference is that he adds two more *pramāṇa*s and he subtracts one or two *prameya*s from the list of categories.

---

[3] *ātmakhyātirasatkhyātirakhyātiḥ khyātiranyathā* ı
tathānirvacanakhyātirityetat khyātipañcakam ıı
— Quoted in *Nyāya-Kośa*, p. 256

What is the ultimate aim of life according to Mīmāṁsā? The ancient Mīmāṁsakas accepted that it is *svarga* or heaven. All the other schools of philosophy in India, they accept *mokṣa* as the ultimate goal, while here it is *svarga*. What is the means to *svarga*? According to Śāṅkara Vedānta, we shall see that *mukti* cannot be attained except by knowledge: *ṛte jñānānna muktiḥ.*

But the Mīmāṁsakas propound very emphatically that only *karma* can lead us to *svarga*. What is *svarga*? *Svarga* is that place where there is no suffering, where we get whatever we desire:

> *yanna duḥkhena sambhinnaṁ na ca grastamanantaram* ।
> *abhilāṣopanītaṁ ca tatsukhaṁ svaḥpadāspadam* ॥
>
> — Quoted in *Nyāyakośa*, p. 1059
>
> Such a pleasure, such a *sukha* where there is no mix of suffering or *duḥkha* — that is *svarga*.

But how do we attain *svarga*? There is a popular Vedic injunction:

> *svargakāmo yajeta* ।
>
> One who wants to attain *svarga*, should perform the *yāga*.

Various rites including the fire ritual, and all the rules and details for this fire ritual, types of fire ritual, these are all enunciated in Mīmāṁsā texts with detail.

What is *śabda*? According to Mīmāṁsā, it is the Veda. The Veda itself is the *śabda:*

> *apauruṣeyaṁ vākyaṁ vedaḥ* — *Arthasaṁgraha*, p. 7
>
> Veda is the *Śabda* or Vedic testimony and each sentence, each syllable of the Veda is significant, it is valid.

There are five types of statements in Vedas which have been listed as *vidhi*, *niṣedha*, *nāmadheya*, *mantra* and *arthavāda*. *Vidhi* is the clear injunctive statement; *mantras* are hymns in Vedas, *nāmadheya* is name or appellation; *niṣedha* is the prohibition; some actions are enjoined to be performed and the others are prohibited because they should not be performed; then there are some statements which are only corroborative statements or explanatory passages. These are known as *arthavāda*.

In brief, *vidhi*, *mantra*, *nāmadheya*, *niṣedha* and *arthavāda* — these are five types of statements which are available in the Veda according to Mīmāṁsā. Details of *vidhi*, details of *mantras* and *nāmadheyas*, details of *niṣedha* and details of *arthavāda* — all these have been given in the Mīmāṁsā texts but what is more important is that Mīmāṁsā deals mainly with *dharma*. In fact, two words are very important in Indian philosophical tradition: *dharman* and *brahman*; both the words are ending with the letter "n" - *dharman* and *brahman*; *dharman* here is duty or obligation but not the obligation which has been inflicted upon me by myself, or by society. These are the duties which have been enjoined for one and all by the Veda, i.e. *dharma*. To quote:

> *dharme pramīyamāṇe tu vedena karaṇātmanā* ।
> *itikartavyatābhāgaṁ mīmāṁsā pūrayiṣyati* ॥

Mīmāṁsā deals with dharma; so what is the prameya of Mīmāṁsā? What is the content of Mīmāṁsā? That is dharma and what is the instrument or the means of knowing dharma, i.e. the Veda. Dharma is enjoined and interpreted in the Veda. The question arises, how to do that, how to interpret and how to comprehend, whatever is said in the Veda, because sometimes, these are not the Veda-mantras only. Mīmāṁsā is also dealing with the Brāhmaṇa texts and there are many statements in the Brāhmaṇas; which are very complex and also seem contradictory at times. As already stated, Vedānta deals with Brahman.

We have introduced ourselves to the Vedic literature already. Each of the Veda has its own Brāhmaṇa. For example, the *Aitareya Brāhmaṇa* is related to the *Ṛgveda*. The *Śatapatha Brāhmaṇa* is related to *Śukla Yajurveda*. Thus, each Veda Saṁhitā is related to a separate Brāhmaṇa and the Brāhmaṇa texts expound the intricacies of rituals and, at various places, we find that there are contradictions or there are inconsistencies. Mīmāṁsā helps us reconcile these inconsistencies and Mīmāṁsā also enables us to comprehend the real import of these. What is the real import or essence of this statement — that is known as *itikartavyatā* (methodology). *Dharma* is the *prameya*, Veda is the *pramāṇa* and Mīmāṁsā provides the *itikartavyatā* or methodology. This methodology incorporates three things which are also relevant to modern day discussion about planning and management. What are these three:

- *Kim bhāvyam*?: First of all, we should decide our course of action; when we intend to do something; say a *yajña* or *yāga* (ritual) it has to be planned well in advance. So, when we plan to do or perform a ritual, we have to decide as to what is to be performed.
- *Kena bhāvyam*?: Who is the agent for this performance, i.e. who will be performing this *yāga.*
- *Kathaṁ bhāvyam*?: What will be the real method or *itikartavyatā*?

These three aspects can be employed in any of the tasks that we undertake. This can be applicable to management; this can be applicable to teaching; this can be applicable to cooking in the kitchen, *kim bhāvyam, kena bhāvyam, kathaṁ bhāvyam*? What is to be done? Who will be doing it? And what will be the method of doing this? These three aspects of ritual are known as *itikartavyatā* in Mīmāṁsā. At another place, it is stated in Mīmāṁsā:

> *dharmākhyaṁ viṣayaṁ vaktuṁ mīmāṁsāyāḥ prayojanam* ।
>
> — *Śāstradīpikā* 1.1.1

> What is the objective of Mīmāṁsā? The objective of Mīmāṁsā is to explain the nature of *dharma.*

What type of *dharma*? Injunctive *dharma*, enjoined duties and the method to perform these duties. Therefore, the ethics of Mīmāṁsā is also very important from this point of view. There are some schools like Buddhism, which emphasized that a real seeker has to be a monk; while Jainism accepts both types of followers: (1) *śrāvaka*, and (2) *śramaṇa* — the householders as well as the monks. But the school of Mīmāṁsā is activistic in approach. It does not impel one to be a monk, rather it emphasizes that duty for duty's sake should be performed. This is the uniqueness of Mīmāṁsā which has given the course of expanse to the *Bhagavadgītā*'s *niṣkāma karma*, although here *kāmanā* of a higher level is also implied: *svargakāmo yajeta.*

Why should one perform the *yāga*? If one wants to attain heaven, one should do one's duty and perform the ritual. Here again Kumārila and Prabhākara differ with each other. According to Prabhākara, there should be no desire. In other words, our activity should be deontological, it just needs to be performed. Whatever is to be done, has to be done for its own sake. On the other hand, it is the desire of the seeker or a performer which is also implied, this is the viewpoint of Kumārila. In this way, we have briefly discussed the epistemology, metaphysics and the ethics of Mīmāṁsā.

Two more points need to be mentioned here which are very important for Mīmāṁsā. First one of these are the types of *karma* because Mīmāṁsā is focusing on the nature of *karma* (action) in the form of *dharma* (duty). In short, there are following four types of *karma* according to Mīmāṁsā:

- There are the *nitya karmas* (daily rituals) like *sandhyā-vandanā.* We should perform these daily duties.
- Then *naimittika karmas*, these are the occasional actions which must be performed on special occasions like *pūrṇimā* or *amāvasyā* — special types of *homa* or *agnihotra* is required on the new moon or full-moon day.
- *Niṣiddha karmas* — there are certain actions which are prohibited, we should never perform them. If we perform them, we accrue sin for ourselves. One might ask here — if we perform the *nitya* and *naimittika karmas*, do we gain anything? To this question, it is said that we may not gain anything, but if we do not do the *nitya* and *naimittika karmas*, then our path may be very difficult, there will be some

complications, some obstructions in our path. Therefore, we should perform the *nitya* and *naimittika karmas* also with faith. But we should never ever do *niṣiddha karmas* as they will bring bad consequences for us.

- Last but not the least are the *kāmya karmas*: desire is also present there. These are optional actions like King Daśaratha performing *putreṣṭi yāga* and begetting four sons; some other king performing the *vr̥ṣṭi yāga* — then rainfall would follow. One would perform these types of *yāgas* and there are proofs that when special type of *yāga* was performed, the desired result was attained. In fact, there may be a scientific reason behind this but there is definitely a traditional reason behind these actions.

Secondly, philosophy of Mīmāṁsā also has an undercurrent of linguistics. We have not dwelt upon it but it must be mentioned here that Mīmāṁsā is a science of interpretation. Mīmāṁsā is known as the *vākyaśāstra* of ancient India. *Vākya* is the sentence, not ordinary sentence but the Vedic sentence (*apauryṣeyaṁ vākyaṁ vedaḥ*). Veda is the impersonal statement and every statement of the Veda is enjoining some kind of *dharma*. The interpretation of these Vedic statements is very important. There are two theories which are very prominent in this regard. One of them is known as Abhihitānvayavāda and the other is explained as Anvitābhidhānavāda. Kumārila is the propounder of Abhihitānvayavāda and Prabhākara enunciated Anvitābhidhānavāda. We might not have thought of it earlier but this is a significant question. When a speaker utters a sentence, do we hear him word by word? Do we come to the meaning of his statement word by word, or is it the collective sense of the sentence that comes at once to our mind — that is the crux of the question? According to Kumārila, it is Abhihitānvayavāda. It means that first, the words are stated — *abhihita*, they are uttered, and then there is this corroboration; *anvaya* or the relation between these words is adjoined later. But according to Prabhākara it is the case of *anvitābhidhāna*. First, there is a relation (*anvaya*) among words, the speaker forms some relation in his mind, then utters the words. In fact, if we go deeper, we will notice that it is one and the same thing, but both of them are looking at it from different places, different points of view. If we think over it minutely, then we would understand that Prabhākara is explaining it from the point of view of the speaker while the view of Kumārila is based on the aspect of the listener. These theories only show how these Mīmāṁsā scholars were also discussing the philosophy of language in intricate details. In fact, very detailed theories have been developed in this regard. Later on, literary circles also expanded these theories for explaining the poetic import. This is sufficient to suggest the significance of Mīmāṁsā philosophy in Indian tradition.

Vedānta

Out of the six *āstika* systems of Hindu philosophy, Vedānta is the sixth and the last school, and the name incorporates two terms *Veda* + *anta; anta* can have many meanings in Sanskrit; *anta* means culmination, *anta* means essence, *anta* also means gist. Hence Vedānta signifies the last portion of the Veda, i.e. the Upaniṣads. It is rightly said:

> *vedānto nāmopaniṣatpramāṇam* । — *Vedāntasāra* 1
>
> Vedānta is the core of Upaniṣads.

Vedānta is based on the Upaniṣads like Mīmāṁsā is based on the Brāhmaṇa texts. Just as Upaniṣads are the last part of Vedic literature, similarly, Vedānta is the last or concluding school of Indian philosophy. It is the essence of Upaniṣads which is presented in the Vedānta school. The *sūtras* of Vedānta are authored by Bādarāyaṇa Vyāsa and they are known as the *Brahmasūtras* because the content of the *Vedāntasūtras* is *Brahman* just like the content of the *Mīmāṁsāsūtras* is *dharma*; *dharma* is duty or *karma* while *Brahman* signifies knowledge. The word *brahman* is derived from the root *bṛṁh* and the verb means: to grow, to expand, but actually it also denotes knowledge since knowledge is ever growing. In other words, *Brahman* is knowledge itself. There are various commentaries on the *Brahmasūtras*, at least ten traditional commentaries are available which have been very popular. Then, there are many more commentaries which have been written after these traditional commentaries.

Śaṅkarācārya is the first and the foremost commentator of the *Brahmasūtras*. He was there in the eighth century. From eighth century to the eighteenth century, for 1,000 years, there have been at least ten different commentaries on the *Brahmasūtras*. There are 555 *sūtras* in the *Brahmasūtras* according to Śaṅkara. Each commentator has listed a different number of *sūtras*; not only their interpretation differs; the number of *sūtras* also differs in their commentaries. Śaṅkara's philosophy or interpretation is known as the *Śārīraka-Bhāṣya*. Why the *Śārīraka-Bhāṣya*?

> *ṣarīre bhavaṁ śārīram śārīram eva śārīrakam* ।
> — *Śāṅkarabhāṣya* on *Brahmasūtra* 1.1.1

> Whatever stays in this body (*śarīra*), that conscious self is known as *śārīra* or *ātman*. That itself is *śārīraka*.

In the *Bhagavadgītā*, *śārīra* is denoted as *dehi:*

> *dehino 'sminyathā dehe kaumāraṁ yauvanaṁ jarā* ।
> — *Gītā* II.13

In other words, the interpretation of Śaṅkara on the *Brahmasūtras* is known as the *Śārīraka-Bhāṣya* and his philosophy is known as Advaita. Śaṅkara propounds that the import of the *Brahmasūtras* is Advaita or non-dualism but there are other commentators who propound an opposite theory on the same source text; for example, Madhvācārya: he says Dvaita is the import of *Brahmasūtras*; duality between *jīva* and *Brahman*. Viśiṣṭādvaita is another theory, propounded by Rāmānujācārya and Śuddhādvaita is the theory of Vallabhācārya. Dvaitādvaita is Nimbārka's theory, Acintya-Behadābheda is the theory propounded by Caitanya Mahāprabhu, Śaivaviśiṣṭādvaita is propounded by Śrīkaṇṭha and Vīraśaivaviśiṣṭādvaita by Śrīkara; Avibhāgādvaita by Vijñānabhikṣu and Bhedābheda by Bhāskara. These are the ten traditional commentaries but, as mentioned above, this is only up to the eighteenth century. Even after eighteenth century, there have been more commentaries on the *Brahmasūtras* and now-a-days it is claimed that there are more than twenty commentaries on the *Brahmasūtras*. This shows how popular the Brahmasūtras have been in Indian philosophical tradition.

In fact, Vedānta philosophy itself is very popular till date and if anybody knows a little bit of Indian philosophy, just ask him and he will name the Vedānta. In this regard, I would like to quote Radhakrishnan (1977, vol. II: 430) who says:

> The Vedānta philosophy deserves closer attention, not only on account of its philosophical value but also because it is closely bound up with the religion of India and is much more alive in that continent than any other system of thought. In one or the other of its forms, the Vedānta determines the world view of the Hindu thinkers of the present time.

This much about the popularity of Vedānta. But what about Śaṅkara, the commentator of *Brahmasūtras,* and Radhakrishnan has to say:

> It is impossible to read Śaṅkara's writings packed as they are with serious and subtle thinking, without being conscious that one is in contact with the mind of very fine penetration and profound spirituality. With his acute feeling of the immeasurable world is studying gaze into the abysmal mysteries of spirit, his unswerving resolve to say neither more nor less than what could be proved, Śaṅkara stands out as a heroic figure of the first rank in the somewhat motley crowd of the religious thinkers of mediaeval India. — Radhakrishnan, 1977, vol. II: 446

It must be mentioned here that we shall only dwell upon Śaṅkara's Advaita while introducing the philosophy of Vedānta as it is not possible to discuss different doctrines of Vedānta at this stage.

As noted earlier, Mīmāṁsā begins with: *athāto dharmajijñāsā* (*Mīmāṁsāsūtra* 1.1.1) while Vedānta begins with:

athāto brahmajijñāsā । — *Vedāntasūtra* 1.1.1

Now therefore the quest to know *Brahman* (has risen).

It is only after the desire to know (*jijñāsā*) *dharma* through Pūrva-Mīmāṁsā (since *karma* precedes *jñāna*, action precedes knowledge), is fulfilled, that we want to know what is the spirit behind these rituals. We have known what type of rituals we should perform and what ritual will yield what type of result, but now we want to know what is the nature of the Ultimate Truth, i.e. *Brahman.*

Significantly, there are four pre-requisite factors for entering into the study of Vedānta. Everybody cannot be given a discourse on the nature of *Brahman* or the Ultimate Truth as this is known as *brahma-vidyā*: *adhyātma-vidyā*:

Brahmavidyā sarvavidyāpratiṣṭhā. — *Muṇḍakopaniṣad* 1.1

adhyātmavidyā vidyānam. — *Gītā* X.32

Obviously, these types of discourses which are propounded in Upaniṣads, they cannot be delivered to all and at once. Some preparations need to be made before one goes into it. Even now, if one wants to seek an admission to MBA, MPhil or PhD, there is an entrance exam. Not to talk of, MA or MPhil — even for nursery admission, it is more difficult to go through the interview. Every admission requires some preparation and some eligibility. Obviously, in admission to a school of learning where the Ultimate Truth of life is being taught, a lot of preparation needs to be done. What are these four prerequisites for this preparation? These are known as *anubandha-catuṣṭaya* (four factors):

- The first is *adhikārī*, a seeker, an eligible seeker. A person who wants to study Vedānta, he should have several qualifications which have been listed out in the *Vedāntasāra*. First of all, his heart should be pure — *nirmalasvāntaḥ* and he should have practised the *yamas* and *niyamas*, he should have studied some Śāstras. Being an *adhikārī* is the first pre-requisite for the one who is eligible to be admitted to the school of Vedānta.
- Then comes *viṣaya*, *adhikārī* does not mean an officer here, *adhikārī* means a *pātra*, he who has an *adhikāra*, a right to

study Vedānta, he is an *adhikārī*. He wants to know, what is the content? Everybody wants a prospectus, when he is going to be admitted. At the time of admission itself prospectus is given and syllabus is handed out. So the seeker wants to know, as to what is the content. Therefore, *viṣaya* is the second factor while *adhikārī* is the first.

- The third one is *sambandha*, what is the relation between the content or the theme, and the teaching that shall be imparted. Is there any connection? Is there any *sambandha* between the theme and the discourse that is being delivered to me. Of course, there is some relation and various types of relations are listed there in the source texts.
- Last but not the least is the *prayojana* or the goal. Why should one study Vedānta? Why should one study Mīmāṁsā? Kumārila has very clearly stated:

> *sarvasyaiva hi śāstrasya karmaṇo vāpi kasyacit* ।
> *yāvatprayojanaṁ noktaṁ tāvattat kena gr̥hyate* ॥
> — *Ślokavārttika* 1.11

No body takes up any action if he is not sure of the objective. If there is nothing to be achieved, why should one labour? Why should One make effort? So *prayojana* has to be listed at the beginning. One should be very clear of the objective for which he has come to study this Śāstra of Mīmāṁsā and Vedānta. These are known as the four prerequisites.

Now, the seeker is admitted to the school of Vedānta because he has fulfilled all the four prerequisites. Again, there is a very tough task waiting for him. What is that? He has to undergo a very strict training here. What is that training? It is *sādhana-catuṣṭaya.*[4] Accordingly the disciple of Vedānta has to prove that he has prepared himself well with the four aspects of studying Vedānta.

---

4 For details, see ShashiPrabha Kumar, 2005, "Significance of Sādhana-Catuṣṭaya in Vedānta", in *Self, Society and Value: Reflections on Indian Philosophical Thought*, pp. 108-25.

The preceptor tells him that if you want to study, you have been admitted, no doubt, but you will be able to understand Vedānta only if you have obtained or mastered these four *sādhanas* or means and these four are even more tough. Śaṅkarācārya has listed these four in his *Vivekacūḍāmaṇi*.

We did not discuss the literature of Vedānta, which is enormously vast. Besides Śaṅkara's commentary on the *Brahmasūtras*, Śaṅkara himself is said to have authored more than fifty texts. We are not very sure whether they are all actually written by Ādi-Śaṅkarācārya. Or it may be that when the name Śaṅkara became popular, many authors started writing in the name of Śaṅkara. Some of these texts are very well-known. The *Vivekacūḍāmaṇi* is one of them. Before Śaṅkara there was his teacher Gauḍapāda, The beginning of Vedānta literature is held from the *Gauḍapādakārikā*. The *Gauḍapādakārikā* or *Māṇḍūkyakārikā* which is another name of the text and this is from there that Śaṅkara took a clue for Advaita theory and he explained the *Brahmasūtras* in his own style.

Coming back to the *Sādhana-catuṣṭaya* or four means of comprehending Vedānta for mastering Vedānta:

- The first one is a discriminating power: *nityānityavastuviveka*. One should inculcate a discriminating power between the permanent and the impermanent. One should always discern what is more enduring and what is not; in other words one should weigh and prioritize. How can one weigh and prioritize, only by discriminating. *Viveka* means *nīra-kṣīra-viveka*. What is more valuable — *nīra* or *kṣīra*? Of course, these days *nīra* is also very valuable but as compared to *kṣīra*, *nīra* is definitely less valuable. We have to always weigh and prioritize and this can be done only on the basis of discrimination between permanent and impermanent, more enduring and less enduring.
- The second one is *ihāmutrārthaphalabhogavirāga*; to explain it in simpler terms, this is the detachment from worldly objects.

How can one develop *viveka*? *Viveka* is the discriminating power. The person who is discerning enough to know that this is evanescent and this is permanent — actually the implied suggestion here is towards body and the soul; body is impermanent and spirit or soul is permanent and the ultimate aim of Vedānta is to realize the self, the *ātman* or *Brahman*.

- Then, the third one is *śamadamādisampat*. There are six virtues that have been listed for controlling the sense organs and for restraining one's mind: Unless the sense organs are under control and mind is restrained, nobody can undertake the serious type of teachings that are being imparted in the school of Vedānta.
- Last but not the least is *mumukṣutva* or a desire to attain *mokṣa*. If one is happy in whatever way he or she is living: eat, drink and be merry; then Vedānta is not meant for them, Cārvāka or Lokāyata is their philosophy. But if one wants to get rid of whatever one is suffering from, if one wants to be released from this suffering forever, then Vedānta is the philosophy. If one wants an intense desire to be released from this suffering, then it is *mumukṣutva*. Śaṅkara says elsewhere:

> *durlabhaṁ trayamevaitat daivānugrahahetukam* ।
> *manuṣyatvam mumukṣutvaṁ mahāpuruṣasaṁśrayaḥ* ॥
> — *Vivekacūḍāmaṇiḥ* 3
>
> These three are difficult to obtain: to be born as a human being, to have an earnest longing for release and the close association with great persons.

Accordingly, following three things are very rare in this world:

- The first one is *manuṣyatvam*, being born as a human being. It is rare; not every being is born as a human being. So value this human birth, which you have got, value this body that you have got as a human being; you have got this body, not for indulging in sensuous pleasures alone, this body is given to you for a greater goal, so try to acquire that greater goal.

- The second one is *mumukṣutva*, no other being in the world can ever desire to attain *mokṣa*, only human beings can do so and we Indians are even more lucky that we are born in India because nowhere else this concept of *mokṣa* is available, it is only discussed in Indian philosophical traditon. In fact this concept of *mokṣa* is the greatest contribution of Indian philosophy to the world thought.
- Therefore *manuṣyatvam*, *mumukṣutvam* and the third is *mahāpuruṣasaṁśraya* or getting close to the great persons like today we are in the company of great minds. So being born as a human being, having a desire to be released and getting along with great sages and saints — these three are rarest of the rare opportunities and fortunately if we have got these three, then it means that God's grace is bestowed upon us. Only divine grace leads us to these three. In this way, the four means for comprehending Vedāntic truth are explained as above.

Now what are the means of knowing or *pramāṇas* in Vedānta epistemology? There are six ways of knowing,[5] according to Vedānta. Just as Kumārila Bhaṭṭa has enunciated, all these six *pramāṇas* are acceptable to Śaṅkara as means of knowing. It is said in Vedānta:

vyavahāre bhāṭṭanayaḥ.

i.e. The philosophy of Bhāṭṭa is acceptable to us in *vyavahāra* or at practical level.

These six ways of knowing are: *pratyakṣa*, *anumāna*, *upamāna*, *śabda*, *arthāpatti* and *anupalabdhi*. We cannot go into details of Vedāntic epistemology due to paucity of time.

As regards Vedānta metaphysics, there is only one single entity and that is:

---

5 For details, see D.M. Datta, 2017, *Six Ways of Knowing*, D.K. Printworld, Delhi.

ekamevādvitīyam । — *Chāndogyopaniṣad* 6.2.1

There is only one entity and that is unparalleled.

That entity is *Brahman*. *Brahman* and *ātman* are not different, *Brahman* is the same as *ātman:*

ayamātmā brahma । — *Māṇḍūkyopaniṣad* 2

This *ātmā* itself is *Brahman*.

Going back to schools of Indian philosophy, Nyāya has listed sixteen entities, Vaiśeṣika six or seven, Sāṁkhya twenty-five; Yoga adds one, so twenty-six, and Mīmāṁsā has propounded five or six. Advaita Vedānta or non-dualism, as the name itself suggests, accepts only one real, as dualism is not to be thought of, there is only one: *ekamevādvitīyam*. *Brahman* is the single Ultimate Truth. All other entities in the world are *asat*. The only *sat* is *Brahman*: What is the nature of *Brahman*? It is *sat*, *cit* and *ānanda*. *Sat* means it exists, *cit* means it is conscious in essence, and *ānanda* means its nature is perfect bliss, no suffering in the nature of *ātman*. In other words *Brahman* is *ātman* and *sat-cit-ānanda* is its nature. These three are not the attributes of *Brahman*. If we explain it according to Nyāya and Vaiśeṣika, then these three are the attributes of *ātman*. *Ātman* is the *dravya* and *sat*, *cit* and *ānanda* are the attributes (*guṇas*). In Vedānta there is no difference in the *dravya* and its *guṇas*; they are one and the same — there is no *dvaita* or duality. So *Brahman* in its essential nature is *sat*, *cit* and *ānanda*; *ātman* and *Brahman* are not different; the only difference is that the word *ātmā* is in masculine gender and *Brahman* is in neuter. Although the word *ātman* is also ending in *n-ātman*. But these differences are only linguistic or grammatical; metaphysically or ontologically, there is no difference, so *Brahman* and *ātman* are one and the same. *Brahman* is *nirākāra*, it does not have a form, it is held to be *nirguṇa*. In its pure nature, it is *nirguṇa*. No attributes are to be attached, but at the empirical level, we ascribe certain qualities to the divine principle like *He* is the creator of the world. *He* sustains the universe, *He* manages our actions at the empirical level. Actually Śaṅkara has elucidated three levels to explain the nature of reality — that is also his unparalleled contribution. There is an empirical level which we all are experiencing and there is a level in between the empirical and the transcendental. That is known as *prātibhāsika* level or the illusory level and the ultimate level is transcendental level: *pāramārthika*, *vyāvahārika* and *prātibhāsika*. Accordingly, *vyāvahārika* is all that we are now seeing, experiencing and enjoying. But is it true? Is it the Ultimate Truth? No. If it was the Ultimate Truth, then we all would have been eternally happy but we are not. That means we are missing something. What are we missing? We are missing to know our self, our true nature. What is our true nature? *Sat*, *cit* and *ānanda* — that is missing. So there is some missing link in between what we feel and what we are; we are *sat*, *cit*, *ānanda*, but we feel that we lack this; we lack that, we do not get this, why are we suffering, why are the others enjoying. Obviously, this is not the true essence of life. This is not the ultimate goal. This is only the empirical level.

As mentioned above, *Ātman* and *Brahman* are not different in Vedānta. There is a third concept and that is of *mokṣa*. *Mokṣa* is also not different from *Brahman* and *ātman*, once we know that we are the true *ātman*, then and there it will be *mokṣa*. *Mokṣa* is not a state to be achieved. It is not different from what we are. It is just a veil of ignorance and that veil has to be removed like the current of electricity goes and everything is enveloped in darkness. When the current of electricity is restored, we do not lift anything. We do not put anything in its place. Everything was there as it is. Only the darkness disappears, light shines and everything appears in its true form. Similarly, when ignorance is eloped, when the veil of ignorance is lifted, then the true nature of the Ultimate Truth is in front of us. So *mokṣa* is also not different from *Brahman* and *ātman*:

> *brahma veda brahmaiva bhavati* । — *Muṇḍakopaniṣad* 3.9
>
> He who knows *Brahman*, he becomes *Brahman*.

> *brahmabhāvaśca mokṣaḥ* । — *Śāṅkarabhāṣya* on *Brahmasūtra* 1.1
>
> *Mokṣa* is realizing the nature of *Brahman*.

One does not go anywhere, one does not change anything. Only the mindset changes. Only the ignorance is gone and the knowledge has manifested itself in its true form.

How to explain *Brahman*? That is the most difficult task. According to Vedānta, it cannot be explained in clear terms, it is *anirvacanīya* (inexplicable); the *Kenopaniṣad* beautifully narrates this fact when it states that the sense organs cannot reach *Brahman*, the mind also cannot reach there. The tongue cannot speak about it. It is only by realizing within ourselves that we can understand *Brahman*. So *ātmasākṣātkāra* or *brahmānubhava* — these are the terms used in Upaniṣads and reused by Śaṅkarācārya to interpret that *Brahman*, *ātman* and *mokṣa* are one and the same thing. They are not different. *Ātman* is *nitya-mukta*, but we think that we are under bondage. Why do we think so? Because it is the veil of ignorance that has covered our pure nature. *Brahman* is self-revealing. We do not need any light to illumine the nature of *Brahman*, light is already there as *cit*, the light of consciousness is already there but only the darkness is to be removed. How can darkness cover the self-revealing consciousness — that is the basic problem and the difficult knot that we have to untie, and that is beautifully explained through the concept of *māyā*.

Māyā is a *śakti* of *Brahman*; *śakti* or *upādhi* means a condition or an imposition. It is also inexplicable like *Brahman*. What is the function of *māyā*, *māyā* covers (*āvaraṇa*) as well as projects (*vikṣepa*); first it covers the nature of truth and then after the cover is lifted, it projects the true nature. *Māyā* is another factor, another entity, another force or power in Vedānta, but it is not the ultimate real. It is only a condition imposed upon the ultimate truth. It is imposed on the nature of reality. As already dicussed, the popular example of the rope and snake is given to illustrate it. Obviously the snake was not there in reality. This was an illusion caused by darkness.

This darkness is ignorance for us (*jīvas*); there is *Brahman* or *ātman*, the Ultimate Truth. But at the empirical level we all are *jīvātmās*, embodied selves and we are different; we seem to be different, reality and appearance are different. There is the appearance of a snake, but in real, it is a rope. Similarly, the whole empirical world is imposed upon *Brahman*.

This is known as *vivarta*, *vivarta* is the theory of causation according to Vedānta. In the Sāṁkhya philosophy, we had discussed that the cause and the effect are identical; in the Nyāya–Vaiśeṣika, cause and effect are held to be totally different; while in Vedānta there is no difference (*abheda*) between the cause and the effect. It is one and the same entity, only a projection is there, only an imposition is there. One appears as many:

> *ekaṁ va idaṁ vibabhūva sarvam* । — *Ṛ̥V* VIII.58.2
>
> The single one has manifested in all.
>
> *rūpaṁ rūpaṁ pratirūpo babhūva* । — *Ṛ̥V* VI.47.18
>
> Divine is one, but manifests in many forms.

Viewed from this angle — this manyness, this plurality is only at the empirical level; at the transcendental level, non-dualism is the Ultimate Truth which is to be realized. It can be realized, according to Vedanta, only through knowledge and not through action while Mīmāṁsā says, *svarga* can be attained by *karma* alone. Śaṅkara says that *mukti* can be realized only through knowledge. Actions are indeed necessary but they are at a lower level as compared to knowledge. *Bhakti* is also helpful but *mokṣa* cannot be realized without the true knowledge. So Vedānta is pure *jñāna-kāṇḍa*, Mīmāṁsā is *karma-kāṇḍa*. There are many more differences between Mīmāṁsā and Vedānta but then many similarities are also there, hence these are known as two sister schools.

In brief, we can say that ultimately all the six schools of Indian philosophy can be reconciled. They are all standing at different stations, looking at the world from different perspectives; they are all trying to explain the reality according to their own viewpoint and every viewpoint has some amount of truth. According to Vedānta, the Ultimate Truth is one and only one: that is *Brahman.* This has been proved on the basis of Upaniṣadic statements, and these statements are also quoted in the form of four *mahāvākyas* which are selected from Upaniṣads related to all the four Vedas. Significantly, these four famous *mahāvākyas*[6] from the Upaniṣads are:

1. *Tattvamasi* (*Chāndogyopaniṣad* 6.9.4)
2. *Ahaṁ brahmāsmi* (*Bṛhadāraṇyaka Upaniṣad* 1.4.10)
3. *Ayamātma brahma* (*Māṇḍūkyopaniṣad* 2)
4. *Prajñānaṁ brahma* (*Aitareya Upaniṣad* 3.3).

Question and Answer Session

SPEAKER: To conclude, this is in brief the introduction to Mīmāṁsā and Vedānta. In fact, it is an endless ocean. And only a few droplets of the vast ocean could be presented here. It is beyond one's capacity to enunciate the whole of the *śāstra* within one hour which is so vast and so valuable. With these words, I thank you all for giving me a patient hearing.

Lt GENERAL SAWHNEY: Thank you so much Dr ShashiPrabha ji. I think it was an amazing introduction and very deep philosophical introduction.

SH PRAKASH SINGH: You said that *mokṣa* is the highest concept. What is the meaning of *mokṣa*? As I understand, it is liberation from the cycle of birth and death, but then what happens to you, we are told that you become part of the *ātmā* or *paramātmā,* and your identity merges into that of the creator, but this concept seems very vague. We do not know who the creator is? And merging your identity into that creator, is that freedom from the cycle of birth and death. What happens really to you? Does it not amount to some

---

6 Although, there are many more *mahāvākyas*, but the above four are most prevalent ones.

kind of permanent death, permanent non-existence, permanent loss of your identity, just see this. Yes. We talk about freedom from the cycle of birth and death. Yes. Human life has its problems, its miseries, its struggles, all kinds of problems are there, but it also has its satisfaction, its sense of fulfilment if you are able to do good to others. If you want to lead a positive life, there is a lot to be said in favour of coming back to life and trying to make your humble contribution for improving the society, improving the neighbourhood, improving the lot of other people. But if you attain *mokṣa*, then it is the end of you. I do not know what happens to you, you cease to exist. I mean I feel slightly confused about this concept of *mokṣa* and then if it is permanent happiness I do not know. What is permanent happiness? When there is no sorrow? This is thinkable to me, but maybe there is a state where only happiness is there. I do not know whether it happens, can also become boring unless, you know, unless you experience sorrow, then happiness has no value.

SPEAKER: This question is the eternal question and all the philosophers in India had grappled with this question, they all have given different answers to this but right now we are talking about Advaita Vedānta. According to it, *mokṣa* is the realization of our own nature and that nature is eternal happiness. Not only *duḥkha* or *sukha*, these are relative experiences, while *ānanda* is the absolute bliss. There is no tinge of sorrow and suffering and the question that you raised is really important: If one is in this state of *mokṣa*, then one is empirically dead. Why cannot there be a *mokṣa* while living. Vedānta and Sāṁkhya, both of them accept *jīvan-mukta/mukti*. You can be liberated while living, so it is not that only after death we can have *mokṣa*, we can be *mukta* while living also. Lord Kṛṣṇa talks of it in the *Bhagavadgītā*; he himself was a *jīvan-mukta*. We have an example of Videharāja Janaka. He was a *jīvan-mukta*, we have Śrī Ramaṇa Maharṣi. There are many seers, many saints and sages in India. They were all *jīvan-muktas*. They were liberated (*mukta*)while living. If we are detached from these bodily afflictions, these mental desires and if we are living only for the sake of doing our duty for others, (i.e. *lokasaṁgraha*). Then this is, *Jivanmurti*. In the *Gītā*, Kr̥ṣṇa says, I do not have to do anything, there is nothing which is left for me to perform, but still I am working for *lokasaṁgraha* (for the welfare of others). So this is a life where one does not have any personal desire. That is the beauty of this concept of *mokṣa*. There are many conceptions of *mokṣa* according to each school, according to Sāṁkhya, it is not only a release from the cycle of birth and death, it is *trividhaduḥkhātyantanivr̥ttiḥ*. If you are liberated from the three types of suffering, *ādhyātmika*, *ādhibhautika* and *ādhidaivika* forever, then it is *mokṣa*. For Cārvāka, *maraṇamevāpavargaḥ*. When you die that itself will be *apavarga*, so enjoy while you are living, who has seen the other life, the permanent liberation from three types of suffering.

Yes, your question is very valid as to what is the purpose of *mokṣa* if we are not going to be there. Some contemporary thinkers, have actually explained the concept of *mokṣa* in these terms. A few of them say that the state of *niṣkāma karma* or *sthitaprajña* that has been enunciated in the *Gītā* is in fact the real state of *mokṣa*.[7] There is at least one modern thinker, Dayananda Saraswati who says that *mokṣa* is not forever; the *jīvas* come back after being liberated also. But for Śaṅkara, it is not going anywhere. It is not attaining anything. It is the self-realization of where we are, what we are, since we have forgotten what we are. Hence, when we realize what we are, that is the state of *mokṣa* according to Śaṅkara *brahmavid brahmaiva bhavati*. I realized the state of being *Brahman*. *Ahaṁ brahmāsmi*. It is not just a statement, it is not just a linguistic utterance. It is the realization of being ever expansive, ever-blissful, ever in the light of knowledge; this is the ultimate state and we cannot doubt this state because we cannot even explain it, but we have to believe it because there have been people who have realized it without studying Vedānta. We have the stories of saints, who had nothing material as their possession, but they were ever fulfilled. They did not want anything. They did not have anything and they did not

---

[7] Varma, Ved Prakash, 1991, *Dharmadarśana ki Mūla Samasyāeṅ*, 1st edn, Delhi: Hindi Mādhyama Kāryānvayana Nirdeśālaya.

want anything. So these were and are the *mukta puruṣas*. *Mukti* is when we do not desire anything. *Mukti* is when we do not crave for anything, when we do not envy anything, when we do not fear anything, i.e. *mukti*; there is only *ānanda*, *moda* and *pramoda*, that is the state of *mukti* according to Advaita Vedānta. Besides, there are the Vaiṣṇava devotees and for them Vṛndāvana is the *mukti-sthala*. So there are various beautiful descriptions of *mukti* in Indian tradition. Thank you for raising this question and let us all find solutions for our own satisfaction. Thank you.

SHRI ANURAG SHARMA: My question is out of curiosity that being born as a human being, we are bound to do *karma*, influenced by the *yoga-māyā* and if human beings are blessed to realize the intellect and attain *mokṣa* through various practices like *bhakti*, *dhyāna* and *yoga*, and go beyond the cycle of rebirth and coming back to this earth. Is there anything that refers to the other species like animals or birds so they can attain *mokṣa*? And my second question is that are *mokṣa* and *mukti* the same concepts coming out of Vedānta? Thank you ma'am.

SPEAKER: Thank you Anurag. Your questions are always very important which show that you keep on studying Indian philosophy. I would first respond to the second question and say that *mokṣa* and *mukti* are the same because both the words have been used in Vedānta. There are other words also, like there is *niḥśreyasa*, there is *apavarga*, there is *kaivalya*, *nirvāṇa* but *mokṣa* and *mukti* have been used interchangeably in Vedānta itself. They have been substituted with each other, so both of these words mean the same; are derived from the same verb, only the suffix changes. So the meaning is also same.

The first question, which you have asked is whether other species or other beings can also aspire for *mukti*, is there any concept of *mukti* for them? Actually, it is said by Śaṅkara himself that this human life is the only opportunity for having a desire to be liberated (*manuṣyatvam*, *mumukṣutvam*), but, yes, we definitely come across the term *sarva-mukti* which means *mukti* for all, so may be that *sarva-mukti* includes all the beings. It has not been elaborated. But *sarva-mukti* may be incorporating all these species, when we say everybody will be liberated, *sarva-mukti* will be there. Then the other species must also get liberated because unless each species or each being is liberated, the ultimate state does not come. But there is another view which believes in *krama-mukti*. There will never be a stage when everybody can be liberated from *karma* because then the world will come to a stop, is not it? So, some souls are getting liberated. The others are getting into this *cakra* but at the end of each creation it is succeeded by a dissolution. It is a *cakra* of *sṛṣṭi* and *pralaya* also. So, after these *cakra*s of *sṛṣṭi* and *pralaya*, there is a *mahāpralaya* when everything just stops. According to Mīmāṁsā, this *cakra* is *anādi*. It will never stop and never begin. But for all other *āstika darśana*s, there is a *cakra* which begins and comes to an end. So, one does not find an explicit mention of the other species being liberated. However, under *sarva-mukti*, we can understand it as the liberation for all beings. Thank you.

Mr SUKANT SARAN: My question is logical. There seems to be some logic involved in this thing when Vedānta says that there is an Ultimate Reality and there is a manifest reality. That the world as we see is a manifestation of that Ultimate Reality and it has also been said that the reality, which we see as the world, is basically a kind of illusion. So my question is: the knowledge which Vedānta is talking about, is also of this world only? So why is that not considered as an illusion?

SPEAKER: This is a question which Śaṅkara himself had anticipated. There are some persons who say that you propound an Ultimate Reality, one single reality, right? And someone says that it is not there, nothing is there. In response to this, Śaṅkara says *ya eva nirākartā sa evātmā*. He or she who says that there is no *ātman*, that person himself or herself is the *ātman*. So, somebody has to be there, some power, some spirit, some force, who says that this is an illusion; maybe this is an illusion, but someone has to give a reason. Also, what about the *śruti-pramāṇa*? That is why whatever Śaṅkara is saying, he is giving a statement from Upaniṣads and Upaniṣads are not ordinary books, which you can discard off like that. This is *śruti-pramāṇa*. Nobody in ancient Indian tradition, at least these six *āstika* schools of Indian philosophy, would reject this *śruti-pramāṇa*. What is common among these six schools is that they all subscribe to *śruti-pramāṇa*. They have different sources, Mīmāṁsā has Brāhmaṇa texts and Vedānta has Upaniṣads. So when Upaniṣads say emphatically and explicitly, not once but many times, that this world is not the ultimate: *neha nānāsti kiñcana* or *neti-neti*. They are negating the whole world, but they are pointing out that there is some reality even after negating everything. Does something remain or not, that is the basic question, you go on negating everything, but who is left there then? Who is negating? He who is denying everything, that itself is *ātman* and that is the ultimate. This is the *śruti-pramāṇa*; the statement is taken from *śruti-pramāṇa* supported by self-realization (*ātmānubhava*), and it is elaborated and explained in different ways.

I am glad that VIF has agreed to publish these lectures. I hope I am able to complete that assignment, which has been given to me by Dr Gupta and I am really thankful to him and to the whole team of VIF, and to all of you who have taken your time out and attended these lectures and enriched my understanding with your deliberations.

Thank you!

Lt GENERAL SAWHNEY: Thank you ShashiPrabha ji for this wonderful discourse and explaining it so beautifully. Thank you!

Epilogue

Typical Trails, Technical Terms and Textual Sources in Indian Philosophy

INDIAN philosophical thought is as old as the *Ṛgveda* and also a rich resource of core concepts such as cosmic creation, human disposition, logical discussion, moral dispensation and spiritual realization. The variety and vastness of Indian philosophy is beyond doubt and description, but a few of its inherent features and paradigmatic practices need to be re-iterated.

II

Accordingly, the most pervasive style of Indian philosophical discourse is as follows:

- to enunciate subtle essence of reality (*sāra*),
- in minimum possible words (*saṁkṣepa*),
- after collecting and presenting all the relevant aspects (*samāhāra*),
- analysing them in crisp classification (*vibhāga*),
- and concluding with one's own viewpoint (*upsaṁhāra*).[1]

Another outstanding feature of Indian philosophy is that philosophy here is termed as *darśana*, which literally signifies the act of seeing or the means of seeing. But more significantly, this seeing is not just physical seeing but an insight or an intuitive vision which provides a right direction to one's life; that is why it is also characterized as *samyagdarśana*.[2]

---

1 *samāhṛtyānyatantrāṇi saṁkṣptaiḥ pratisaṁskṛtaiḥ* ।
sampūrṇāmucyate vargaiḥ nāmaliṅgānuśāsanam ।। — *Amarakośa* 1.2

2 *samyagdarśanasampannaḥ karmabhirna nibadhyate* ।
darśanena vihīnastu saṁsāraṁ pratipādyate ।। — *Manusmṛti* 6.74

Significantly, philosophy in Indian tradition is classified as *śāśtra*, a term which can be derived from two roots as follow:

√*śams* (शंस्) = to describe

√*śās* (शास्) = to prescribe

From this point of view, all the philosophical schools in Indian tradition are descriptive as well as prescriptive.[3] It is not without reason then that philosophy in India is not just a view of life but also a way of life.

The approach of almost all the Indian philosophical schools is comprehensive rather than exclusive. Therefore the proponent (*siddhāntī*) invariably presupposes an opponent (*pūrvapakṣī*), and it is only after examining all the possible arguments and counter arguments that one's own position is put forth.[4]

In addition to above, Indian philosophical thought is unique in the sense that almost all the schools here in (barring the Cārvāka) posit the *summum bonnum* as an ultimate goal of life and guide their respective students on the path leading to this everlasting good. It is not without reason then, that Indian philosophy is also known as Mokṣaśāśtra; although the concept of *mokṣa* and the means to achieve it are visualized differently in several schools.

Accordingly in Nyāya school of Indian philosophy, it is enunciated as *apavarga* (absolute freedom) from all types of pains[5] to be obtained through the knowledge of sixteen categories.[6]

---

3 *pravr̥ttirvā nivr̥ttirvā nityena kr̥takena vā* ।
puṁsāṁ yenopadiśyeta śāstraṁ tadabhidhīyate ।।
— *Ślokavārttika*, Śabdapariccheda 4

4 *śodhayet pūrvapakṣantu yāvannottaradarśanam* ।
uttareṇāvaruddhasya nivr̥ttaṁ śodhanaṁ bhavet ।। — *Ajñātakartr̥ka*

5 *tadatyantavimokṣo 'pavargaḥ* । — *Nyāyasūtra* 1.1.22

6 *pramāṇaprameyasaṁśayaprayojanadr̥ṣṭāntasiddhāntavayava-tarkanirṇayavādajalpavitaṇḍāhetvābhāsacchlajātinigrahasthānānāṁ ṣoḍaśapadārthānāṁ ā tattvajñānānniḥśreyasam* । — Ibid. 1.1.1

The Vaiśeṣika describes it as *mokṣa:*

> the non-existence of conjunction with the body when there is at the same time, no potential body existing and consequently rebirth cannot take place.[7]

The same is also expressed as *niḥśreyasa* (overall accomplishment), the supreme aim beyond *abhyudaya* (material gain) and is said to be obtainable through the real knowledge of six categories propounded in Vaiśeṣika system.[8]

The Sāṁkhya school of Indian philosophy explains the final aim of life as *mukti*, the release from all types of sufferings obstacles forever and for sure.[9] For the Yoga stream of Indian philosophy, *kaivalya* is the ultimate aim of life in which *kevala puruṣa* remains in isolation (*Yogasūtra* 4.34). For both these schools a discriminatory understanding of *prakṛti* and *puruṣa* is necessary for accomplishing the ultimate goal (*Saṁkhyakārikā* 68).

Mīmāṁsā system of Indian philosophy accepts *svarga*[10] as the highest goal of life which can be attained by performing right kind of action in the right manner as ordained by the Veda.[11]

Last but not the least, Vedānta school of Indian philosophy presents the knowledge of *Brahman* (supreme consciousness) as the highest goal of life. Although it is also termed as *mokṣa* like in other schools of Indian philosophy, yet the difference lies in its conceptualizing. According to Vedānta, this is not an external state to be arrived at, rather it is the true nature of one's own self; so it has

---

7 *tadabhāve saṁyogābhāvo 'prādurbhāvaśca mokṣaḥ* ।
— *Vaiśeṣikasūtra* 5.2.18

8 *yato 'bhyudayaniḥśreyasasiddhiḥ sa dharmaḥ* । — Ibid. 1.1.2

9 (i) *trividhaduḥkhātyantanivṛttiratyantapuruṣārthaḥ* । — *Sāṁkhyasūtra* 1.1 and (ii) *muktirantarāyadhvasterna paraḥ* । — Ibid. 6.20

10 *yanna duḥkhena sambhinnaṁ na ca grastamanantaram* ।
abhilāṣopanītaṁ ca tatsukhaṁ svaḥpadāspadam ।। — *Ṭupṭīkā* 6.1.1

11 *codanālakṣṇo 'rtho dharmaḥ* । — *Mīmāṁsāsūtra* 1.1.2 and *Śābarabhāṣya*

to be realized by each one of us in our own being, which in turn is not different from the supreme consciousness in real sense of the term.[12]

As a corollary to the above, there is one more significant trait of Indian philosophy which permeates throughout the vast spectrum of Indian thought traditions; doctrine of *karma* and rebirth is an underlying concept of all these varied ideas. According to it, the metaphysical structure of the world is rooted in one's *karma* as a cause and moral retribution is affected by the same. So, the doer of any action is bound to face the respective consequences — good or bad.[13] In this way, variety of worldly situations is not accidental, it is due to the deeds done by an agent, hence it not only explains the cause of visible differences among human beings, but also propels them to follow the path of good actions in future. The fruits of one's actions are not available in this birth alone as the idea of rebirth is also related to the theory of *karma*. The above-mentioned ideal of *mokṣa* is in fact to be attained only after the successive chain of *karma*s performed by oneself is broken forever. That in turn is made possible by practising non-attachment to the fruits of action and performing one's duty as an offering to the Supreme. Notably, all the schools of Indian philosophy (except Cārvāka) accept the theory of *karma* and rebirth.[14]

III

As already mentioned, brevity is the crux of Indian philosophical tradition which reaches its culmination in the form of *sūtra*, a style adopted by all the sages and scholars who propounded different schools of Indian philosophy. In fact, this is one feature of Indian philosophy which distinguishes it from the other form of Sanskrit

---

12 *brahma veda bramhaiva bhavati* । — *Muṇḍaka Upaniṣad* 3.2.9

13 *yasyāṁ yasyām avasthāyāṁ yat karoti śubhāśubham* ।
tasyāṁ tasyām avasthāyāṁ tat tat phalaṁ samupāśnute ।।
— *Mahābhārata*, Strī Parva 2.33

14 For details, see *Doctrine of Karma and Rebirth*, ed. ShashiPrabha Kumar, Delhi: Upasana Publications, 2018.

literature, i.e. *kāvya* and qualifies it as *śāstra*. It is also worth noting in this regard that it was in the concluding part of oral tradition of Vedic literature that these cryptic statements in the form of *sūtras* were delivered directly by the preceptors to their disciples. But later on, when the direct contact between the preceptor and the disciple was on a decline, then understanding of these *sūtras* became a bit difficult and the need for detailed interpretation of terse philosophical statements arose. It is in this process that not only a lot of commentary texts (Kapoor 2005) were written but they were also classified and defined in different categories such as *sūtra, bhāṣya, vārttika, saṁgraha, ṭīkā, ṭippaṇī, pañjikā, vṛtti, vyākhyāna, prakaraṇa* and *paribhāṣā*,[15] etc.

In the rich repository of source material in different schools of Indian philosophy all these types of texts[16] are abundantly available.

IV

As regards the methods perused in Indian philosophical tradition, it would be interesting to glance through the following details:

- It is worth mentioning that although it does not directly deal with philosophy, yet in the *Nāṭyaśāstra* of Bharat Muni, several methods of elucidation are not only counted but also defined such as *saṁgraha, kārikā* and *nirukta*,[17] etc.
- Similarly in the very beginning of *Arthaśāstra*, Kauṭilya enumerates thirty-two types of *tantrayuktis*, which are in fact the methods employed by him in his treatise.[18]

---

15 Details about these technical terms of Indian philosophical traditions are appended herewith in the form of Annexure A.

16 Details about these types of texts from different systems of Indian philosophy are enclosed in Annexure B.

17 *sthāpito 'rtho bhavedyatra samāsenārthasūcakaḥ* ।
dhātvarthavacaneneha niruktaṁ tatpracakṣate ।। — *Nāṭyaśāstra* 6.13

18 *taddvātriṁśadyuktiyuktam* । *adhikaraṇaṁ vidhānaṁ yogaḥ padārtho hetvartha uddeśo nirdeśa upadeśo 'padeśo 'tideśaḥ pradeśa upamānamarthāpattiḥ saṁśayaḥ prasaṅgo viparyayo vākyaśeṣo* →

- The Nyāya school of Indian philosophy enumerates four modes of objects[19] and three kinds of methods to comprehend these objects.[20] Accordingly, there are four modes of philosophical analysis, namely: subject, object, means and the result while three methods need to be adopted for a logical understanding of these, i.e. enumeration, definition and examination.
- The propounder of Vaiśeṣika school of Indian philosophy has mentioned that a proper knowledge of six types of categories is a means to the ultimate goal and the same can be attained through twin methods: by ascertaining the similarities and dissimilarities among these categories.[21]
- The Sāṁkhya and Yoga schools of Indian philosophy proclaim that just like the science of medicine (Āyurveda), their *śāstra* is based on four aspects: *heya* (objects to be rejected), *heyahetu* (cause of these), *hāna* (rejection) and *hānopāya* (ways of rejection).[22] Obviously this fourfold treatment of a topic is akin to the well-known four noble truths of Buddhism.

← *'numataṁ vyākhyānaṁ nirvacanaṁ nidarśanamapavargaḥ svasaṁjñā pūrvapakṣa uttarapakṣa ekānto 'nāgatāvekṣaṇamatikrāntāvekṣaṇaṁ niyogo vikalpaḥ samuccaya ūhyamiti* । — *Arthaśāstra* 15.1.5

19 *pramāṇāni, prameyaṁ, pramātā, pramitiśceti catasr̥ṣvetāsu vidhāsu arthatattvaṁ parisamāpyate* । — *Nyāyabhāṣya* (*Nyāyasūtra* 1.1.1)

20 *trividhā cāsya śāstrasya pravr̥ttiḥ-uddeṣo lakaṣaṇaṁ parikṣā ceti* ।
— Ibid.

21 *dravyaguṇakarmasāmānyaviśeṣasamavāyānāṁ ṣaṇṇāṁ padārthānāṁ sādharmyavaidharmyābhyāṁ tattvajñānānniḥśreyasādhigamaḥ* ।
— *Vaiśeṣikasūtra* 1.1.4

22 *yathā cikitsāśāstraṁ caturvyūham-rogo rogaheturārogyaṁ bhaiṣajyamiti, evamidamapi śāstraṁ caturvyūhameva* । *tadyathā-saṁsāraḥ, saṁsāra-heturmokṣopāya iti* । *tatra duḥkhabahulaḥ saṁsāro heyaḥ* । *pradhāna-puruṣayoḥ saṁyogo heyahetuḥ* । *saṁyogasyātyātyantiki nivr̥ttirhānam* । *hānopāyaḥ samyagdarśanam* ।
— *Yogasūtravyāsabhāṣya*, p. 78

In other words, the sister schools of Sāṁkhya and Yoga begin with discussing the objects which need to be rejected along with their respective causes because everything is produced by a cause. Thereafter, the process of rejection as also the means of rejection are elaborated so that the final freedom from the cause of bondage is obtained. Unless all these four aspects are known in details, everlasting release from all types of pain is not possible.

- As far as Pūrva-Mīmāṁsā system of Indian philosophical tradition is concerned, its methodology is three-pronged as follows:
    - the object (*kiṁ bhāvyam*).
    - the subject/agent (*kena bhāvyam*).
    - the method (*kathaṁ bhāvyam = itikarttavyatā*).[23]
- Thereafter a fivefold process of discussion is described in Mīmāṁsā texts:
    1. Raising a doubt (*viśaya*).
    2. Identifying a dubitable topic (*viṣaya*).
    3. Examining arguments of the opponent (*pūrvapakṣa*).
    4. Positing one's own argument (*uttarapakṣa*).
    5. Conclusion (*nirṇaya*).[24]
- In earlier (Upaniṣadic) Vedānta, triple process of comprehending the reality is prescribed:
    - Listening intently (*śravaṇa*).

---

[23] *dharme pramīyamāṇe hi vedena karaṇātmanā* ।
itikarttavyatābhāgaṁ mīmāṁsā pūrayiṣyati ।।
— *Kullūkabhaṭṭa quoted in Musalgaonkar 2008: 10*

[24] *viśayo viṣayaścaiva pūrvapakṣastathottaram* ।
nirṇayaśceti pañcāṅgaṁ śāstre 'dhikaraṇaṁ smṛtam ।।
— *Sarvalakṣanasaṁgraha*, p. 7

- Rumination (*manana*).
- Contemplation (*nididhyāsana*).[25]

- While in the later Vedānta, four factors (*anubandhacatuṣṭaya*) are enumerated in the very beginning which are necessary for undertaking the study:
  - Eligible student (*adhikārī*).
  - Theme of study (*viṣaya*).
  - Relation between the topic and the text (*sambandha*).
  - Purpose of study (*prayojana*).[26]
- Besides, four means of preparation are prescribed for the true seeker of Vedānta, which are as follow:
  - Discrimination between eternal and non-eternal (*nityānityavastuviveka*).
  - Detachment from the enjoyment of fruits of here and hereafter (*ihāmutrārthabhogavirāgaḥ*).
  - Possession of tranquillity and self-restraint, etc. (*śamadamādisādhanasampat*).
  - Desire for liberation (*mumukṣutvam*).[27]
- The Jaina school of Indian philosophy presents its own sevenfold style of discussing an issue:
  - Under certain conditions, "A" exists (*syādasti*).
  - Under certain conditions, "A" does not exist (*syānnāsti*).
  - Under certain conditions, "A" is inexpressible (*syādavaktavyam*).

---

25 *ātmā vā 're draṣṭavyaḥ śrotavyo mantavyo nididhyāsitavyaḥ* ।
— *Bṛhadāraṇyakopaniṣad* 2.4.5

26 *tatrānubandho nāma-adhikārīviṣyasambandhaprayojanāni* ।
— *Vedāntasāra* 4

27 *sādhanāni nityānityavastuvivekehāmutrārthaphalbhogavirāgaśama-damādiṣṭkasampattimumukṣutvāni* । — Ibid. 8

- Under certain conditions "A" exists but under certain other conditions, does not exist (*syādasti ca nāsti ca*).
- Under certain conditions "A" exists and is inexpressible (*syādasti cāvaktavyam*).
- Under certain conditions "A" does not exist and is inexpressible (*syānnāsti cāvaktavyam*).
- Under certain conditions, "A" exists, does not exist and is also inexpressible (*syādasti ca nāsti cāvaktavyam*).[28]

V

What follows from the above is that Indian philosophical tradition not only has certain unique traits of its own but has also devised certain specific terms and typical techniques for deliberating upon the basic issues in a logical manner. Therefore, it is not proper to presume that research methodology is a recent phenomenon in Indian intellectual tradition. In view of the brief outline presented in the foregoing pages, it is obvious that each system of Indian philosophy had its own methodology suitable to its metaphysical orientation; besides, there were also some underlying traits and overriding terms and techniques which were commonly adopted and used in all the schools of Indian philosophy, including Buddhism and Jainism.

In brief, while there were strong divergences and long debates among all the schools of Indian philosophy, yet due to some of their common characteristics and general presuppositions, they were constantly engaged in enriching each other via healthy dialectics; this is one extraordinary feature of Indian philosophical thought which is worth emulating in contemporary times as well. In fact, it was due to these broad generic trends that Indian philosophical tradition could sustain itself for such a long duration of more than two millennia.

---

28 *Jainendra Siddhāntakośa*, part 4, p. 315.

Annexure A

Definitions of Technical Terms with Examples of Texts

- **Sūtra**

(a) *alpākṣaramasandigdhaṁ sāravadviśvatomukham* ।
astobhamanavadhyañca sūtraṁ sūtravido viduḥ ॥[28]

(b) *laghūni sūcitārthāni svalpākṣarapadāni ca* ।
sarvataḥ sārabhūtāni sūtrāṇyāhurmanīṣiṇaḥ ॥[29]

For example, *Nyāyasūtra, Vaiśeṣikasūtra, Sāṁkhyasūtra, Yogasūtra, Mīmāṁsāsūtra* and *Brahmasūtra*, etc.

- **Bhāṣya**

(a) *sūtrārtho varṇyate yatra padaiḥ sūtrānusāribhiḥ* ।
svapadāni ca varṇyante taṁ bhāṣyaṁ bhāṣyavido viduḥ ॥[30]

(b) *ākṣipya bhāṣaṇād bhāṣyam* ।

For example, *Nyāyabhāṣya, Praśastapādabhāṣya, Vyāsabhāṣya, Śābarabhāṣya, Śāṅkarabhāṣya, Mahābhāṣya*, etc.

- **Vārttika**

uktānukttaduruktānāṁ cintā yatra pravartate ।
taṁ granthaṁ vārtikaṁ prāhuḥ vārtikajñāḥ manīṣiṇaḥ ॥
For example, *Nyāyavārttika, Yogavārttika, Ślokavārttika, Tantravārttika*, etc.

- **Saṁgraha**

vistareṇopadiṣṭānāmarthānaṁ sūtrabhāṣyayoḥ ।
nibandho yaḥ samāsena saṁgrahaṁ taṁ vidurbudhāḥ ॥
— *Nāṭyaśāstra* 6.11

---

[28] *Madhvabhāṣya* 1.1, Introduction, p. 3 (*Nyāyakośa*, p. 1030).

[29] *Bhāmati*, p. 47, quoted in Musalgaonkar 2008: 12.

[30] *Parāśara Upapurāṇa*, ch. 18, quoted in Musalgaonkar 2008: 10.

For example, *Padārthadharmasaṁgraha, Yogasārasaṁgraha, Siddhānta-leśasaṁgraha*, etc.

- **Ṭīkā**

  yathā sambhavamarthasya ṭīkanaṁ ṭīkā ।

For example, *Vyomavatī, Kiraṇāvalī, Sāṁkhyatattvakaumudī, Ṭupṭīkā, Bhāmatī*, etc.

- **Ṭippaṇī**

  ṭīkāyāṣṭīkā ṭippaṇī ।

For example, *Nyāyakandalī 'ṭippaṇa'*, etc.

- **Pañjikā**

  viṣamapadabhañjikā pañjikā ।

For example, *Nyāya-Pañjikā*, etc.

- **Vr̥tti**

  śābdabodhahetupadārthopasthityanukūlaḥ ।
  padapadārthyoḥ saṁbandhaḥ vr̥ttiḥ ॥

For example, *Nyāyasūtravr̥tti* and *Māṭharavr̥tti*, etc.

- **Vyākhyānam**

  padacchedaḥ padārthoktirvigraho vākyayojanā ।
  ākṣepeṣu samādhānaṁ vyākhyānaṁ pañcalakṣaṇam ॥

- **Prakaraṇam**

  śāstraikadeśasaṁbaddhaṁ śāstrakāyāntare sthitam ।
  āhuḥ prakaraṇaṁ nāma granthabhedaṁ vipaścitaḥ ॥

For example, *Tarkabhāṣā, Tarkasaṁgraha, Arthasaṁgraha*, etc.

- **Kārikā**

  alpābhidhānenārtho yaḥ samāsenocyate budhaiḥ ।
  sūtrataḥ sā tu vijñyeyā kārikārthapradarśini ॥
  — *Nāṭyaśāstra* 6.9

For example, *Kārikāvalī*, etc.

- **Paribhāṣā**

  padārthavivecakācāryāṇāṁ yuktiyuktā vāk ।

For example, *Vedāntaparibhāṣā* and *Mīmāṁsāparibhāṣā*, etc.

Annexure B

Types of Texts in Six Schools of Indian Philosophy

1. Textual Sources in Nyāya Philosophy

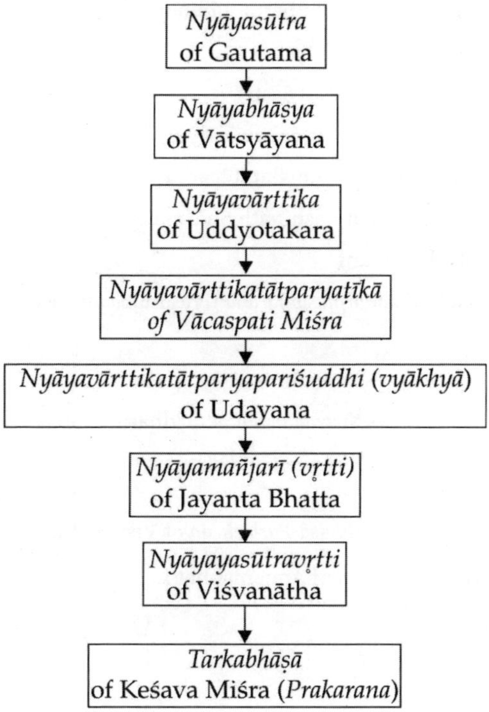

2. Textual Sources in Vaiśeṣika Philosophy

Vaiśeṣikasūtra of Kaṇāda

↓

Commentaries of *VŚ*:

- *Praśastapādabhāṣya* of Praśastapāda
- *Upaskāra* (*Bhāṣya*) of Śaṅkara Miśra
- *Vaiśeṣikasūtracandrānandavr̥tti* of Candrānanda
- *Vaiśeṣikasūtra Ajñātakrtr̥ka Vyākhyā*
- *Vaiśeṣikasūtravārttikam* of Bhaṭṭa Vādīndra
- *Vivr̥tti* of Jayanārāyaṇa
- *Vaidika Vr̥tti* of Haraprasād Śāstrī
- *Rasāyanabhāṣya* of U. Vīrarāghavācārya
- *Sugamā Vr̥tti* of Deśikatirumalatātācārya
- *Vedabhāskarabhāṣya* of Kashinath Sharma
- *Bhāṣya* of Brahmamuni

Padārthadharmasaṁgraha (*Praśastapādabhāṣya*)

↓

Commentaries of *PDS*:

- *Vyomavatī* of Vyomaśiva
- *Nyāyakandalī* of Śrīdhara
- *Kiraṇāvalī* of Udayana

Prakaraṇa:

Kārikāvalī or *Bhāṣā-Pariccheda* of Viśvanātha

Tarkasaṁgraha of Annamabhaṭ ṭa

3. Textual Sources in Sāṁkhya Philosophy

Sāṁkhyasūtra of Kapila

↓

Sāṁkhyapravacanabhāṣya of Vijñānabhikṣu

↓

Sāṁkhyakārikā of Īśvarakr̥ṣṇa

↓

Sāṁkhyatattvakaumudi of Vācaspati Miśra

↓

Sāṁkhyakārikābhāṣya of Gauḍapāda

↓

Māṭharavr̥tti of Māṭhara

↓

Sāṁkhyaparibhāṣā of Kr̥ṣṇa Miśra

4. Textual Sources in Yoga Philosophy

Yogasūtra of Patañjali

↓

Yogasūtrabhāṣya of Vyāsa

↓

Tattvavaiśāradī/Vyāsabhāṣyaṭīkā of Vācaspati Miśra

↓

Rājamārtaṇḍavr̥tti of Bhojadeva

5. Textual Sources in Mīmāṁsā Philosophy

Mīmāṁsāsūtra of Jaimini

↓

Mīmāṁsābhāṣya of Śabara

- *Ślokavārttika* (on *Śābarabhāṣya* 1.1) of Kumārila Bhaṭṭa
- *Tantravārttika* (on *Śābarabhāṣya* from 1.2-3) of Kumārila Bhaṭṭa
- *Ṭupṭīkā* (on *Śābarabhāṣya* from 4-12) of Kumārila Bhaṭṭa

- *Bṛhatī Ṭīkā* ⎤ of Prabhākara Miśra
- *Laghvī Ṭīkā* ⎦

Mīmāṁsāparibhāṣā of Śrī Kṛṣṇayajvan — *Paribhāṣā*

6. Textual Sources in Vedānta Philosophy

Brahmasūtra of Vyāsa

↓

Brahmasūtrabhāṣya of Śaṅkara

↓

- *Bhāmatī* (*Ṭīkā*) of Vācaspati Miśra
- *Advaitasiddhi* of Madhusūdana Sarasvatī
- *Upadeśasāhasrī* of Śaṅkarācārya
- *Pañcadaśī* of Vidyāraṇya
- *Vedānta-Parimala-Kalpataru* of Appayadīkṣita

Bibliography

Primary Sources

Abhidharamakośa of Vasubandhu, 4 vols, ed. Dwarkadass Shastri, Bauddha Bharati, Varanasi, 1970-74.

Allopaniṣad, Pandit, pandit project.org/entity/108586/work>

Amanaskayogaḥ, by Guru Gorakhnath, ed. Yoganath Swami, Poona, 1967.

Amṛtabindūpaniṣad, *Iśādyaṣṭottaraśatopaniṣadaḥ,* Rashtriya Sanskrit Sansthan, New Delhi, 2003.

Āptamīmāṁsā of Samantabhadra, Bharatiya Jnanapitha. New Delhi 2010.

Arthasaṁgraha of Laugakṣī Bhāskara, ed. A.B. Gajendra Gadkar and R.D.Karmakar, Motilal Banarsidass, 1998 (repr.)

Arthaśāstra of Kauṭilya, translated by R. Shamasastry, 4th edn, Sri Raghuveer Printing Press, Mysore, 1951.

Arthaśāstra of Kauṭilya, (ed.) R.P. Kangle, Bombay: University of Bombay, 1969 (2nd edn).

Aṣṭādhyāyī of Pāṇini, Vols I-II, ed. S.C. Vasu, Motilal Banarsidass, Delhi, 2017.

Bauddha Tarkabhāṣā of Mokṣākara Gupta, ed. Raghunatha Giri, Varanasi, 1969.

Bodhicaryāvatāra of Śānti Deva, ed. Paramanand Sharma, Aditya Prakashan, New Delhi, 1990.

Brahmasūtras (*Vedāntasūtras*) of Bādarāyaṇa with Śaṅkara's Commentary, ed. M.M.A.K. Shastri, Nirnaya Sagar Press, Bombay, 1938.

Brahmavaivartta Purāṇa, Anandashram Sanskrit Series, Anandashrama, Poona. 1935.

Bṛhajjābālopaniṣad, Īśādyaṣṭottaraśatopaniṣadaḥ, Rashtriya Sanskrit Sansthan, New Delhi, 2003.

Bṛhatī of Prabhakaramisra, University of Madras, Madras, 1934.

Kauṣītaki Upaniṣad, Īśādyaṣṭottaraśatopaniṣadaḥ, Rashtriya Sanskrit Sansthanam, New Delhi, 2003.

Kena or *Talavakāra Upaniṣad,* with Śāṅkarabhāṣya, Gita Press, Gorakhpur 2011.

Kena Upaniṣad, Eng. tr. Sitanath Goswami, Sankrit Pustak Bhandar, Calcutta, 1954.

Mahābhārata of Vyāsa, vols. I-VI, Gita Press, Gorakhpur, *Saṁvat 2072.*

Majjhima-Nikāya Buddist Publication Society, Sri Lanka, 1995.

Mānameyodaya of Narayaṇa, 2nd edn, Adyar Library, Madras, 1973.

Manusmṛti, ed. Surendra Kumar, Delhi: Arsh Sahitya Prachar Trust, 2000.

Manusmṛti of Manu, Eng. tr. Ganganath Jha, Calcutta, 1924.

Milindapañha of Nāgasena tr. T.W. Rhys Davids, The clearendon Press Oxford, 1890.

Mīmāṁsā Ślokavārttika of Kumārila Bhaṭṭa, ed. Varadācārya, New Delhi: Rashtriya Sanskrit Sansthan, 1987.

Mimāṁsā Ślokavārttika of Kumārila Bhaṭṭa, vols I-II, Eng. tr. Ganganath Jha. Sri Satguru Publications, Delhi, 1983.

Mīmāṁsāsūtra of Jaimini with the Commentary of Śabara (7 vols), Pune: Ānandāśrama, 1981.

Mīmāṁsāsūtra of Jaimini, Eng. tr. N.V. Thadani, Delhi, 1952.

Nāṭyaśāstra of Bharatamuni with the commentary of *Abhinavabhāratī* of Abhinavagupta (vol. 1), Delhi: Parimal Publications, 2003 (repr.).

Nighaṇṭu and *Nirukta* of Yāska, Laksman Sarup, Oxford University Press, London, 1920.

Niyamasāra of Ācārya Kundakunda, Eng. tr. Uggar Sain, Lucknow, 1981.

Nṛsiṁhottaratāpiṇī Upaniṣad, Īśādyaṣṭottaraśatopanisadaḥ, Rashtriya Sanskrit Sansthanam, New Delhi, 2003.

Nyāyabhāṣya of Vātsyāyana, Eng. tr. Ganganath Jha. Mothilal Banasidass Delhi, 1912.

Nyāyakośa, Bhīmācārya Jhalkikar, Bhandarkar Oriental Research Institute, Poona, 1996.

Nyāya-Kusumāñjali of Udayanācārya, Eng. tr. E.B. Cowel, Varanasi, 1936.

Nyāyamañjarī of Jayanta Bhaṭṭa, parts I-II, ed. S.N. Shukla, Varanasi, 1998.

Nyāyasūtras of Gautama: With the Bhāṣya of Vātsyāyana and the Vārtika of Uddyotakara (4 vols), Eng. tr. Ganganatha Jha, Delhi: Motilal Banarsidass, 1999.

Nyāyasūtras of Gautama, ed. and trans. S.C. Vidyabhusana, Sacred Books of the Hindus, vol. 8, Allahabad, 1913.

Nyāyavārttika of Uddyotakara, ed. Anant Lal Thakur, Indian Council of Philosophy Reseach, New Delhi, 1997.

Nyāyavārttika-Tātparya-Ṭīkā of Vācaspati Miśra, ed. Anant Lal Thakur, Indian Council of Philosophy Reseach, New Delhi, 1996.

Nyāyavārttika-Tātparya-Ṭīkā-Pariśuddhiḥ of Udayanācārya, ed. Anant Lal Thakur, Indian Council of Philosophy Reseach, New Delhi, 1996.

Padārtha-Dharma-Saṁgraha (*Praśastapādabhāṣya*) on *Vaiśeṣikasūtra,* Eng. tr. Ganganath Jha, Chowkhambha Orientalia, Varanasi, 1982.

Padārthatattvanirūpaṇam of Raghunātha Śiromaṇi, ed. Karl H. Potter, Harvard Univesity Press, 1957.

Pañcāstikāyasāra of Ācārya Kundakunda, ed. A. Chakravartinayanar, Arrah The Central Jaina Publishing House, 1920.

Pañcāstikāyasāra of Kundakunda: Building of the Cosmos, ed., tr. and Comm. Jagdish Prasad Jain, D.K. Printworld, New Delhi, 2024.

Pāraskara Gṛhyasūtras, ed. Brahmananda Tripathi, tr. Jagdish Chandra Mishra, Chaukhamba Sanskrit Pratishthan, Delhi, repr., 2010.

Prabodhacandrodaya of Kṛṣṇa Miśra, Nirnaya Sagar Press, Bombay 1916.

Pramāṇamīmāṁsā of Hemacandra, Tara Publications, Varanasi, 1970.

Pramāṇavārttika of Dharmakīrti, ed. R.C. Pandeya, Motilal Banarsidass, Delhi, 1989.

Pramāṇavārttikam of Ācārya Dharmakīrti, including *Manorathanandivṛtti* of Ācārya Manorathanandī, critically edited with Hindi tr. by Kashinath Nyaupane, D.K. Printworld, New Delhi, 2022.

Pravacanasāra of Ācārya Kundakunda, Rajachandra Ashram, Agas, 1984.

Raghuvaṁśa of Kālidāsa, with Mallinatha's Commentary, Cantos I-X , ed. M.R. Kale, 3rd rev. edn, Bombay, Gopal Narayan & Co., 1922.

Rāmāyaṇa of Vālmīki. Gita Press, Gorakhpur, VS 2072.

Ṛgveda Saṁhitā, with Sāyaṇabhāṣya, ed. F. Max Müller, 6 vols, London: Oxford University Press, 1849-74.

Ṛgvedādibhāṣyabhūmika, Dayananda Saraswati, 8th repr., Ārṣa Sāhitya Pracāra Trust, Delhi, 1993.

Śābara-Bhāṣya on Mīmāṁsāsūtras, Eng. tr. Ganganath Jha. Oriental Institute Baroda, 1933.

Ṣaḍdarśanasamuccaya of Guṇaratna Sūri. ed. Mahendra Kumar Jain, Bharatiya Jnanapith, New Delhi, 1997.

Sāmaveda Saṁhitā, ed. Satyavrat Samashrami, Munshiram Manoharlal, New Delhi, 1983.

Sāmavidhāna Brāhmaṇa tr. A.C. Burnell, Trubnar & Co., London, 1873.

Samayasāra of Ācārya Kundakunda, ed. Balabhadra Jain, Eng. tr. Vijay Kumar Jain, Vikalp Printers, Dehradun, 2012.

Sāṁkhyapravacanabhāṣya of Vijñānabhikṣu, ed. R. Garbe, Harvard Oriental Series, Cambridge, 1943.

Sāṁkhyasūtra, Eng. tr. J.R. Ballantyne, Parimal Publications, Delhi, 2021.

Sāṁkhya-Tattvakaumudī-Ṭīkā on Sāṁkhyakārikā of Vācaspati Miśra, Eng. tr. Ganganath Jha, 1st edn, Varanasi/Delhi, Chaukhamba Sanskrit Pratishthan, 2004/2021.

Śāṅkhāyana Āraṇyaka ed. A.B. Keith, Royal Asiatic Society, London, 1908.

Śāṅkhāyana Brāhmaṇa, Anandashram Sanskrit Series, Anandashrama, Poona, 1898.

Sāṅkhyakārikā of Īśvara Kṛṣṇa with the Commentary of Gauḍapāda, Translated into English by T.G. Mainkar, Poona: Oriental Books Reprint Corporation, 2nd edn, 1972.

Śārīraka-Bhāṣya of Śaṅkara on *Brahmasūtras*. Eng. tr. V.M. Apte, Popular Book Depot, Bombay, 1960.

Sarvadarśanasaṁgraha of Mādhavācārya, ed. E.B. Cowell and A.E. Gough, 7th edn, Varanasi: Chowkhamba, 1978 (retypeset edn published in 2016 by D.K. Printworld, New Delhi).

Sarvadarśanasaṁgraha of Madhvācārya, or Review of the Different Systems of Hindu Philosophy, ed. E.B. Cowell and A.E. Gough, Chowkhambha Sanskrit Series Office, Varanasi, 1961 (retypeset edn published by D.K Printword, New Delhi, 2016).

Sarvalakṣaṇasaṁgraha of Swami Gaurishan Bhiksu, Chaukhambha Sanskrit Series, Varanasi, 2010.

Sarvānukramaṇī of Kātyāyana. ed. A.A. Macdonell, The Clarendon Press, Oxford, 1886.

Sarvasiddhāntasaṁgraha of Śaṅkarācārya, Eng. tr. M. Rangacharya, Ajay Book Service, Delhi, 1983.

Śāstradīpikā of Pārthasarathi Miśra, Eng. tr. Venkataramaiah, Goekwad Oriental Series, Baroda, 1940.

Śatapatha Brāhmaṇa, Eng. and Hindi tr. Motilal Shastri, Rajasthan Vaidik Shodh Sansthan, Jaipur, vs 2015.

Śatapatha Brāhmaṇa, vols I-V, Sacred Books of the East, vols 12, 26, 41, 43 and 44, Clarendon Press, Oxford, 1882-1900.

Śatapatha Brāhmaṇa, Vijñāna-Bhāṣya (Hindi), Motilal Śāstri, Vols. I-II, Rajasthan Vaidik Tattvaśodhana Sansthan, Jaipur, vs 2015.

Ślokavārttika of Kumarila Bhaṭṭa, Eng. tr. Ganganath Jha, vols I-II, Sri Satguru Publications, Delhi, 1983.

Śukla Yajurveda, ed. V.L. Shasti Pansikar, Nirnaya Sagar Press, Bomboy, 1929.

Suttanikāya, ed. Dwarkadas Shastri, Bauddha Bharati, Varanasi, 2000.

Śvetāśvatara Upaniṣad, ed. Swami Tyagisananda, Sri Ramakrishna Maṭh, Madras, 1949.

Syādvāda-mañjarī of Malliṣeṇa, Sri Rajchandra Ashrama, Agas, 1979.

Tarkasaṁgraha of Annambhaṭṭa, ed. Y.V. Athalye, Bhandarkar Oriental Research Institute, Poona, 1974.

Taittirīya Brāhmaṇa, vols I-III, ed. Narayan Śāstri, Anandashrama Sanskrit Series, no 37, Anandashrama, Poona, 1934-38.

Taittirīya Saṁhitā, Anandashram Sanskrit Series, Anandashrama, Poona, 1940.

Taittirīya Upaniṣad, Anandashrama Sankrit Series, Anandashrama, Poona, 1889.

Taittirīyasaṁhitā-Bhāṣya, Anandashrama Sankrit Series, Anandashrama, Poona, 1940.

Talavakāra Āraṇyaka, or *The Jamanīya Brāhmaṇa*, Pandit Rama Deva,

Dayanand Mahavidyalaya, Lahore, 1921 (*e-book* available on Vedic Heritage Portal, IGNCA).

Talavakāra Upaniṣad, see *Kena Upaniṣad*.

Tantravārttika of Kumārila Bhaṭṭa, Eng. tr. Ganganath Jha, vols I-II, 2nd edn, Sri Satguru Publications, Delhi, 1983.

Tarkabhāṣā of Keśava Miśra, Eng. tr. S.R. Iyer, Chowkhambha Orientalia, Varanasi, 1979.

Tarkabhāṣā of Yaśovijaya Gaṇi, ed. Sukhlalji Sanghavi, Singhi Jain Granthamala, Calcutta, 1938.

Tarkadīpikā, Commentary on Tarkasaṁgraha of Annambhaṭṭa ed. Y.V. Athalye, Bhadarkar Oriental Research Institute, Poona, 1974.

Tattva-Cintāmaṇi Dīdhiti of Raghunatha Śiromaṇi with Prakāśa of Vardhama Upadhyaya ed. Tarkadarshanatirtha, The Asiatic Society of Bengal, Kolkatta, 1910.

Tattva-Cintāmaṇi of Gaṅgeśa Upādhyāya, ed. Kamakhyanatha Tarkavagisa, Baptist Mission Press, Calcutta, 1888.

Tattvārthasūtra of Umāsvāti, Sambodhi Prakashan, Delhi, 2017.

Tattvasaṁgraha of Śāntarakṣita, Bauddha Bharati, Varanasi, 1981.

Tattvopaplavasiṁha of Jayarāśi, ed. Sukhlal Singhvi, Gaekwad Oriental Series, Oriental Institute, Baroda, 1940.

Ṭupṭīkā of Kumārila Bhaṭṭa, ed. Gaṅgādhara Śāstrī (Benares Sanskrit Series), Benares: Braj B. Das & Co., 1904.

Vākyapadīyam of Bhartṛhari, ed. K.V. Abhyankar and V.P. Limaye, Sanskrit and Prakrit Series, University of Poona, Poona, 1965.

Vaṁśa Brāhmaṇa ed. B.R. Sharma, Kendriya Sanskrit vidyapeetha, Tirupati, 1983.

Vedāntasāra of Sadānanda, Eng. tr. M. Hiriyanna, Oriental Book Agency, Poona, 1962.

Vedāntasāra of Sadānanda together with the commentaries of Nṛsimhasarasvati and Ramatirtha, ed. Colonel G.A. Jacob, 5th edn, Bombay: Nirnaya Sagar Press, 1934.

Vivekacūḍāmaṇiḥ of Śaṅkarācārya, Eng. tr. Swami Madhavananda, Advaita Ashrama, Calcutta, 1995.

Vyākaraṇamahābhāṣya of Patañjali. ed: Charudev Shastri, Motilal Banarsidass, Delhi, 1968.

Yājñavalkyasmṛti, Anandashram Sanskrit Series, Anandashrama, Poona, 1903.

Yajurveda with Subodha Bhāṣya (in Hindi), S.D. Satavalekar, Swadhya Maṇdala, Paradi, 2010.

Yogasūtras and Vyāsabhāṣya along with Tattvavaiśāradī of Vācaspati Miśra, Anandashram Sanskrit Series, 47, Anandashrama, Poona, 1932.

Yogasūtravyāsabhāṣya, Ānandāśramasanskritgranthāvaliḥ, Granthāṅka 47, Pune, 1904.

Yogavārttika of Vijñānabhikṣu. ed. Keshav Shastri, Medical Hall, Kashi, 1884.

Secondary Sources

Aurobindo, Sri, *The Secret of the Veda,* Pondichery: Sri Aurobindo Ashram, 1998.

Bengali Baba, 1979, *Yogasūtra of Patañjali,* Delhi: Motilal Banarsidass.

Bhide, Nivedita Raghunath, 2022, *Indian Culture: Challenges and Potentialities,* 2nd edn, Chennai: Vivekananda Kendra Prakashan.

Bloomfield, M., 1906, *A Vedic Concordance,* Cambridge: Harvard University Press.

Bodas, M.R., 1974, "A Historical Survey of Indian Logic", Introduction to *Tarkasaṁgraha of Annambhaṭṭa,* Poona: Bhandarkar Oriental Research Institute.

Bodas, M.R. and Y.V Athalye, 2003, *Tarkasaṁgraha of Annambhaṭṭa,* Pune: Bhandarkar Oriental Research Institute.

Bothlink, Roth Otto and Rudolf Roth, 1855, *Wörterbuch, Sanskrit Wörterbuch,* (*Sanskrit-German Dictionary*), vols I-VII, St. Petersburg: der K. Akademic der Wissenschaften.

Chattterjee S.C. and D.M. Dutta, 1939, *An Introduction to Indian Philosophy,* 7th edn, Calcutta. University of Calcutta.

Chinmayananda, Swami, 2013, *Muṇḍakopaniṣad,* Mumbai: Central Chinmaya Mission Trust.

Dandekar, R.N., 1946-2004, *The Vedic Bibliography,* vols I-V, Poona: Bhandarkar Oriental Research institute.

Dasgupta, S.N., 1975, *History of Indian Philosophy*, vols I-V, Indian edn, Delhi: Motilal Banarsidass.

Datta, D.M., 1960, *Six Ways of Knowing*, second revised edn (retypeset edn published by D.K Printworld, New Delhi, 2018).

Faddegon, B., 1918, *The Vaiçeśika System, Described with the help of the Older Texts*, Amsterdam: Johannes Müller.

Frauwallner, Erich, *History of Indian Philosophy*, vol. II, Motilal Banarsidass, New Delhi, 1973.

Halbfass, Wilhelm, 1993, *On Being and What There is?* (1st Indian edn) Sri Satguru Publications, Delhi.

Hiriyanna, Mysore, 2005, *Outliness of Indian Philosophy*, Delhi: Motilal Banarsidass (first published in 1932 by George Allen & Unwin Ltd., London).

Ingalls, H.H., Daniel, 1951, *Materials for the Study of Navya Nyāya Logic*, Harvard Oriental Series, 90, Cambridge: Harvard University.

Jhalkikar, B., 1978, *Nyāyakośaḥ*, Poona: Bhandarkar Oriental Research Institute.

Kant, Immanuel, 1956, *Critique of Pure Reason*, New York: Mcmillan.

Kapoor, Kapil, 2005, *Text and Interpretation: The Indian Tradition*, New Delhi: D.K. Printworld.

Katju, (Justice) Markandeya, 2013, *The Mīmāṁsā Rules of Interpretation*, Allahabad: Modern Law Publication.

Kumar, ShashiPrabha, 2005, "Significance of Sādhana-Catuṣṭaya in Vedānta", in *Self, Society and Value: Reflections on Indian Philosophical Thought*, pp. 108-25, Delhi: Vidyanidhi Prakashan.

Kumar, ShashiPrabha, 2009, "Persona of Women in the Vedas", in *Women in Ancient and Medieval India*, History of Science, Philosophy and Culture in Indian Civilization, PHISPC, vol. IX, part 2, ed. Bhuvan Chandel, pp. 31-42, New Delhi: Centre for Studies in Civilizations.

Kumar, ShashiPrabha, 2013, *Classical Vaiseṣika in Indian Philosophy*, London and New York: *Routledge*.

Kumar, ShashiPrabha, 2013, *Vaiśeṣika Darśana meiṅ Padārtha-Nirūpaṇa*, 2nd edn, New Delhi: D.K. Printworld (1st edn, 1992).

Kumar, ShashiPrabha (ed.), 2018, *Doctrine of Karma and Rebirth*, Delhi: Upasana Publications.

Kumar, ShashiPrabha, 2019, "Vaiśeṣika Studies Across the World", in *Categories, Creation and Cognition in Vaiśeṣika Philosophy*, pp. 171-86. Singapore: Springer Nature.

Kunhan Raja, C., 1974, *Some Fundamental Problems of Indian Philosophy*, 2nd edn., Delhi: Motilal Banarsidass.

Maneewong, P., 2015,"The Sautrāntika School of Buddhism", in Academia. edu. (this is an e-journal) .

Matilal, B.K., 1981, *Central Philosophy of Jainism,* Ahmedabad: L.D. Institute of Indology.

Monier-Williams, 1899, *Sanskrit-English Dictionary*, Oxford: Clarendon Press.

Mookerjee, Satkari, 1997, *Buddhist Philosophy of Universal Flux*, Delhi: Motilal Banarsidass.

Mukherjee, Satkari, 1978, *The Jaina Philosophy of Non-Absolutism,* Motilal Banarsidass, New Delhi.

Müller, Max, 1860, *A History of Ancient Sanskrit Literature*, London/ Edinburgh: Williams and Norgate.

Murthy, T.R.V., 1955, *Central Philosophy of Buddhism*, London: George Allen & Unwin.

Musalgaonkar, Gajanana Shastri, 2008, *Śāstradīpikā* (*Tarkapāda*), ed. Vijay Sharma, Varanasi: Chaukhambha Surbharati Prakashan.

Nyaupane, Kashinath, 2000 (vs 2056), *Mīmāṁsātarkabhāṣā*, Kathmandu, Nepal: Jayatu Samskrita.

Paranjpe, Vasant, V. 2020, *Homatherapy: Our Last Chance*, Maheshwar, Madhya Pradesh: Fivefold Path Publications.

Payne, E.F.J. (Eng. tr.), (1851/2000), *Parerga and Paralipomena* of Arthur Schopenhauer, Oxford: Clarendon Press.

Radhakrishnan, S. 1968, *The Principal Upaniṣads,* 2nd Impression, London: George Allen & Unwin.

Radhakrishnan, S. and Charles A. Moore (eds), 1957, *A Sourcebook of Indian Philosophy,* Princeton, NJ: Princeton University Press.

Radhakrishnan, S., 1953, *The Principal Upaniṣads*, London: George Allen & Unwin Ltd.

Radhakrishnan, S., 1977, *Indian Philosophy*, vol. I & II, London: George Allen & Unwin, reprinted in India, Tenth Impression, Bombay.

Saraswati, Satya Prakash (Swami), 2005, "Introduction" to *The Holy Vedas*, 7th repr, New Delhi: Clarion Books.

Satavalekar, Sripada Damodara, 2007, *Ṛgvedasaṁhitā* with Subodha bhāṣya, vols I-II, Swadhyaya Maṇḍala, Pardi, Surat.

Shakya, Milan, 2000, *Essentials of Sautrāntika Philosophy*, Academia-edu, e-Source.

Sharma, Arvind, 2020, "Contrasting Indian and Western Philosophy", *Times of India*, 2 March.

Sharma, I.C., 1991, *Ethical Philosophies of India*, 2nd edn, Ghaziabad: International Publishing, Duhai.

Shastri, Dharmendranath, 1976, *Critique of Indian Realism: The Philosophy of Nyāya-Vaiśeṣika and Its Conflict with the Buddhist Diṅnāga School*, Delhi: Bharatiya Vidya Prakashan.

Shastri, Dwijendra Nath, 1956, *Sanskrit Sahitya Vimarsaḥ*, Meerut: Bharati Pratishthan.

Sinha, Jadunath, 1968, *Indian Philosophy* (*Bhāratīya Darśana*), Hindi tr. G.P. Bhatt, 2nd edn, Agra: Lakhmi Narain Agarwal Educational Publisher.

Sinha, Nand Lal, 1911, *Vaiśeṣikasūtra of Kaṇāda*, Eng. trans. Panini office, Allahabad.

Stcherbatsky, T., 1976 (1st edn, 1930), *Buddhist Logic*, Repr., Delhi: Motilal Banarsidass.

Tilak, Bal Gangadhar, 1893, *Orion or The Antiquity of the Vedas*, Bombay: Radhabai Atmaram Sagoon.

Upadhyaya, Baldev (Hindi), 1966, *Bhāratīya Darśana*, 7th edn, Kashi: Sharada Mandir.

Upadhyaya, Baldev, 2015, *Vaidika Sahitya aur Saṁskriti*, 7th edn, Sharda Sansthan, Varanasi.

Vidyāraṇya, Swami, 1997, Pancadaśī, ed. K.P. Tripathi, Lucknow: Uttar Pradesh Sanskrit Sansthan.

Zimmer, H., 1978, *Philosophies of India*, ed. J. Campbell, tr. J.M. Simone, Paris: Payout.

DICTIONARIES AND ENCYCLOPEDIAS

Amarakośa of Amara Siṁha, Bombay: Nirnaya Sagar Press, 1961.

Amarakośaḥ (*Nāmaliṅgānuśāsanam*), of Amara Siṁha, 4th edn, Chowkhamba Surabharati Prakashan, Varanasi, 1992.

Jainendra Siddhāntakośa of Jinendra Varṇī, part four, 6th edn, New Delhi: Bharatiya Jnanpeeth, 2000.

Sanskrit Vaṅmayakośa of Śrīdhara Bhāskara Varṇekara, Lokabharati Prakashan, Allahabad, 2nd edn, 2001.

Index